Restoring & Collecting
Antique
Reed Organs

To Lorena—my long-suffering wife who certainly didn't know what she was getting into when she innocently mentioned that she would like to have an old pump organ to play.

Restoring & Collecting
Antique
Reed Organs

By Horton Presley

Vestal
Press

THE VESTAL PRESS, LTD.
VESTAL, NEW YORK   13850

First edition: July 1977, TAB BOOKS
Copyright (c) 1977 by TAB BOOKS

Original Library of Congress Cataloging in Publication Data:

Presley, Horton.
    Restoring and collecting antique reed organs.

    Bibliography: p.
    Includes index.
    1. Reed-organ. I. Title.
ML597.P73   786.9'43   77-2756
ISBN 0-8306-7911-1
ISBN 0-8306-6911-6 pbk.

Second edition: November, 1986
The Vestal Press
320 N. Jensen Road, PO Box 97
Vestal, NY 13850

Vestal Press edition ISBN 0-911572-5 6-2 pbk.

Appendix (Sources of Supply and Bibliography) revised by
publisher March, 1992. New CIP listing applied for.

The author. with two unrestored organs

Contents

Introduction

This is a book designed primarily for the amateur craftsman who wants to know the nuts and bolts of restoring an antique reed organ. While I know that it has useful information for anyone interested in organs, its basic assumption is that the person most likely to use it is someone having an old organ, or intending to get one, in very poor condition, with parts missing, and that the owner will have no source of detailed information concerning what to do. As anyone knows who has researched this field, there are very few books of any kind about reed organs, and those that do exist just have snatches of information here and there about restoration. Consequently, I have tried to be as comprehensive as possible. The good antique furniture restorer may already know much that is in here concerning restoration of organ cases, just as the experienced organ restorer already knows what to do about faulty vox humanas. The typical owner of an old organ most likely does not know it all and would like a single book that includes as much as possible of what he is going to need to get the job done.

The primary purpose of this book is to help the amateur craftsman get the organ into working condition, with a reasonably acceptable appearance. This purpose may conflict at times with the preferences of the purist who wants nothing but faithful restoration of the organ to its original condition. Of course, this restoration is preferable where possible. I recommend, for instance, that the restorer rebuild the bellows as originally designed rather than install an electric blower unit. I prefer a *pump* organ (before you disagree, read on, friend; a well-restored organ is not hard to pump.) Yet, often, faithful restoration of these organs is not possible. The canopy top, so often prized today, may be missing, having been thrown away years ago; stop faces may have fallen off and the style of the originals is simply not replaceable; cut-outs in the keyslip (located below the keyboard) may be so splintered as to be beyond recognition; the bellows may be gone. In cases such as these, and others that will be dealt with as we go along, the restorer must do with what he has and use his creativity when no pattern for the missing part exists.

After all, the organ was not designed as a museum piece. It was an instrument which, for the most part, was purchased by families and churches with modest incomes for use in their everyday enjoyment of music. If the organ can be restored so that it serves its primary function again, with its appearance pleasing enough so that it is an enjoyable addition to someone's living room, I'm satisfied—even though we all know it may not be faithful to its unknown original appearance. A major part of my satisfaction in restoration has been the resurrection of sad piles of stuff that were sold to me as spare parts, too far gone to remake into an organ. If that's your intention and you have (or can get) an old instrument with sorrow peering out of its weepy stops, then this book is for you.

Do I consider myself the dean of restorers who knows it all and therefore can spread the good word? Good grief no. By raising the question, I am reminded of the story of the young second lieutenant, with a specialty, who was assigned to teach in the General Staff College at Fort Leavenworth. On the first day of class he peeked into the classroom and saw high brass all over: none were less than colonel. He began to sweat but then straightened up, strode into the room and on to the platform. "There are probably a thousand men in this army who know more of this subject than I do," he began, paused a moment, then continued. "But I see none of them here so I will proceed with confidence." So the story goes, with the side note that he had the brass well in hand from then on.

I know for a fact that there are many craftsmen who have restored many more organs than I have, but as yet none has taken time to write anything comprehensive. So I might as well start the ball rolling. I depart significantly from my military analogy, however, in that I have asked several much more experienced restorers than I to read this text making criticisms and suggestions. They are John Kejr, of Wilson, Kansas; Harlan Fisk, of Lubbock, Texas; and certainly not last, my very good friend Walter Butler of Butler's Music Store here in Ottawa.

The latter gent deserves special mention. In 1960, after I had bought a beautiful old Beckwith organ which was moldering away in a vacant house, I ran to Walt crying "help," which he promptly gave in abundance. He still does. He really ought to have written this book but he is kept too busy repairing virtually any instrument made, particularly in his capacity as a master luthier. You ought to see the job he does on smashed guitars, mandolins, and the like. But that is another book, I hope by him. Thanks Walt.

Two other important acknowledgments. A lot of photography went into this project. While I did the camera work, I got lots of help from a former student of mine, Carl Spencer, who did the darkroom work. He has been a tremendous help. Richard Turner, of Turner's Antiques, has often helped me to find organs, parts, and what-not. He is a real master of furniture restoration to whom I regularly run when I don't know what to do with some aspect of woodworking or refinishing. Without Walt and Richard this book just wouldn't exist.

In a sense, everything that follows is an expression of psychologist Carl Rogers' comment, "Experience is the highest authority." Everything in this book comes out of actual experience, most of it mine. This certainly is not to say that there are no better ways of doing things: I just know that the techniques detailed here WORK. I fully expect that some readers will know of better ways to do certain steps; others will devise means of solving problems I haven't faced. Since there were many hundreds of brands of organs manufactured, it is presumptuous of me to assume that my techniques fit all conceivable needs. In fact, you will find blank pages at the end of each construction chapter so that you can record any additional information you uncover which goes beyond what the chapter gives. If it is practical, I would like to hear from you about your discoveries; who knows, another edition of this thing may be called for and I would like to include your ideas, properly acknowledged in the text, of course. Have fun.

Horton Presley

Chapter 1
A Brief
History
of the Reed
Organ in America

In various forms, reed organs have been around for centuries. They probably began millenia before the Christian era, with the Chinese *sheng*, or *sho*, a kind of mouth organ. Tracings of the organ's development continued through the European *Regal* to the *pressure harmonium* made in France and England in the early years of the nineteenth century. These all made use of free reeds: that is, reeds having one end free to vibrate in response to air pressure or suction. Such reeds had been in use even before the nineteenth century in certain ranks of pipe organs, but there is question as to whether anyone actually put together a full reed organ before 1800.

THE SUCTION PRINCIPLE

The debate continues over who first actually used the suction principle, so dominant in American organs. Milne, a British writer, stated that the suction principle was first used by a Frenchman, Alexandres of Paris, about 1835; but the writer is so wrong when he says that the suction organ first came to America in the 1850s that his prior date is also suspect.[1] The best candidate evident at present is a Mr. Aaron Merrill Peaseley of Boston, who patented an organ using free reeds in 1818. The most significant note in the patent is the statement that his principle may be used either with a force bellows or a suction bellows.[2] The problem is that instrument makers of the period often made individual instruments either from whim or demand, so exact dating of the construction of the first suction organ may never be settled for certain. Research is continuing however, and it is hoped more accurate information will be forthcoming.

Regardless of all that, the fact is that before 1846 very few such organs were manufactured.[3] The big impetus toward a mass market came with the work of Jeremiah Carhart who patented a suction organ on December 28, 1846. The date appeared on many organs made for years after that, and is often erroneously taken as a date of manufacture. His patent was used by George Prince, his employer, by himself, to make an organ under his own name (restoration of one is discussed later in this book) which looked like the Prince, and by several other manufacturers. Ironically, the patent was declared void quite some time later. It apparently had been allowed in 1846 because a patent office fire in 1836 had destroyed the records of Peaseley's earlier invention, and a copy of the original did not surface until years later.[4]

THE REED ORGAN

The fact remains that Carhart's efforts, and those of George Prince, began the big swing to reed organs. The petite little one-pedal organ shown in Fig. 1-1 was made in late 1847 or early 1848 (more of the dating problem later) making it probably one of the oldest of its kind in existence. By unscrewing two brass wing-screws, one under each set of legs, the owner could fold up the legs and carry the organ around quite easily. The Smithsonian Institution has one organ identical to this, but with a higher serial number. Theirs also has the original rough-lumber carrying box in which it came. The Musical Museum of Deansboro, New York has an almost identical Carhart with a very low serial number. Not knowing how serial numbers were assigned, I cannot be sure whether the Prince or Carhart is older.

The organ has a rosewood veneered case with a single *stop*—the small pedal visible at the bottom of the left front leg. The instrument is pumped with the single pedal that hangs down from a leather strap. The organist must hold down the heel plate while operating the rest which pivots at the side of the heel plate. Some time ago a friend and I took the Prince to a rural church for an old-fashioned sing and attempted to teach the congregation to line-sing in the manner so often used when these organs were first introduced. After accompanying the congregation for just one hymn, I have profound respect

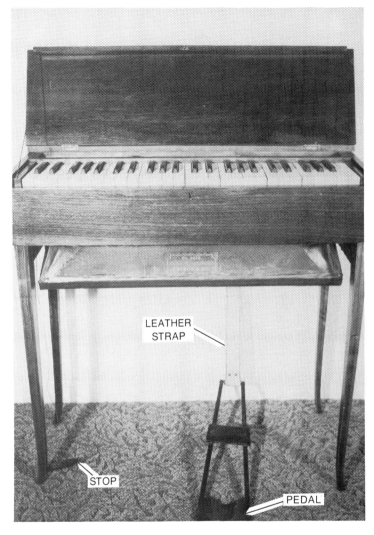

LEATHER
STRAP

STOP

PEDAL

Fig. 1-1. 1847/48 Prince one-pedal melodeon. (Author's collection.)

for those organists so long ago who could pump the thing for a three-hour revival. One song almost paralyzed my leg.

From 1846 on, the organ rapidly gained the dominance of small churches and parlors. Monster reed organs were made for large church uses, but they never seriously challenged the pipe organ in that market. The graceful parlor melodeon shown in Fig. 1-2 was in use by 1849 and was made in increasing abundance until about the time of the Civil War.

Fig. 1-2. Eldredge parlor melodeon, about 1850. (Author's collection.)

Soon the double-pump exhauster bellows was invented, more ranks of reeds and associated stops were added, and the organ began to take on the more familiar appearance of the upright parlor organ. The 1875 Prince is a good example of its early appearance. (Fig. 1-3).

THE PIANO

The heyday of the standard upright parlor organ continued into the 1890s at which time the piano began to challenge its hold on the home market; the organ began to be thought of as old-fashioned. In order to combat rising resistance to reed organs, manufacturers began to make them increasingly ornate (to the irritation of musicians who rightly pointed out that an elaborate canopy does nothing for musical quality) and

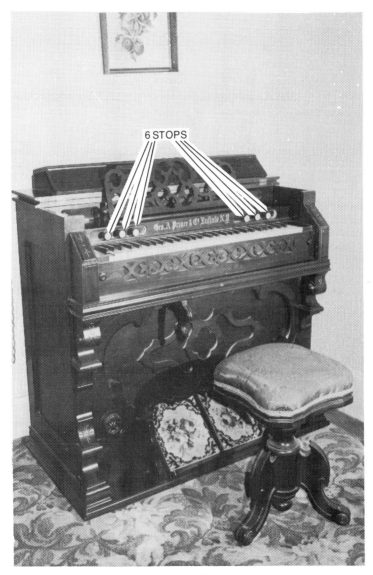

Fig. 1-3. Prince six-stop organ, 1875. (Owned by Turner's Antiques, Ottawa, KS.)

Fig. 1-4. Crown Concert Roller Organ, 1901. (Author's collection.)

to disguise them as something else. Gellerman documents strange combinations such as a sewing machine and organ in the same case. For those lacking money for a standard instrument, space to display it, and even talent to play it, the little Crown Roller Organ was made about 1900 (Fig. 1-4). It sold for as little as $3.95 and the changeable rollers sold for 18¢ each.

Fig. 1-5. Beckwith Concert Grand Piano-cased Organ, 1908. (Author's collection.)

THE PIANO-CASED ORGAN

The 1908 Beckwith piano-cased organ (described in detail later in this book) is a good example of the attempt, beginning about 1885, to stem the tide of sentiment for the piano by putting the organ in a piano case and, by very ingenious means, achieving multi-stop capabilities without having the stops prominently visible (Fig. 1-5).

Even so, because pianos were so much more expensive and difficult to play, organs continued to be made, with manufacturers continually adding features to keep them attractive to buyers. The Windsor of 1914, sold by Sears

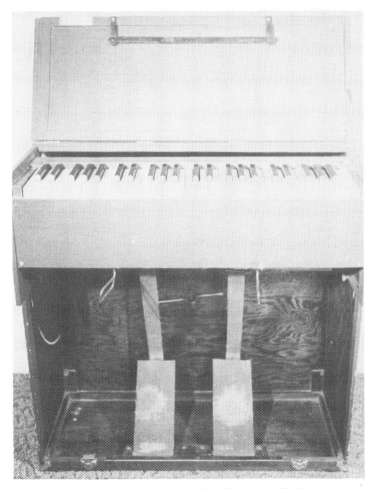

Fig. 1-6. White folding organ, 1944. (Author's collection.)

(several shots of its action can be seen in this book later) had four ranks of reeds and seventeen stops. Reed organs continued to be made in smaller quantities through the 1930's.

RETURN OF THE REED

The instrument stubbornly refused to die, though, and returned to its original form. Many Salvation Army street meetings have been led by organists playing a folding organ similar to the one in Fig. 1-6, which was formerly owned by my

Fig. 1-7. Wurlitzer church organ. (Owned by Walt Butler, Butler's Music Store, Ottawa, KS.)

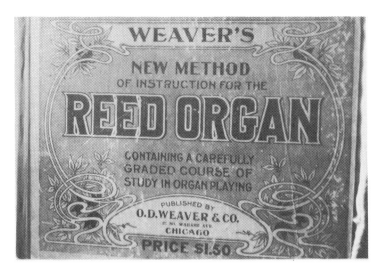

Fig. 1-8. Cover of Reed Organ Instruction Book. Author's collection.

mother and bought in 1944. The Wurlitzer church organ in Fig. 1-7, restored and owned by Walt Butler, is a reed organ, electronically amplified. Music stores still sell cheap reed organs with a simple electronic amplifier attached. The familiar accordion, of course, makes use of free reeds similar to those of the old organ. Who knows? Maybe the home reed organ will, like the Phoenix, rise again.

The musical development of any culture is often a reflection of the instruments in use and our culture is no exception. For that reason I am surprised at the lack of information (at least the lack of information that I have been able to find) on the influence of the reed organ on American music. With the possible exception of the guitar, and I have some doubts even there, no instrument seems so widely used throughout the country during its formative years as was the reed organ. Harmonies such as are so common in nineteenth century Protestant church music and in barbershop quartets are very common in the reed organ books so often given with the organs (Fig. 1-8). I disclaim any authority as a music historian, but it would seem to me that the influence of this dulcet-toned instrument on America's musical development is a subject crying for detailed study by someone.

Notes For Chapter One

1. H.F. Milne. *The Reed Organ. its Design and Construction.* London. 1930. p. 10.

2, 3, 4. *The Musical Courier.* Oct. 15, 1884. quoted in *The American Reed Organ* by Robert Gellerman. Vestal Press, Vestal, N.Y., 1973., p., 5, 7, 9.

Chapter 2
Terminology

The reed organ is really not an extremely complicated piece of machinery though there are some rather specialized terms which apply to some parts of it. To make matters muddy, the few texts in existence often use differing terms to apply to the same mechanism or function. This brief glossary is intended to clear up such problems. When more than one term is in use, the first term of the definition will be the one ordinarily used in this book.

> **beat note**—When two notes are sounded continuously, unless they are an exact octave apart, a *beat note* will be heard. This refers to the faint but distinct rising and falling of sound intensity that will vary in exact proportion to the harmonic relationship of the notes. A full discussion of the definition of many terms associated with *beat note* would take too long, so check the chapter on tuning for a bit more discussion. It is sufficient to say here that if the *beat note* frequency is not correct for a given combination of notes, the organ is out of tune.

> **concert pitch**—This refers to the American standard tuning pitch which dictates that the note of A above middle C should vibrate exactly 440 cycles per second. Since this standard came to be established long after reed organs were already a fixture in musical America, many organs were tuned to other standards. Commonly you can expect to find A435 (lower than

concert pitch) and A452 (higher than concert pitch) in organs. This is why many organs cannot be played in tune with a piano or with any other instrument that cannot be tuned considerably off concert pitch.

coupler—This is a mechanism that connects two notes together so that when the lower of two octave notes in the upper half of the keyboard is sounded, the octave above it sounds also. In the lower part (bass), it operates the opposite way: when the upper of the two notes is played, the octave below sounds also.

cypher—This is a very irritating condition in which a note sounds when it is not supposed to. It may sound all the time that the organ is being pumped whether any key is depressed or not, or it may only sound when a nearby note is played.

exhauster—Also known as pump bellows, feeder bellows, and suction pump.[1] The exhausters are the portion of the bellows directly connected to the pedals (usually two). Their job is to draw air out of the main bellows, thus creating the partial vacuum on which the organ operates (Fig. 2-1).

guide pins—These are mainly to be found in two important locations. Each key on the keyboard has two guide pins: a round one at the rear which goes all the way through the key and is designed to allow the

Fig. 2-1. Typical exhauster bellows.

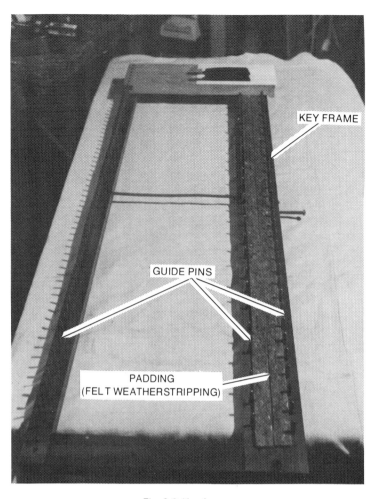

Fig. 2-2. Key frame.

key to pivot up and down but not sideways. Then at the front of the key is a larger guide pin, oval in cross section (well, not always), which goes up inside the key (but not through it) in a felt-lined opening (earlier organs may not have the felt.) Again, this permits free up-and-down motion but not side-to-side. Similar functioning pins (though smaller) are found under the reed pan where they perform the same functions for each pallet.

harmonics—This complicated term is well-known to musicians and mathematicians but difficult to explain.

Basically it refers to the fact that any vibrating element produces not only its fundamental frequency but, under many circumstances, produces also fractional multiples of its fundamental. An under standing of how harmonics "beat" together is necessary for anyone wishing to tune an organ.

key frame—This is the wooden structure which holds the keys. It must be free of warps, its guide pins firmly set, clean, and perfectly vertical (Fig. 2-2).

keyslip—This is the panel, frequently with cloth-backed cut-outs, that is positioned directly below the keyboard. Its removal is usually necessary for one to have access to the front rank of reeds.

mutes—These are the spring-loaded pieces (usually triangular in cross section) which seal the reed cells for a given group of reeds. When the mute is shut (as it normally is when a given stop is pushed in), no reed in any cell it closes should sound even if the key associ ted with it is depressed. In Fig. 2-3 the mute is still installed. Figure 11-10 in Chapter 11 shows an organ thats mutes and reeds have been removed to show the reed cells.

octave—Notes exactly twelve half-steps apart are said to be an octave apart. In practice these always have the same key designation (such as C, A, etc.) Some

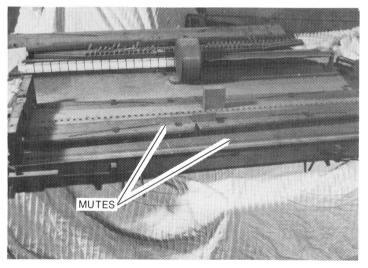

Fig. 2-3. Packard action, unrestored and partially disassembled, showing mutes.

writers[2] will describe the octave relationship by starting with the octave beginning with middle C and designating each related octave with a numeral (thus middle C is C1) the octave above it being C2, the octave below it being tenor C, the octave below that being CC.

pallet—Also called the reed valve. See Figs. 11-13 and 11-14 in Chapter 11 for a full set of pallets. This is a piece of wood approximately six inches long (the size varies) which covers the reed opening under the reed pan. In the standard organ each pallet covers two reed openings, each reed tuned to the same note and controlled by the same key. Pallets are usually covered by a layer of felt and then by a layer of soft leather. When a spring pushes this leather covered piece snugly against the openings to the reed cells, no air can be drawn through the reed.

pitman—Also called push pin, plunger, sticker, pallet rod, and tracker pin. Organs with octave couplers have two kinds of pitmans: one that is simply a straight dowel and one that has an additional small section of a much larger dowel (usually about 1/2-inch diameter) glued on it about a third of the way from the top. This larger dowel section is called the *coupler collar* and has a circular piece of felt on it that is exactly the same diameter as the collar. The pitman is the connecting rod between the organ key and the pallet. When the key is depressed, it pushes the pitman down causing the pallet to open, allowing air to be drawn through the reed. The coupler collar is the connection to the pitman for the octave coupler, enabling the player to depress a single key but have two notes of the same octave to sound.

reeds—These are the brass pieces that vibrate when air passes over them causing them to sound (Fig. 2-4). They are more fully described in the section on tuning. The part of the reed frame nearest to the outside opening of the cell it is inserted in is called the *heel*. It also contains the shallow slot in which a *reed hook* is inserted in order to pull the reed from its cell. The front (usually rounded) is called the *toe* and the vibrating part is called the *tongue*.

reed cell—This is the small opening in the block of wood mounted on the floor of the reed pan in which the reed is inserted. This block of wood *must* be very securely fastened to the bellows platform, and must be completely airtight as any leaks here drastically affect the operation of the organ.

reed pan—Also called the reed chest or sound board. This is the shallow box made like an inverted pan (hence the name) on which the reed cells sit.

registers—This refers to specific groups of reeds such as treble (high pitch) and bass (low pitch.) Usually a single mute controls all the reeds in a given register; this is not true, however, with organs having four complete sets of reeds (such as the Windsor later referred to). These will have several registers of a given range of notes.

springs—Certainly a common term, but it is listed here because the restorer needs to know that an organ contains quite a variety of springs. The most powerful are those inside the main bellows (though they are sometimes located outside). These may be made of quarter-inch brass spring rod or of flat, curved springs that look like inside-measuring calipers. Other springs control the pallets; a different type yet controls the mutes (it acts like a miniature torsion bar); and

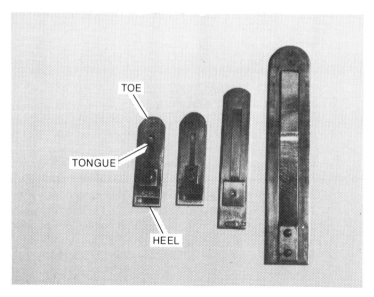

Fig. 2-4. Reeds: one-rivet, two-rivet, melodeon, sub-bass (reading left to right)

springs similar to the old screen-door spring even get into the act (in the piano organ, for instance). Since springs often break and drop off their original position, the restorer should be well aware of the many varieties and their uses so that he can infer what kind might have been used where, in case something obviously is missing or cobbled up.

swell—This is usually a hinged, flat panel that covers the entire front or back set of reeds. Its main function is that of volume control.

temperament—This is a term used in tuning. When the temperament is properly set, the instrument is in tune.

tremulo—See vox humana.

valves—The term applies to any device specifically controlling the air supply to any part of the organ. *Main chest valves* control the air drawn out of the main bellows (or chest); *exhauster valves* control air drawn out of the exhauster or pump bellows; *pallet valves* control air to individual reeds; the *relief valve* is a safety device on the main bellows which allows air to be admitted to the main bellows if it is pumped up too tightly, thus endangering the seals at any point where too much suction might cause the bellows to tear loose.

vox humana—This means "human voice" and describes the function which causes the tone of a rank (or two) or treble reeds to waver somewhat like the vibrato of the human singing voice. *Tremulo* is another name often used for the same function, though the two terms are usually applied to different types of mechanisms.

Notes For Chapter Two

1. I have chosen to stay with *exhauster* as the term for the bellows part that is directly attached to the pedals since it is the one used by both Milne and Gellerman. I see some advantage in trying for some uniformity. However, John Kejr strongly prefers *suction pump* for the following reason: "The Player Piano is a vacuum-operated instrument in which the bellows pumps become *exhausters* with the intent that the atmospheric balance in the pneumatics be destroyed so that gravity immediately and rapidly snaps shut the pneumatic without further help from some other mechanical device, and activates the pneumatic with its linkage to the strings of the piano as rapidly as the traveling valve (the music roll), with its perforations, mates with the perforations on the tracker bar. The pump organ is a suction-operated instrument. The suction pump together with the spring-operated reservoir sucks the air through the reed as the pallet valve is opened by the mechanical device of the key operated by the human finger, thus sounding the reed."
2. Milne, p. 19.

Chapter 3
Finding and
Buying an Organ

The easiest means of getting an organ is, of course, to find one stashed in some relative's back room when he wants it out. Most organs are not particularly small. They do take up room, and can be smelly old vermin attractors. They clutter up that back bedroom, the basement, barn, or even the chicken-house. A few years ago all you had to do was to hear of one so located and you were welcomed with open arms if you offered to take the thing off the relatives' hands. Not so today.

SOURCES

The antique market has so raised people's consciousness of the value of old items that few giveaways can be found now. Even if you are offered one by a relative, I would go so far as to suggest that you make a discreet search to be sure that someone who might inherit the thing is not going to be upset to find that you have it. A little precaution here can save much unpleasantness later.

Antique Dealers

Barring such easy sources, you are going to have to look elsewhere. The easiest place to start with is your local antique shop. At least at this writing, many shops, particularly those country shops specializing in original-condition furniture, will have unrestored organs; some will have several. A typical one is shown in Fig. 3-1, which was taken recently in a local shop. A factor affecting your quest will be the part of the country

Fig. 3-1. Unrestored organ in Main Street Antiques, Ottawa, KS.

where you are searching. Stores in western states are less likely to have organs than are those in mid-western or eastern states since the former were settled after the heyday of the parlor organ. Those you may find in western shops have been shipped in, and the price usually reflects the trouble the dealer had in getting the thing.

I might mention the interesting practice of dealers who try to latch onto some item that lends class to the shop, then put such an impossible price on it that there is no chance of its being sold. Sometimes that item is an organ. I know of a particularly striking organ, unrestored, that had a price on it seven years ago of $550—a price I thought at the time to be absurd. Recently I was in the same shop and noted that the price is now $1850. I have a hunch that the price would rise still higher if I tried to buy it. Unless you have unlimited funds and just must have that particular organ, forget it.

Better be aware of a fact of life concerning antique dealers: They most often learn their trade by the grapevine, and get prices by nosing through other dealers' shops or by reading *The Antique Trader*. As a result, some dealers see a fantastic price on an organ in Joe's Antiques, note with horror that they have a much lower price on that one they just got at a farm auction, and run home to raise the price. Now this doesn't hold for all dealers; I have some very good friends who have a fixed policy of selling at a fair mark-up regardless of how low their purchase price was. In such shops you can often find an organ at a very reasonable price. Even here you should try to do some bargaining, particularly if you know that the organ has been taking up valuable space for some time. Recently I had a dealer urge me to make him an offer on a real monster: artificial pipes rising over eight feet, and all that. I didn't do so, afraid he'd accept. He wanted it out. The organ had no price on it anywhere (a practice I am suspicious of in any shop) so I don't know where he started his price from. The same dealer had a Packard in very poor shape. It was minus the top, stop faces gone, evidence of severe weather and vermin damage, with a price clearly marked at about five times what I had paid a few months before for another make in similar condition.

If you make regular rounds of antique shops, as I do, you soon will get to know dealers and their stock so you can have an idea of what might be available. Conversely, the dealers can get to know you and might be able to get an organ for you. Some dealers are reluctant to buy poor-condition antiques since they tend to sit in the shop tying up capital and space, but they would be willing to keep on the look-out for something for you.

Private Owners

If you are actively searching for organs, the word has a way of getting around; therefore private owners might be your best bet. I have a habit of talking about my hobby (my wife says that must mean that I have a heck of a lot of hobbies!) and this talkativeness has led me to some reed organs. Not long ago I was at a banquet at the college where I teach (English), and many non-college guests were present. I got into a discussion about antiques with the person on my right and soon, as you might imagine, we were discussing organs. The people across the table broke in to ask if I wanted to buy an organ in poor condition; they wanted to get rid of one that was cluttering up the back porch. I bought it the next week. (It is one of the two organs I am leaning on in the book's first photo.)

Don't be afraid to let people know that you are in the market. The antique grapevine is very efficient. Frequently dealers are very helpful here. They may not wish to buy a given organ, knowing that it may not be exactly what you want, but they will tell a seller that you are in the market. A note posted on a bulletin board in a dealer's shop may also pay off.

A note of caution about buying from anyone: Except in the rare instance when the seller really knows the history of the organ, owners know only what they have been told. Their information on dating, condition, previous restoration, all may be correct—or totally and honestly wrong. *Always* make your own independent judgments about condition and value. Of course, if you buy a very high-priced organ that is said to be in perfect condition, you can insist on having that in writing with a buy-back agreement within a specified period. This book is written for those buying less-than-perfect organs that need tender loving care; you should keep in mind that once you buy it, all of its problems are yours alone, regardless of what you have been told.

Auctions

Auction sales are another prime source for finding organs. Here the condition of the organ case is of considerable influence on the price it will bring. An organ in obviously poor condition may just be a tremendous bargain for you. An organ that looks good but needs all sorts of work internally may sell for a ridiculously high price. Also, the whim of the auction crowd is a major factor. The important thing is that you should keep an eye on auction notices and attempt to arrive on the scene early enough to do a thorough job of personally inspecting the organ well before the auction begins. You should do so without letting those with financial interests in the sale know you really are serious. (I have had dealers run up bids against me when they were actually the ones trying to sell through the auction.)

There are times when you may be permitted to see the organ before auction day. If you can't be at the auction, you may be allowed to leave a bid. Take your time; think about the organ; make good use of the suggestions in this chapter. Be sure that you are able to live with the price if you are the successful bidder, or live with yourself if you don't get it.

A final word about auctions: Consider the problems of getting the thing home immediately after the auction. Some auctioneers can make arrangements for reasonably priced hauling for successful bidders. You might be able to disassemble it enough to get into the back seat and trunk of a large car, but I doubt it. Even if you could, I don't recommend it, as such action would be an easy way to lose parts.

Other Sources

Don't be afraid to contact collectors in your area if you know of any. They might have some organs they purchased years ago with ideas of restoration, but no longer want to go to the trouble. They also might know where organs are. Frequently I have people call me, wanting to sell. Not being in the business, I just can't afford to take all those that are good buys. I keep a list for a while of those people who want to sell, just in case I can pass the good word on.

Ads in area papers can also be useful in locating organs, both those ads you put in and those others insert. I frequently see such ads in the *Kansas City Star*. Classified ads in antique journals are also possible sources. In our area it has become fashionable for even supermarkets to have bulletin boards for free use by patrons. Your notice placed there certainly can't hurt. In all of these ads, try to be as general as possible unless, of course, you are looking for a particular organ or one within a given price range.

PRICE

You may have noticed that so far I have said nothing concerning what you should have to pay. It is impossible for me to indicate, even in the broadest terms, what a fair price should be. I hope that this book will be useful for several years, and antique prices have a habit of becoming outdated quite rapidly. Further, the price I think is reasonable might not appear so to you. Then, the condition of any organ is such a decisive factor that two organs looking almost identical may have real values quite far apart. Thus, do your homework: Check the organ carefully, know exactly how much money you have available for the restoration process as well as the initial purchase price, then be prepared to stick to your decision.

Price Guides

What about price guides? I have found the published antique price guides almost useless. Of course, if you find an organ for $25 and you know that all the guides show prices of over $200, you know that you have a bargain; but you didn't need a guide to tell you that.

The main thing to know is that often dealers use those guides as benchmarks for setting their own prices. If you occasionally check one of the lists you will know what to expect as a minimum in the shops. I might add that these publications are the one area I have found where the price guides are generally low. Of course, the guides are supposed to reflect actual prices paid rather than prices asked—all of which means, don't hesitate to dicker with a dealer.

Private Owners

Probably the most sensitive problem is that of establishing a price with a private owner who knows nothing of antiques (or, worse, thinks he knows it all), and who has been told that he has a priceless organ. I have seen prices of over $1000 on instruments I would not pay a small fraction of that for. When such an outlandish price is asked of you, your only real response is, "It's really a fine organ," followed by a graceful decision, reluctantly rendered of course, not to buy just now. Above all, don't try to convince the owner that he is out of line. Every time I have opened my big mouth to educate such a person, I have just convinced him that I am a con man out to steal his gold mine.

The same holds true when the owner refuses to quote a price but asks me to do so. I have really insulted people by offering a realistic price when they were secretly sure that the organ was rare and valuable. I have simply stopped offering a price. If the owner wants to sell, it is up to him to set the price. If the organ really fascinates you and you just must make an offer, better make it as high as you really know you can go, or reasonably close, and hope that you don't get into trouble.

Playing Condition

An additional problem: if the organ will wheeze and play at all with furious pumping, that usually makes the average owner consider it to be in perfect condition. He won't believe you when you say that it still needs a lot of interior work. Recently I tried playing one in a shop—the organ had a $1000 price tag—only to find that the bellows was in very poor condition. The case was not bad, though one lamp bracket was missing, and the stopboard had not been touched. The shop owner assured me that it was in perfect condition, having just had an expensive restoration. I don't want to know by whom.

Intended Purpose

A final consideration: Why are you buying? If strictly personal hobby interests are at stake, your resources and the challenge the instrument presents are the only considerations. Buy what you want. The more problems it has, the more fun you have fixing them. The Cornish in Fig. 3-2 needed *everything*. Furthermore, the completed organ can grace your living room as evidence of your skill, a working hobby that returns fun with living music as well as visual enjoyment.

If you are buying for resale, you must decide if you want to be able to make a fair return for your hourly labor, or just enough to make your hobby self-supporting. In either case, you must do much more thorough checking before buying so that you can estimate just what will be involved in terms of time and materials—or even if the organ is restorable at all. If word gets around that you restore organs, you will undoubtedly have requests to do such work for others (more on that later). For now, however, I strongly urge that you do *not* make your first attempt at restoration a job whose product is intended for someone else—good way to ruin a beautiful friendship. Recently a local dealer asked me to restore a player piano for her. I want to try such a job sometime, but not for someone else the first time. Be sure you know what you're getting into before going into the business.

EVALUATING ORGAN CONDITION

Some decisions on buying organs are easy: the thing is so high-priced that there's no way you're going to get it. Or, the owner wants to get rid of the thing so he gives it to you, or nearly so, and it's worth what you pay if only for parts. Few decisions are that easy. Following is a checklist for evaluating condition and restorability. If you can't do what you intend with it, it's no bargain at any price.

Fig. 3-2. Cornish, 1904, now owned by Mr. & Mrs. Keith McAdoo, Ottawa, KS.

Condition of the Case

First, but by no means most important, is the condition of the case. I say this is less important simply because a badly damaged case can be restored in almost amazing fashion.

Other less obvious problems pose more difficulties. A good share of my fun has come from taking a gunked up hunk of wood and making it into something that shines in the living room. You do, however, need to make sure that you can do whatever is needed to repair the case.

First, check to make sure that all parts are present. Even if the parts are in virtually unusable shape, they can be models for reproduction. Here you must keep in mind your capabilities. If major wood turnings are missing and you have no lathe, or no access to one, you had better pass up the organ. Even here, though, you may have an out. In my community the high school offers courses in adult education (I took welding) and wood-working is commonly taught. In such courses you can learn to do almost any woodwork an organ needs.

Be particularly alert for major sections that are missing. Many organs had a large canopy top. If so, you will probably find a slot about 1 × 1 inches all across the back of the top of the main case. The canopy top extended down into this slot for stability. If the canopy is missing you can still probably restore the organ and fill in the slot with wood like the rest of the case. The organ will then appear like a cottage style which didn't have the canopy in the first place. You need to know, however, that an organ so restored is not as valuable on the antique market as is one that is reasonably complete. Other organs show evidence of having had something on top (such as a railing or some low carvings) that is now gone. Here you may be able to find something in a book like *Michel's Organ Atlas* to guide you in reproducing the missing part. Be careful, though, of buying organs without the top when the top contained the music rack. In such an event you must depart even further from the original appearance of the organ to come up with something that will make the instrument serviceable.

Check very carefully for evidence of screw holes in peculiar places on the case. This usually indicates that something was there but is long gone. Often the handles at the side are gone. Before deciding that handles have been removed, make sure that screw holes or outlines in old varnish indicate they originally were there. Some organs did not have the side handles. If pieces of decoration, carvings, and the like, are missing, does there seem to be a counterpart somewhere else on the organ that you can use as a pattern? If not, can you deduce from an outline in the old varnish what the missing part probably looked like?

Check the entire case, including the back, very carefully for loosening glue joints, warps, and rot. Particularly check the feet of the organ since often they have been sitting for years in damp places. You may have to replace a lot of wood. Check all veneers: are they lifting or bubbled up? Are pieces gone? All of these problems can be solved to a degree, but veneers are particularly hard to piece and match. If the organ seems to have a recent coat of finish (usually hastily slapped on), but has places that are quite dark, be suspicious of large rot spots that have been plugged with plastic wood then deliberately crudded over to mask the stuff. (I know of a wholesale furniture dealer who will do this.)

Condition of the Playing Action

Now for the action. Again, are all parts present? Can you work all the stops and determine what each does? If not, can you figure out what may be missing? This particular little job is one difficult to do in a short time unless you have restored several organs and know exactly what to look for—but in that case, you probably won't be reading this book. Anyway, here is where you often must make some snap judgments without hard-and-fast guidelines. If you pay a stiff price for a nice case but just can't get things hooked up so it will play, you're in real trouble. Better be reasonably sure of what needs to be replaced. Use a flashlight and probe into the case as well as you can, checking at the sides of the action to see what's what with the connecting shafts between the mutes, swells, and stops. Are they all there? Can you figure what was supposed to be connected?

Always have a screwdriver with you (doesn't everyone?) so that you can remove the keyslip under the front of the keyboard. Put something under the swell and the mute so that you can see the reeds. Using a flashlight, examine each reed as much as possible. By far the best approach is for you to pull each reed and examine it. Cracks that can make a reed unusable are almost invisible except close up. Realistically, few people have time to pull all reeds or even have the reed hook available if they did. If you don't, though, be advised that you run a real risk of having some cracked or otherwise unusable reeds. New ones are expensive, if even available. So—check as far as you can and have fervent hope. Do the same for the rear rank(s) of reeds though here the problem is even greater, You can't get as close for examination as you can to the front rank and, seriously, you run the risk of running into little beasties. I once opened the back of an organ only to have a whole family of mice jump out. Check into special boxes on the rear (Fig. 3-3); they may hold extra ranks of reeds.

While looking at reeds, check the condition of the reed cells. Any cracks? Check where the cell block is glued to the reed pan. Any sign of separation? If so, that poses a very ticklish and time-consuming repair job though by no means impossible. Any evidence of vermin damage to the cells? Just having a lot of insect nests in the cells may not be damaging. In fact, one organ I got was full of mud dauber's nests, but was in beautiful interior condition otherwise. The insects had kept moths and mice and everything else out!

Water damage is another matter. If there is evidence of warping be sure you can correct it. Also, if water has been standing inside the reed cells it has probably ruined a number of reeds: that means trouble. Water can also go through the finish and damage wood to the extent that more than stripping

Fig. 3-3. Unrestored Hunt organ action, box removed from sub-bass.

will be necessary if the case is to look like anything. If you know what to do and have the time, go to it.

Stop faces frequently are missing. If even one is gone, be prepared to replace the whole set. New ones are available but in a very limited style. I have had the fantastic luck of matching a set of irreplaceable ceramic stop faces, but don't you plan on doing likewise. Before deciding that you must replace them, however, look very carefully down inside the organ and all around the floor where it has been sitting for years to see if you can find the one or two that have dropped off. While the keyslip is off, check to see if anything has dropped down between the keys. You just may find them and rejoice.

Keep notes of all of these points plus any others that may occur to you. If possible, take some time to mull over the implications of what you found before you finally decide. I am much too prone to make snap judgements for my own good; know your own weaknesses and take proper precautions.

OK, so you got one, maybe even in spite of your better judgment. Welcome to the club. Now follows, I hope, what you need to know to do something with it. Take your time. You have a lot of enjoyment ahead.

Chapter 4
Principles of Organ Operation

It is important that a restorer know certain information about how an organ operates so that he can deduce what might be needed to replace a missing part on an organ he buys. Often all he has to know is just what a desired operation is or how parts are supposed to perform. With that information he can remake the part or even improve on its operation. The following section will detail not only the main principles of organ operation, which are really quite simple, but describe some actual organ actions that accomplish the same task in a variety of ways.

THE REED

The reed itself is just a small brass frame with a tuned, flexible brass strip that can vibrate when air is moved nearby it. When a key is depressed, a pitman pushes down on a pallet below the opening in which the reed is placed. When the pallet is open, vacuum in the main bellows causes air to be drawn through the reed, causing it to sound. Figure 2-4 showed typical reeds from both organs and melodeons. Figure 4-1 shows typical keyboard action. The key must move without binding either at the front or rear guide pins; the pitman must fit smoothly in the hole that goes through the reed cell block without binding; and the pallet must fit snugly up against the opening in the bottom of the reed cell, securely sealing it off from any air. It must also move smoothly without binding

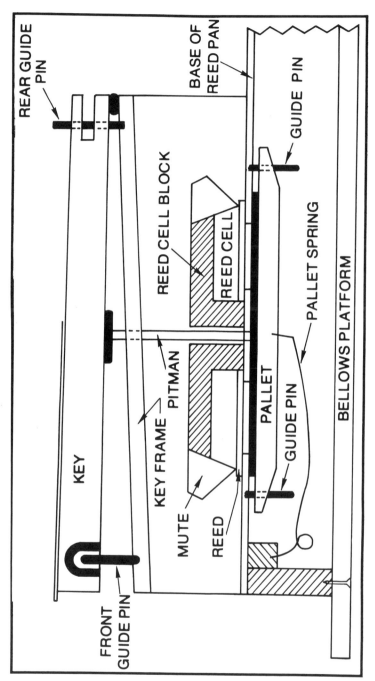

Fig. 4-1. Principles of keyboard action.

44

either on the two guide pins at either end or against pallets on each side. While this operation is really quite simple, there are, in fact eight points relevant to *each note* where binding can take place and cause trouble.

THE STOP

The term *stop* might better be called *opener* since its main function is that of opening various mutes and swells in order to allow a particular rank of reeds to sound, or to combine ranks, or to modify the amount of air drawn through a given rank. Various organ books distinguish between *speaking stops*—those that actually control air to any rank of reeds—and *mechanical stops*, which are secondary controls (such as the vox humana and the swells.)

The function of the stop is simple. It mechanically provides a linkage from the pull above the keyboard to the desired function element. But the means of accomplishing that job may vary widely. Differing styles of linkages are illustrated in Figs. 4-2,4-3, and 4-4. You may expect to find numerous other styles as you rummage around in the innards of these things since this seems to have been one way a given manufacturer justified his attempt to sell his organs, or, more likely, the only way he could get into the business without facing a patent infringement suit. It is not likely that you will find a totally destroyed stopboard, so if enough of it exists for

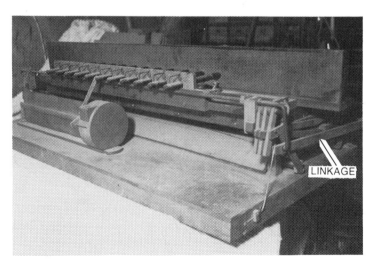

Fig. 4-2. Unrestored Packard action, rear view.

45

Fig. 4-3. Restored Cornish action, rear view.

you to know how one or two stops operate, you can figure out the rest.

THE GREAT SWELL

"Great Swell" or "Grand Organ" are terms given to the mechanism that literally "pulls out all the stops" of the organ.

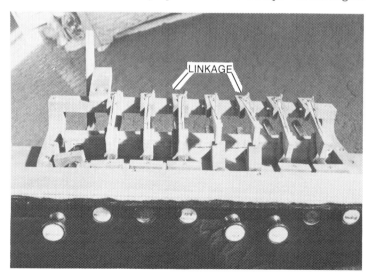

Fig. 4-4. Unrestored New England Organ stopboard, bottom view.

(Vox humanas are usually excepted.) The principle is simple: Arrange a mechanism by which any stops that are not pulled out initially are effectively brought into play. For instance, in Fig. 4-5 the function is performed by the left knee swell which connects to a rod that activates the block shown. Note that all

Fig. 4-5. Typical ''great swell'' mechanism, unrestored.

of the shafts on the floor of the rear of the stopboard have a cam-like bend in them near the side of the stopboard. When the knee pedal is pressed, the block of wood presses down on all of those raised cams and uniformly depresses them, effectively activating all stops on that side. A similar arrangement controls stops on the other side of the stopboard. These two mechanisms must be linked together if a full "great" is to be achieved, and often a restorer will find that the wood or metal shaft linking the two is missing. If you know that they must be connected, you can probably devise a substitute. This feature is common on the standard organs from roughly 1880; these organs have two knee swells. Those having only one knee pedal either do not have a "great" pedal or accomplish the job with a stop on the stopboard.

Organs having a vibrato have a means of varying the air supply to the treble reeds. If it is a vox humana of the rotating-vane type (Figs. 4-2 and 4-3), only the rear rank of reeds is affected. If it is of the tremulo type, involving a weighted spring inside a box (See Fig. 11-7 in Chapter 11) it will work on all treble reeds. While these will be treated in detail later, it is necessary now to point out that openings at the rear center or at a rear corner of the reed pan are usually there to accommodate some kind of vibrato. If the mechanism is missing, you can still restore the organ to full playing condition (though without the vibrato) by sealing off the openings. More on this later.

THE MUTES

The mutes control which reeds can sound when a key is depressed. Usually, a given key can be affected by the operation of at least two mutes. The tone of the note will be determined by the number of mutes open and, therefore, the number of reeds sounding when each key is played. Some stops open a mute only very slightly in order to give a very soft tone while others open it fully. Since wear and tear and other problems can alter the exact degree to which a mute opens, this operation is one that is frequently out of adjustment. Also note that the mute must *completely* seal *all* reed cells under it. If not, when a key is played you will hear a cypher from the rank of reeds not completely sealed. In some cases this may cause little difficulty because the notes in front and back will be in tune with each other, and a slight tone modification may not be objectionable. In other cases such as when one rank is a voix celeste, the other rank is tuned two or three cycles differently and the result is a real dissonance if the wrong one sounds. This is one part of restoration where you cannot settle for a half-way job; those mutes must fit well.

THE SWELLS

The swells are volume controls and the usual organ has two: one in front and one in back, running the full length of the keyboard. When the swell is shut the reed will still sound (if its associated mute is open, that is) but its volume will increase when the swell is open.

Unlike the mute, the swell does not need to seal the reeds under it completely; indeed, it shouldn't. Some sound needs to escape when the swell is closed, and air must be available to supply the reeds. Consequently, don't worry when you find some gaps at the end of each swell, for example. In some organs the swells are individually controlled by stops but in others they are operated entirely from the right knee swell. In the piano organ there is no front control of the swell at all; it is mechanically connected to the bellows in such a manner that when the bellows is pumped up at least half way, the swells open automatically.

THE OCTAVE COUPLER

The *octave coupler* is a very common device that, when activated, enables two notes an octave apart to sound simultaneously when a given note is played. It was described in some detail in Chapter 2. It is sufficient to mention here that the coupler requires some means of raising and lowering the coupler table so that it can be brought into operation. In some cases there is a U-shaped bend in a long rod extending to the side of the action; the bend is so positioned under the coupler table that when the rod is rotated a few degrees, the "U" raises the coupler table the necessary amount for activation. In other actions, a wedge-shaped block of wood is so positioned under the table that when it is pulled straight back (when the coupler stop is pulled out) it wedges under the table, raising it the needed amount.

Couplers can cause real difficulties if they are not adjusted rather precisely. While the photos in the book show the type most commonly used, there are many other types serving the same function. Here again, a coupler is not an absolute necessity for organ operation. If yours is simply falling apart and cannot be repaired, just remove it (keeping it, of course) and restore the rest of the organ. Some day you might be able

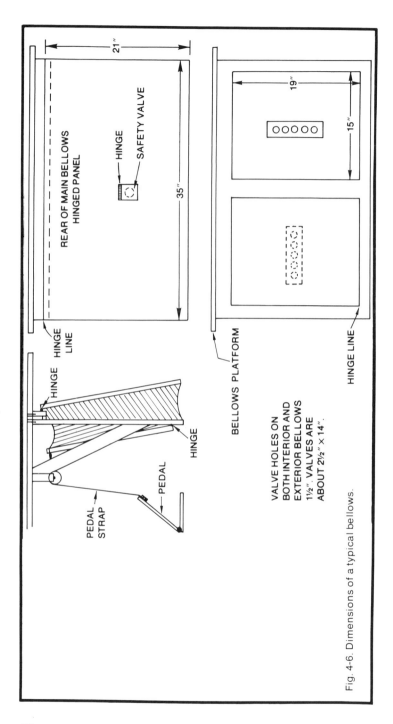

Fig. 4-6. Dimensions of a typical bellows.

50

to go the rest of the way either with another one or with the original you finally figured out how to restore.

THE BELLOWS

The term *bellows* is a misnomer because it usually signifies a blower of sorts. Indeed, in the European organ and in a few made in this country, reed organs were made which operated from a pressure bellows; often the name *harmonium* applies to such organs, though I have heard it applied to the suction organ as well. The vast majority of American organs made since 1846 operate on the suction principle, giving a mellower, though softer, tone than is characteristic of the European harmonium. The bellows consists of two main parts: the main vacuum reservoir and the exhauster bellows that are activated by the foot pedals. Figure 4-6 shows the essential features of the usual bellows. As the foot-pedal is depressed, the exhauster is drawn out, causing the exhauster valve to close and the inside valve to open. This action allows air to be drawn out of the reservoir. When the pedal is released, a spring forces the exhauster back against the reservoir; the valve on the reservoir closes, thus retaining the vacuum it has, and the valve on the outside of the exhauster opens allowing the air it has drawn out of the main reservoir to escape. Now the cycle is ready to be repeated.

While you will have to determine the exact dimensions needed for your organ in case a bellows is missing, Fig. 4-6 plus the photos in the bellows restoration section in Chapter 10 ought to be enough for you to be able to make a new one. It is not uncommon to find old organs with nothing but the bellows platform remaining below the action, with a hole cut in that for the insertion of the hose from a vacuum cleaner which functioned as a source of vacuum. (What a sound combination that must have made! I was told by a friend just a few days ago that forty years ago he did this to an organ but kept the vacuum cleaner in the *basement* and ran a hose through the floor to the organ in order to avoid the noise. I still don't recommend it.)

These principles of operation are remarkably uniform for American organs. It is a measure of manufacturing ingenuity (or deception?) that so many different mechanisms were devised to accomplish such a simple operation.

Chapter 5
Dating Organs

Really, we should all be interested only in the quality of our organ regardless of when it was made. But let's face it, we are all eager to have "an old one" despite what that may mean to the performance of the organ. I am just as snobbish about it as anyone else, being very proud of the fact that the Prince I own may be one of the oldest organs in the country. So, your efforts to find the date and history of the organ you now own can be as rewarding as the restoration efforts themselves, and can influence your attitude during the restoration work.

Organ dates are sometimes difficult to determine. First, try to find out if your organ is listed in *Michel's Organ Atlas*. While this book has its limitations (some of the information is not accurate), it is the only such publication available at this time concerning organ types and serial numbers. The book lists hundreds of makes of organs though sometimes only the brand name is given. With many, however, the author gives serial numbers with approximate dates of manufacture, place, and a little history. Thus it is useful to know that the Crown organ was made by George Bent, an important manufacturer who made organs under many labels. Research concerning George Bent might tell you much about your Crown.

CATALOGUES

Reproduction catalogues from early mail-order houses are a real help. The houses sold organs by the thousands. I have restored two organs like those pictured in the 1902 Sears Roebuck catalogue and the piano organ whose restoration is described in some detail later is fully detailed in the Sears Catalogue of 1908 (Fig. 5-1). Both of these catalogues are available, at this writing, at nominal cost. I know also of some Wards reproductions, as well as publications reproducing early magazine ads. All of these could have some use for you.

Fig. 5-1. Page from a Beckwith ad in a 1908 Sears catalogue.

A caution: The fact that the picture of an organ may be in a given catalogue does not indicate the exact date of manufacture, just a close one. I don't know exactly when those models of organs first were sold by Sears or when they were changed. For instance, the Windsor occasionally referred to later in this book is pictured on a booklet put out by Sears (currently reproduced by Vestal Press) in 1910, but the organ itself has an internal date of 1914.

NEWSPAPERS AND MAGAZINES

Another source is that of newspapers and magazines from the period in question. If *Michel* said that the organ was made between 1875 and 1890, try to find magazines from that period that carry organ ads. Here many antique dealers can help. They frequently have stacks of old magazines you can browse through. Of course, your local library may be an invaluable source of old publications, possibly stacked in an attic where the general public just doesn't know of their existence. Be prepared to spend a lot of time leafing through musty pages, with every likelihood of coming up with nothing.

In particular, try to find magazines that you know were published in the area where the organs were manufactured or at least sold. Religious journals of the period would also be good since so many churches used these gems. One organ, the Epworth, was even named after the longtime youth group in the Methodist Church, the Epworth League.

DATES IN THE ORGAN

As you look over your purchase, be very careful to examine everything you find. Slips of crumpled paper may turn out to be sales tickets or other identifying aids. However, just finding a date on a piece of paper without further indication of significance may mean something as unrelated to dating as the fact that someone was trying to remember his wife's birthday.

Attached Dates

Dates attached to the organ are, of course, of much more significance. Even here you need to exercise caution. A dated card tacked to the inside of the case may indicate only when later work was done on it or when it was sold second-hand. Usually, however, repair dates will be so identified. A date located on the back of the action may be the date when the action was manufactured, not when the rest of the organ was built. The same holds for a date only on the case. Even so, you can assume that those dates are probably near what could be termed a manufacturing date.

Newspaper Scraps

Newspaper scraps that may have been used for patterns are of great help here. Inside the bellows of my Prince melodeon I found an apparent paper pattern made from uncut sheets of *The Western Literary Messenger*, including most of the date. It read "---mber 1847." Since the paper includes a poem dated October, 1847, I am assuming that this mutilated date is November or December, 1847. Even this doesn't prove that the organ was made in 1847; the paper is obviously scrap, so it might not have been used in this fashion for some time after it was printed. Thus, I am claiming very late 1847 or early 1848 as the date of probable manufacture.

A word here about such paper patterns that may be glued to a given surface. If you have the time and are interested, you may try soaking the paper *very* carefully in water and then trying to peel it off to see what's on the other side. Even if a printed date is not to be found, the stories you can find or other information might lead you to complete files of that paper so that you can then determine the date.

Pencilled Names and Dates

As you further disassemble your organ, watch very carefully for other pencilled names and dates. For instance, inside Turner's little Prince is the name G.V. and F.G. Schotte, Agents, of some town in Pennsylvania (Fig. 5-2). The latest patent date listed on the label beside the signature proves the earliest possible manufacturing date (Fig. 5-3). The Carhart Melodeon had the label of the original agent (Fig. 5-4) plus his signature (Fig. 5-5). Even though these names may mean nothing to you now, they might mean something later or you might find out from some historical society something about the person whose name appears. Many of the old towns in the east compiled very early city directories and you may be able to find out from them when these organ salesmen were in business. I follow the practice of copying all markings I find, even when they don't seem to make sense, particularly when they are in a location that will not be possible to get at again withoug taking things apart. Then I can look at the information later when I have reason to believe it might fit a piece in the puzzle.

Fig. 5-2. Signature inside the Prince of Fig. 1-3.

My most useful information has come from pencilled dates I have found on the raw wood on the upper back part of keys, the part normally covered by the stopboard of the standard parlor organ. For some reason, many organs have a date on about the tenth or eleventh key from the base side, though I recently found such a date faintly visible on the center key. This fact calls for a strong note of caution: *Don't* get in a lather to clean off the dirt that inevitably will be on that part of the

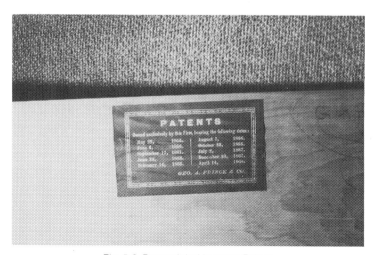

Fig. 5-3. Patent label in same Prince.

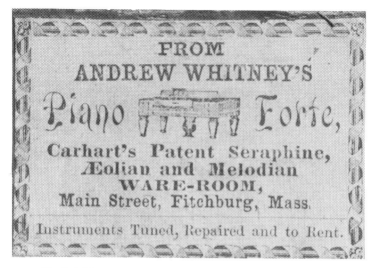

Fig. 5-4. Whitney label inside the Carhart pictured in Fig. 21-1.

keyboard when you remove the stopboard. You can easily destroy forever the only evidence of your organ's antiquity. *Carefully* wipe off the accumulated dirt with a soft, clean cloth. Examine each key in light that is as non-directional as possible so that reflections do not mask faint pencil lines. Wipe very lightly with just a damp cloth to take off the rest of the

Fig. 5-5. Whitney's signature.

surface dust. Again, examine each key. If you find something on one key, don't stop; there may be more on others. When you do find something, try to copy it, even if it doesn't make sense. Draw the lines exactly in relationship as they are on the key. You might then be able to figure out what connecting line has faded out and then, in true Sherlock tradition, fill in the missing data.

ORGAN MANUFACTURERS

Some companies that formerly made organs are still in existence, such as Mason and Hamlin. They may be able to help you date your instrument. In many public libraries you will find books giving dates of pianos; a date book about the piano built by a company that, in the early days, also built organs, might give you some help.

MUSEUMS

Increasingly, museums both public and private are accumulating extensive organ collections. If you know of these collections and can stop by, they might be able to help. In the midwest, the Miles Mountain Musical Museum of Eureka Springs, Arkansas is excellent. The Musical Museum of Deansboro, New York very graciously gave me information about my Prince and Eldredge melodeons some time ago when I found out that the museum had instruments similar to mine. A most authoritative source is the Smithsonian Institution of Washington, D.C., which has a superb collection and a fabulous restoration shop. If you happen to take the *Smithsonian* magazine (as I do— a beautiful publication) and are therefore a Smithsonian Associate, by all means take photos of you organ with you when you visit the Smithsonian. Ask to talk with the people in the musical instrument department of the Science and Industry section. They will treat you with the utmost consideration and be of very real help on many aspects of instrument history and restoration.

A note about writing for such information, particularly from private sources: Always enclose as much information as you can. Don't just ask "what date is my Crown organ" since that doesn't give the authority anything to work on. Enclose a good picture, give serial numbers, names you found in the instrument, the works. *Always* enclose a stamped, self-addressed envelope. People will be glad to help if they can do so very quickly, but don't expect them to do primary research for you.

HISTORICAL SOCIETIES

Local historical societies may be of help, particularly those in the vicinity of the original manufacturing plant. Again, don't expect them to do your research. Few such societies have full-time paid employees; their work is a labor of love so be considerate of their time. They may be able to give you only clues to where information might be found, but be grateful for that. If you want to go to some expense, you can at times buy microfilms of newspapers published in a given period. If you know for sure that your organ was made by a given company, you might try to find out if papers from the period are available for purchase or on interlibrary loan (or at least the microfilms; seldom are original paper files allowed out of the library.) Check with your local public or college librarian for possibilities here.

THE SELLER

Of course you should find out as much as possible from the person you bought your organ from, even if all he can say is that he bought it at an auction in Podunk. You can then sometimes check with the Podunk auctioneer who may know who brought it to the auction, who may know where he got it. I bought a Packard from a dealer who got it from another dealer who bought it at an auction of the estate of some people from Iola, Kansas. I wrote to them and found that some members of the family are still living and were willing to give me what little information they could about the organ. All I know at the present is that it came from Iowa sometime around WW I or before (that's my impression), but nothing more. In pursuing such leads you should be very aware of people's sensibilities here. They might not like to be reminded that sentimental family treasures had to be sold at auction. Don't insist on information if they are reticent. I sent a good color picture of the restored organ to its owner, mentioned how much I was enjoying it, and invited the lady to stop by and see it when she is in Ottawa. In this case I received a very gracious letter expressing her gratitude that the organ had fallen into friendly hands and a promise to come by sometime. I'm looking forward to her visit.

Don't make yourself obnoxious, but don't give up. Keep adding to your fund of knowledge about your instrument and you might be surprised what you can find out in years to come. You will also be pleasantly surprised to find out all the information you weren't looking for. Researching all I can find out about the antiques my wife and I have collected (we have more than reed organs—we're packrats) has led us to fascinating information we didn't suspect. That "child's warmer plate" we bought turned out to be made of Sheffield silver which is a fascinating story in itself. Such research can be a hobby within a hobby.

If you like to take vacations with a destination, try going to areas where organs were made. Someday I'd like to get to Cherry Valley, New York where a lot of melodeons seem to have been made, and to Brattleboro, Vermont, the home for years of the Estey Manufacturing Company. The Packard was made in Ft. Wayne, Indiana so I just might get there a bit quicker. At any rate, there are many locations where you might have a lot of fun. Use your ingenuity and go digging. Research can be a ball.

In the meantime, on to restoration work...

Chapter 6
Tools

The exact tools you will need to restore your organ depend, of course, on the extent of restoration necessary on your instrument. If much case work is to be done you will need power woodworking equipment plus a generous supply of bar clamps, "C" clamps, and handscrews. A number of small tools I have found useful, none expensive, are illustrated in Fig. 6-1. It may be well for you to make them available before getting underway. I will be describing them from left to right.

The first tool on the left is a very small, narrow-blade saw I got from Brookstone Tools. It is particularly useful in getting into very narrow spaces as you repair or reproduce carvings. It has replaceable blades, one of which I keep taped to the handle.

Next are two (from a set of five) inexpensive jeweler's screwdrivers which I picked up on a bargain counter of cheap tools. They are useful, of course, on some of the very small screws you may encounter, but also for cleaning out small areas such as the slots the reeds fit into.

Above the screwdrivers is a small (1 3/4 oz.) squeeze bottle of white glue. For a long while I used a larger bottle since I don't particularly like to fill glue bottles. However, I was forever cleaning up spills from the big nozzle. I find this little one much easier to manage.

Next is a reed hook which will be frequently mentioned later. These were always given to buyers with the organ when sold, but were easily lost. They are available very reasonably

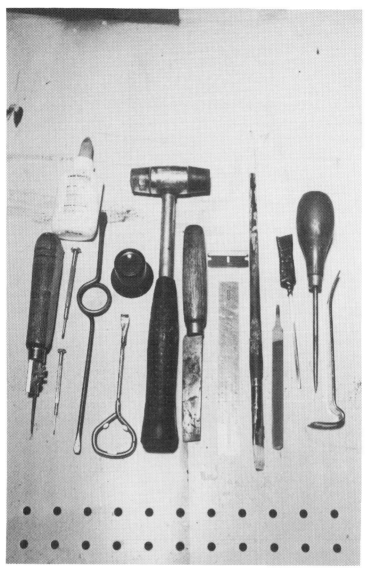

Fig. 6-1. Small tools useful in organ work.

from suppliers listed in the Appendix. Next to it is a common paint can opener which, I found, makes a beautiful reed hook for the melodeon reeds that have a bump at the rear for pulling (or require that you pull on the rivet holding the reed tongue). As is, the bent portion of the opener is not bent quite enough; you will need to put it in a vise and bend it exactly 90°. It then even *looks* remarkably like the reed hooks given with earlier organs (See Fig. 6-2).

Above the opener in Fig. 6-1 is an inexpensive, plastic jeweler's eye loup, available for about a dollar. I got this one from a large electronics supply company. Anyone working on printed circuits has to have one. It is very good for examining reeds, particularly the little ones.

The hammer, also a bargain table item, has both rubber and plastic faces. You will find many uses for this all the way from securing the bellows cloth to the bellows, to gently tapping the case in spots where you just can't run the risk of dents.

The flat-bladed knife is another Brookstone product, having a thin, very sharp blade. This is quite useful in trimming bellows cloth. Next is a metal, six-inch ruler with a slot (faintly visible at the bottom) which is calibrated for use as a wire gauge. It is useful in determining the size of wire springs.

Above the ruler is the familiar single-edged razor blade, absolutely perfect for cutting pallet leather and felt.

Next is the 1/2-inch flat bright oil painting brush that I use for applying contact cement to bellows cloth.

Then comes two cheap files (again from that gold mine, the cheap tool counter) which just happen to fit the slots in reed cells. Note that the end of the flat file has been ground to

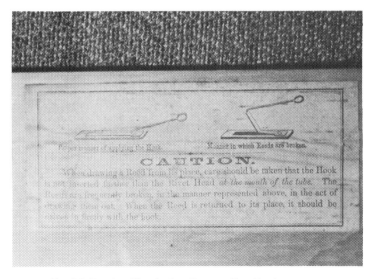

Fig. 6-2. Reed-pulling instructions on New England organ.

fit the rounded end of the reed cell. The narrow file next to it has been ground to a square cross section so that it is exactly the size of the slot in a reed cell.

Next is the awl. It is particularly useful in lining up screw holes when you are installing the action on the bellows platform.

Finally is the miniature prybar. I use that thing almost daily for everything from pulling tacks to smoothing down bellows cloth. It is one of my most useful tools.

A final tool mentioned by Walt recently: see your friendly doctor and ask for a throw-away hypodermic. It is very useful in getting glue into difficult areas.

Chapter 7

Logical Order of Restoration

It might seem that the way to go about restoring organs is simply to take things apart and start fixing; not so. All things being equal, there is a method, which I will shortly go into, that will make things much easier for you and minimize the problems a hobbyist is most likely to have. The point needing stress right now is that you should first determine what your most serious problem is going to be and solve that problem *first*, regardless of where it might ordinarily fit in the logical order of work. What doth it profit, my friend, for you to get half-way through a restoration only to find out to your horror that you can go no further? Thus, check the reeds very thoroughly before doing anything else; if many are bad you will want to get replacements from somewhere before investing time and money on an instrument that may never play.

Other problems can also arise. Are action parts missing? Can you reproduce them? Not only make sure you *can* reproduce them, better do so before you disassemble things. Are parts broken beyond your expertise? Be sure you can get them done by a competent craftsman, preferably having it done right then. Be warned that if large pieces of veneer are gone you might have to replace a whole panel. Are you sure that matching replacement veneer is available? Can you do the job well if it is? If special types of wood must be replaced, are you sure you can find them or ate least fabricate a reasonable facsimile? Making a copy can be done but it takes

Fig. 7-1. Packard carving in process of duplication with tools.

some tricky brush work at times. If major carvings or turnings are missing, can they be reproduced? The Packard featured in this book was minus a major carving and some turnings when purchased. It was that omission which made it possible for me to get the organ so reasonably in the first place. When I started restoration, the very first job I did was to reproduce that carving (Fig. 7-1). I knew that if I could do that job I could handle all the others. Even here, you may have some options. I had decided that if I just couldn't come up with an acceptable carving, I could design a simpler substitute that would do the job of holding up the mirror. I would, of course, keep the original carving that was present and would make no structural changes in order to install the replacement brackets. That way if I were able at a later date to reproduce the original, I could put things back. Well, the carving came out OK (after about 35 hours of work!) and I then proceeded with normal restoration.

After you have solved the most nagging problems you can proceed on a logical program. Subsequent chapters will detail the procedures for each step, but for now, let me give you an overview of the procedure.

After the organ has been disassembled as suggested in the next section, restore the case first. The reason for starting here is that unrestored parts tend to get scattered around, and old wood, with deteriorated finish, attracts moisture. When the case is done, put it in a safe place and cover it with plastic. Another reason: If you work on something else first, say the action, you run the risk of getting sawdust, paint overspray, etc., on the action while you finish other elements. With the case done, you can install each component as it is completed.

Next, then, would be the bellows. This should be immediately installed in the case, including pedals and pedal pads (unless you have not obtained the pedal pads and cloth for cut-outs. More of that in the chapter on the case.) If you install the bellows right away it not only protects the new fabric from possible punctures, but it also secures the bellows platform in its normal position, thus minimizing the possibility of warping. Next is the action, then the keyboard, finally the stopboard. As each is completed it is installed.

You might well alter the order because of the peculiar needs of your organ or, frankly, because of your own whims. After all, we are still talking about a hobby. Thus, while something is setting up on the bellows, you may want to work on that badly chipped stopboard. I have found, however, that such a haphazard procedure multiplies the individual parts that are scattered around the workshop at any given time, subsequently multiplying the chances of their getting lost. If you plan to work full-time on the job, you may not have trouble. If you are an average hobbyist you may take a year or more to complete a job. I actually took almost two years to complete the Packard, what with the various and sundry other projects that kept continually getting in the way. Believe me, in such a case, parts boxes can really crawl into the most unlikely places.

I strongly suggest using the order previously described. If you have reason to depart from it, by all means do so, but have a reason that is thoroughly thought out. Thorough anticipation of coming problems can make restoration a lot more fun.

Chapter 8

Disassembly Procedure

Hear the restorer's tale of woe:
Where the heck does THIS thing go?

Yes, I know that you are itching to get at that jewel you just rescued from the burning, but please, friend, go slow. There is a procedure for dissassembling the standard parlor organ that will save you manifold headaches. The approach will also work for other organs, but since you are most likely to be working with a relatively common type, that will be the focus of the first part on this book.

PREPARATION

If your shop is like mine, it is horrendous: stuff all around, other projects (assigned by you-know-who) stacked in various stages of completion. Restrain yourself and don't start on the organ until you have made some order of the chaos. I once spent some time rebuilding a part I was sure did not come with the original organ, only to find the same part some time later in a pile of other items. To prevent such agonizing experiences, clear a space for the organ work and reserve space for parts storage. Lay in a supply of boxes of various sizes plus several sizes of manila envelopes for small parts. Three-quarter inch masking tape will be useful many times in storing parts.

Drawings and Pictures

Decide at the outset *not* to trust your memory even though you are quite sure you are going to get the job done quickly. Even the simplest mechanism can be a fooler when you try to reassemble it after some weeks. Make a lot of measurements and drawings; have a Polaroid camera handy so you know you have the picture. Do *not* use scraps of paper for notes on drawings; they get lost too easily. Use a full-sized notebook. Don't worry about taking too many photos; take pictures from several angles, particularly of the stop action. Flash is not good for close-ups so have a photoflood handy. I keep two clipped to a rafter and find them easy to use without time loss.

Coding System

Devise some sort of coding system for the parts, envelopes, and boxes. Walt recommends marking parts using a system of two numbers; the first referring to the sub-assembly (e.g., keyboard), and the second referring to the order number in which the part was removed. Thus if the keyboard was assembly #5, the wooden keeper holding keys in, which would be removed first, would be labeled 5-1. You may also wish to add T for top, B for bottom, LS for left side, and so on. Harlan uses a system of small dots of white paint to indicate locations. Thus the first mute to be removed would have a dot; a matching dot would appear on the part the first one connects to. Two dots would appear on the next to be removed, and so on. This makes the parts permanently identifiable for reassembly.

Plan to make good use of masking tape to keep sets of screws and the like together. You should keep all sets of screws together after you remove them even though you know that some are so far gone that you will have to replace them. You need to know exactly what came from where. *Don't* put all screws in a box, thinking that you can always find the right one when you need it; believe me, you can't.

Cleaning

As you clean the organ before disassembling it, be very careful what you do with the dirt you take out. Sometimes you will take stuff out by the handful. Even so, sort carefully through the dirt and make sure no small part has fallen in it. Keep even slivers of wood since they may be key pieces to the restoration of something you can't see as yet. I have found stop faces, parts of the stopboard, pitmans, guide pins, and the like, in the most improbable spots. It would be best to clean the worst out by hand before vacuuming; more than once I have sorted through a vacuum cleaner bag and found the part I had misplaced. I often wonder how much I have lost in this manner.

While mentioning vacuum cleaners, I should suggest that you have available an old tank-type cleaner which has the capability of blowing through the hose when it is connected in reverse. It really comes in handy in a shop.

DISASSEMBLING MAJOR UNITS

The initial disassembly is really only a partial one; major units should be kept intact to avoid problems if too much is scattered around. Thus, if you haven't already done so, remove and set aside the large canopy top. If the mirrors in it seem shaky, temporarily tape them in so they won't get damaged. Next remove the top of the main case, including the music rack, if your organ can be so disassembled; some can, some can't. Remove the sliding keyboard cover by unscrewing the hinged guides from the back edge of the cover. Some covers do not have such a guide but are held in by screws inserted into the inside of the case that double as stops for the cover. Be careful in taking the cover out; I have had some come apart in my hands. If the glue is poor, you should tape the unit together. Do not assume that parts apparently identical (such as right and left frame pieces of a five-piece keyboard cover) are interchangeable. Better play safe and keep them in original order.

The Stopboard

If you have access to the stopboard from above, you may be able to remove it without taking out the entire action as a unit. This can be an advantage since the whole action is a bit cumbersome to handle. If you do remove the action in pieces, be *very* sure to diagram the exact connections between the rods from the stopboard and their associated mutes and the like. You will want to reassemble things after they are out and *before* restoration so you don't forget how they go together.

Many stopboards are held in place by two large flat-head screws on each side, easily accessible from above. You will, of course, first remove all connecting shafts between the board and mutes, swells, and vox humana. Some stopboards are held only by a pivoting sickle-shaped catch that is located on either side. I assume that the initial idea of using these "dohickeys" was to make stopboard removal easier; just swing the catches back, lift it up off a couple of guide pins, and that's it. But it isn't that simple. Those catches often are covered with dirt, the guide pins become swollen so that they don't come loose properly and everything gets difficult to see, much less reach.

Unless those catches move easily, you may have to wait until the whole action can be removed before you get to them.

The Reed Pan

The reed pan is held to the bellows platform by a number of long screws that go through the reed pan at the back and up through the bellows platform at the front. Check carefully for at least one long screw going through the reed pan from the top at each side near the center; this screw is usually at least partially hidden by the connecting rods from the stopboard, making it hard to find and harder to remove. Further, the spot is often a good one for dirt to accumulate so that even after you have found the screw, you may then find that the slot in the head is full of rust. I have always managed to get the things out, but only at the expense of much sweat and exasperation with knives, screwdrivers, and the like. Also check for similar screws in the side of the reed pan from the bottom. Most of the time the bottom screws will hold only the front of the reed pan, but not always.

While you are under the front of the thing, remove the knee swells if they hinder your removal of the action. Some knee swells are attached to the action, some to the bottom of the bellows platform, others to the panel covering the pedal straps. Remove them at the most convenient time.

The Action

If all action screws seem out and the thing still doesn't lift off, check carefully for missed screws. If you have them all and the action still sticks it might be just that the seals are tight. Carefully pry up at the back by inserting a sturdy knife or thin chisel between the reed pan and the bellows platform. *Don't* apply heavy pressure. If things don't come loose, look for odd fastenings or even such horrors as nails someone drove in years ago trying to stop a leak. Also look for glued-down actions.

When the action is free, carefully lift it up from the rear, holding it as near the middle as you can so that you can lift the front high enough for the knee-swell actuating rods to clear the front of the bellows platform. If your stopboard is on the action, this may require you to have help in handling the awkward package. If you are setting things on a bench, be sure you don't bend the pallet springs under the reed pan since they come down close. Harlan prefers to set the action on two short lengths of 2 × 4 to protect the springs. Now take those pictures of the action. There are so many types of actions it is impossible in a book of this nature to describe them all, but several are pictured in the text. One caution: Don't turn the action upside down if you can avoid it. Things can fall out or get caught in strange ways, so keep things upright.

If you were able to remove the stopboard before taking out the action, I suggest that you reinstall it now while you still remember which goes where and take those pictures, particularly of the end linkages of the stopboard. (See Figs. 11-1 and 11-2 in chapter 11). Do not disassemble further at this time. Cover with plastic and set aside.

The Case

With most of the weight gone, you will find the case easy to handle. Before going further, take off the panel above the pedals and remove the springs that keep the exhausters compressed on the main bellows. Then carefully lay the case over on its back so that you can get to the underside of the pedals. Each pedal strap will be held by one or two screws through a small block of wood. Some organs have a thin piece of wood covering the bottom of the case as a kind of dust and vermin protector. This should be removed at this time also. After you have removed the pedal straps you can usually remove the pedals as a unit by taking out the two countersunk screws on each side of the bottom plate beneath the pedals. Turn the organ back upright and remove the two or three screws on each side of the case; they are usually easy to get to by now. Remove the bellows, lifting it out from behind the case and set it aside. This completes the usual disassembly.

Just a word of warning about disassembly: Don't try shortcuts. If the bellows seems to work well you will be tempted to leave it as is. If the organ was playing when you bought it, you might feel that there is no reason to pull the reeds. My experience has been that I always have to go back and do the job anyway. The instrument is from 60 to 130 years old; in spite of good care, it probably needs the works. Even when you know that some restoration has been done on the organ in years past, test things very carefully before bypassing any step. It is rather discouraging to find that you have to disassemble and start over.

Now lets get down to cases.

DISASSEMBLY NOTES

Chapter 9
Case Restoration

What you do with the organ case depends, of course, on the condition it is in and your philosophy of restoration. Let's take the latter problem first. Assuming that the organ is not in totally disastrous condition, you need to decide if full disassembly of glue joints, stripping of finish, and the like, is an absolute necessity. Don't be hasty in jumping to the conclusion that all is lost with the original finish; much can be done, if you have the time and patience, to restore chipped or crackled finish. You can, for instance, soften existing finishes, add to them, and come up with a pleasing finish that is still largely original. For the restorer who prizes original condition, this is the route to go even though the result will still show many imperfections.

Others feel that a crackled finish is not attractive; obviously the organ wasn't like that originally, and some owners want it like the original. That too is a perfectly legitimate approach. More will be said later about overzealous stripping and sanding, but within limits the full job is often quite justified. Those who restore antique furniture have so many ideas about what should be done to an antique that there is really no firm guideline. You do what you can accomplish with your own skills and can live with when done. One overriding principle: do as *little* as you think you may be satisfied with; then if it proves to be not enough, you can do more later. Once you have the whole thing stripped, though, you can't go back to the original finish.

PLANNING

Following is a kind of checklist you can use for planning case work:

CONDITION	WHAT TO DO ABOUT IT
Case in good condition; glue joints all firm; finish good except for minor cracking and peeling.	Carefully clean. With small brush and stain try to match chips where they appear. Possibly needed: a light, thin coat of semi-gloss or satin finish varnish to give a uniform sheen and to form a protective coat to seal in the patina of the old finish.
Case good, glue joints good (will survive pressure tests), but finish poor in spots (e.g., has sun damage on one side).	Depends on your skills. Try redoing damaged area to match the rest, particularly if the bad area is less exposed to view. Then give an overall protective coat. Otherwise do as suggested next.
Case good, glue joints good, finish badly peeling, stains evident in several spots.	Needs full stripping of finish, thorough cleaning, sanding, stain treatment or blending, and refinishing.
Case wood OK, some poor glue joints, though finish is seemingly good.	Don't assume that stripping is automatically called for. Carefully clean cracks, glue and clamp, and touch-up.
Case wood OK, but glue joints poor, finish poor.	Knock poor joints apart where possible, clean out others, reglue and clamp, then refinish.
Very poor shape all around: glue bad; wood warped, cracked, or missing; finish just gone.	Restore missing or badly damaged parts; glue all joints until you are sure case is in good, sturdy condition. Strip, sand, refinish.

78

The important thing in all of this is that you adopt a systematic approach which doesn't cause you to backtrack. My furniture restorer friend, Richard Turner, has emphasized over and over to me the necessity of making *sure* that all glue joints are really tight, not just apparently so. Many of the old glues are quite subject to deterioration from moisture or heat and they often just powder off upon the slightest pressure. He strongly advises the judicious use of a rubber mallet in testing all joints.

Let us now assume that you have an organ in very poor condition, properly disassembled as in the last chapter, and you are ready to start on the case.

GLUING

First: what glues are you planning to use? You really need to have at least three kinds readily available. The easiest is the familiar white glue often called *Elmer's Glue*. I once saw the results of a test that showed that white glue is the best glue commonly available for holding power. Contrary to what you may have heard, it is better than the water-mix plastic resin glues. However, it has one very serious problem; it is vulnerable to moisture. If you have such a problem, use the plastic resins which require longer clamping time but are not subject to moisture. Walt prefers to use *Franklin Tite Bond* since it is not subject to moisture as much as *Elmer's*, and has high tensile strength.

I use contact cement extensively in restoring bellows, but it is also quite useful in case work where I have very small pieces of veneer to work on or small slivers of stuff to insert here and there. Contact can be bought in tubes so that application is also made easier. There are also specialty products such as *Chair-Lok*, a chemical that can be injected into a loose joint that cannot be disassembled without damage It causes swelling of wood to the point that an otherwise unrepairable part might be at least made more sturdy. As with finishes, new products are coming on the market all the time so adhesives like those applied with the new glue guns might be very useful to you. Just be sure you know what you are doing with them.

Start testing all of those glue joints, removing all glue from questionable joints, knocking apart all that you can. If you must remove rather intricate decoration, be sure you have taken pictures detailed enough to enable you to replace it correctly. Occasionally you will find a piece so badly chewed or fragmented that you need to make a pattern of it before removing it since you must fill in parts of the design by inferring what probably fit that vacant spot. Be sure to look closely at the condition of the finish around the part. You may find outlines in old varnish that will tell you the shape of the missing part. At this time, reproduce it and make sure it fits before doing further disassembly. If it is not a part that is ordinarily to be disassembled, you will want to use wood that matches the original as closely as possible and install it before you proceed further. When I had to reproduce the carving on the Packard shown in Fig. 7-1, I was lucky enough to find an oak board about 100 years old. Even here the exact character of the grain and the coloration of the wood did not match the original. I had to make some attempts at matching. More of that later.

After making the reproduction piece as good as you can, properly sanding it, filling, etc., glue it in place. By this means, when you strip the finish off the rest of the organ, you can let the strippings stand on the new piece. Do this even if the piece is not glued to the piece being stripped. I did so with the carving; when I stripped the main case, I just dumped stripping gunk on the carving and let things set. This does a remarkable job of helping to match new wood to the patina of the old. You probably will still have to do some careful work with stain to get a perfect match, but this technique helps.

REPRODUCING MISSING PARTS

This is as good a place as any to discuss the reproduction of missing carvings and turnings. Your problem is simplified if you have at least a picture of what your organ looked like, even better if there is a model to work from (like a piece from the other side of the organ.) In addition to the missing mirror bracket, my Packard was minus two turnings. They were cut off from *both* sides so that I had no model. From the appearance of other decorative turnings on the organ I had a hunch of what those missing parts looked like so I chucked some oak in my little lathe and went to it. Happily, I later found an advertising picture of the original organ and my guess proved to be virtually identical with the original.

But if you have even less opportunity to figure what the missing piece probably looked like, then what? Well, you can either let the thing stand without the part until such time that you *can* be sure of proper reproduction (see earlier suggestions about research concerning your organ), or you can do your best to fit something in that harmonizes.

In fitting your piece in, do not alter the case in a manner that can't be changed if at some future time you do unexpectedly find out what the original was like and want to redo things. For example, the music rack of the Cornish seen in Fig. 16-5 of Chapter 16 is strictly my idea. Nothing was on the organ as purchased except holes where the hinges attached to the top of the case. I designed what to me was a harmonizing size and edge design and picked up the cut-out design from the keyslip to make things appear to match. If I ever find out what the original was really like, it will be easy to make another and replace this one.

Reproducing missing pieces can be very simple or quite complicated, requiring special tools. For instance, a carving-duplicating device to which a router is fitted may be just what you need. Try a tool rental shop to see if you can get one. The most common tools you will need are a lathe and a saber saw or heavy-duty jigsaw. In addition, a power hand-grinder such as the *Sears* I have (shown in Fig. 7-1) or a *Dremel*, if you prefer smaller tools, are both good.

The wood required is ordinarily not a very expensive item, so if time is no object don't be afraid to experiment. The carving in Fig. 7-1 took me over 30 hours to make, so I can't say it would have been a financial success had I been restoring the organ on contract. I must confess to a lot of satisfaction that I got the thing to come out so well.

FIXING CRACKS AND WARPS

You will frequently find many hairline cracks that are probably going to cause you no trouble. In fact after you strip the original finish and properly fill any wood needing it, most of those small cracks will disappear.

If a crack appears at a glue joint, you need to proceed with more caution. Try to press it farther apart. If the joint is weak, you need to get it apart so that you can clean, glue, and clamp. If you have wood handscrews you may not need case protection but it is still safest to use pads. In all clamping with "C" or bar clamps, be careful not to dent the case.

Your most ticklish problems will come with warped pieces. For instance, a decoration on the side of my Packard had come partially off, the loose portion warping so that it stood about 1/4 inch away from the part of the case it was supposed to be glued to. Your first impulse will be to run some sandpaper down there, slop on the white glue, then clamp. If the glue on the rest of the piece is really tight and if the gap isn't very large, clamping the loose end may work. In my case, I was afraid that I would get either a cracked carving or one where the newly glued area would be firm but at some future date the *other* end would come loose—and after refinishing, yet.

In such doubtful cases, try to remove the entire piece. Using a very thin knife, work around the glue joint that seems to be tight, all the while applying some *gentle* pressure through the crack side with a small screwdriver or sturdy knife (like an old kitchen knife.) If you work at it patiently, you can probably get the thing off. John suggests the use of hot water as a means of softening the old glues. Just be sure you don't soften more than you intend. Be alert for small brads or even glue-pegs that hold the carving on. In the latter case you may have to go so far as getting a thin saw blade in to cut the peg.

When you have the carving off, you have to decide what to do with it. Sometimes you can soak the thing for several days, then put it under weights or clamps so that it gradually comes back flat (the technique I used.) The other possibility is that of sanding the back so that you have a flat area to reglue. A thick carving can be so treated, but a thin one might just show the treatment too much. You'll just have to be the judge.

Warps in the main case should be similarly treated with caution. Above all *don't* try to pull things together with clamps. A crack most often opens up because a piece of wood has shrunk and warped away from itself. If you do manage to get things jammed back together, expect soon that more cracks will appear. To correct such conditions, you just have to add wood and try to match the rest by hand work with stains.

Frequently you will find situations where a thin panel of solid wood (often about 1/4 inch) is framed by heavier wood, the panel fitting into a slot. Keyboard covers and case sides often are made this way (Fig. 9-1). Do NOT—repeat, do NOT—glue the thin panel into the slots. Take a good look; it probably was not originally glued in. The four pieces comprising the frame around it should be securely glued. The reason is that the panel must have some room for swelling and shrinking. A good finish will shift with this very gradual wood movememt so you will never notice any change. If you do glue all things together, expect cracks to appear in the panel. If the panel has shrunk so much that it really rattles in the slots, you may have

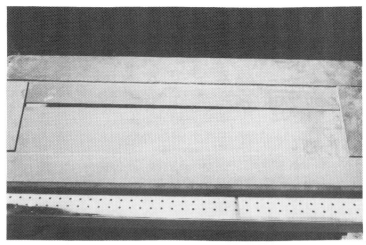
Fig. 9-1. Unrestored keyboard cover, coming apart.

to add a thin piece to a couple of sides to make it fit better. The added pieces should be small enough that they will be hidden in the panel slots. Even here, don't try to get a snug fit. Leave moving room and try to keep glue from the outside frame from seeping into the panel slot.

One reason for doing the glue jobs before you strip the case is that glue spills will come off with the old finish. In the event you have glue seeping on new or cleaned-off wood, do your best to get it all off because you will have trouble getting stain to take to the wood evenly over glue.

STRIPPING

The next step is, of course, stripping. Here you can get arguments that won't quit about which stripper to use. Following are some guidelines I would suggest:

Be careful of vat stripping. Of course this is the easiest to do and I know of an organ restorer some years ago who would do nothing else. The trouble is that there are many methods and materials used in vat stripping and there are operators with widely varying competencies. In general, avoid operations using a lye solution; it bleaches the wood and horrendously raises the grain. It also totally destroys what original patina had developed on the wood. The restorer I just mentioned produced organs with very harsh-looking wood. Above all, don't use lye with veneered pieces: it leads to ruination. I have seen ads for different methods using ''secret'' chemicals that are guaranteed not to raise grain, bleach, or damage delicate veneers. All I can say is, be sure you talk to someone you trust who has used the service you may be contemplating before consigning that irreplaceable piece to its tanks. Don't trust the ads to be all that accurate.

Doing Your Own

Most likely you will want to do your own stripping. Here again, you have a variety of products to choose from. I suggest that you avoid products requiring a water wash for clean up, particularly if you have veneers to work on. What can happen is that small amounts of water can get under the veneer, showing up only months later as a bulge. Choose products with proven track records and then *follow directions*. Most often, the inexperienced restorer doesn't use enough stripper or doesn't give it time to work. Usually you should attempt to work on surfaces you can put in a flat position, cover them with the stripper you use, then *leave them* for a while. For instance, I use *Kutzit*. I flow on a liberal amount, let it set for at least ten minutes, then flow on more. After a while the finish will start coming off with the brush. The novice commonly puts on a thin coat then immediately begins to dig in with a putty knife or scraper. This method takes a lot of time and effort in addition to being the cause of many gouges left in the surface.

If the organ has its original finish, you will find that it usually comes off very easily. If it has had subsequent coats of gunk plastered on it (I have had some with four coats of varnish or enamel) you may have to go at it in a couple of sessions. Put stripper on until you have a gooey mess on the surface. Using a putty knife, lift off as much as you can (don't dig for it, just lift the loose stuff off) and wipe it on scrap newspaper. Then wipe off the remaining goo on the piece and start in with stripper again. This time you ought to get down to bare wood.

Reaching Tricky Areas

So far I have been talking about relatively large, flat areas like the top of the main case, the sides, or the keyboard cover. What about the carvings and the like? The same procedure should be used with variations. Put the stripper on, let it stand, then take it off. However, you will need some very small brushes to use for getting into cracks and small crevices of carvings. I use some very small oil-painting brushes (available at any art store) and old toothbrushes, particularly the stiff, two-row kind. A word of caution about using metal instruments to dig into carvings: They can dig too far. I certainly use them—small screwdrivers, knife blades, even an awl; really, anything that will go where I want to get to. Remember, though, that the stripper softens the surface of the wood and you can come up with deep gouges that may be impossible to conceal when you refinish.

When you have removed the largest portion of the old finish, put a fairly uniform coat of stripper back on, let it set for a short while, then wipe it off with rags. I have had good success using sawdust from my radial saw or joiner when cleaning off relatively flat pieces (Excelsior also) but ran into trouble using such on carvings. The stuff gets down in the carving and takes more time to dig out than the process is worth. When doing final clean-out of carvings, use clean rags and work them in on the end of small screwdrivers and the like, changing cloths frequently.

Taking Proper Precautions

Be sure to take proper precautions when using most strippers. They are usually flammable, toxic to breathe, and murder on skin. However, new products are coming out all the time which may make things easier. A new product *Hope's Instant Furniture Refinisher* seems to be much easier to use, according to a close friend who is very enthusiastic about it. Another is *Woodcrafters Finish Remover*. I have seen it demonstrated and just bought a quart but haven't used it as yet. It has none of the problems I just mentioned and can be used over and over again (after letting the old finish settle out.) It is expensive, by comparison with other removers, but in the long run may be worth it. Whatever you use, be sure it will do the job before you try it out on that delicate veneer. If you are not sure, try it on some obscure spot first.

REMOVING STAINS

The stripper will usually take care of problems with old finish. Stains are another matter; water or other stuff that has stood on the case for some time will discolor it deep down. You must either sand below the stain (definitely *not* recommended unless the stain is superficial), or make some other effort to remove or disguise the thing. If you sand too much you well may remove the stain, but you then uncover new wood below the patina of everything around it and the result is worse than if you had left things as they were. Some wood bleaches are available in hardware stores and might be good to use. Again, be careful of bleaching a spot that just can't be brought to match. The Packard had organic stains on a couple of spots by the music rack; leaves had moldered there for no one knows how long. My friendly druggist and I were discussing the possibility of my using some peroxide hair bleach to remove the stain when he happened to think of a product called *Gartsides Rust and Stain Remover*. It worked wonders! The stain completely disappeared to the point that I honestly can't find where the spot was. It caused no bleaching of the surrounding wood or anything. I heartily recommend it for organic stain removal. I don't know how it would work on other types of stain but I would not hesitate to try it since it seems to have no adverse effect on the wood. I don't know what it might do to a good finish since I used it after the Packard had been stripped.

You have a lot of judgment calls to make when it comes to deciding what to do about difficult stains as well as other imperfections such as deep dents, scratches, small edge chips, burned spots, patches on the wood, and the like. Even original imperfections pose problems. I once restored a Sears organ on which the case work was originally done rather shoddily: saw marks were still clearly visible, and such. These evidences of age are thorny; one dealer-refinisher I know wants the whole shebang cleaned up as much as possible. Another, horrified at the thought, insists that such practices destroy all evidence of antique genuineness. One writer I know contemptuously refers to stripping and thorough sanding as "skinning."

Obviously I'm not going to be able to solve all philosophical and practical problems for you. My rule of thumb is, do nothing that might make matters worse. If that dent bothers you, try first to lift it up by means of a damp cloth plus a hot iron (or soldering iron for use with small dents.) If that doesn't work, try at least to blend the dent a bit by judicious sanding around the edges, but be very careful not to go too deep. Be particularly careful when using power sanders; they can leave marks that are horrendous, particularly rotary disc sanders. Personally, I find some imperfections intriguing. On a dresser I restored some time ago I left the burned spots where someone a long time ago turned some kerosene lamps up too high and burned wood slightly at the top. For some romantic reason, everytime I see those spots I think of those people a century ago. Not everyone has to be so inclined.

So far I have stayed away from the rather distasteful topic of cash value. I work with reed organs because I enjoy them, not because of their salability. However, you should not ignore the fact that some modifications may reduce the value should you wish to sell yours sometime. Dealers, for the most part, desire those signs of use and antiquity as long as they are not so damaging as to impair looks or utility. You may prefer to sand the case until it looks almost like it did when new (the "skinning" earlier referred to) and that's your privilege; I honestly don't want to imply that you are wrong. Interestingly enough, such a total restoration to absolutely "like new" condition is apparently considered great for antique cars but bad for furniture. You be your own judge.

PATCHING VENEERS

Patching damaged veneers can be tricky business. If pieces are gone, it is even more difficult. Of course you can usually buy new veneer of the same type of wood that is gone (some very good supply houses are listed in the Appendix), but that only begins your solution. In the first place, old veneers were thicker: 1/20 inch to 1/8 inch, where modern pieces are usually 1/28 inch. You can, of course, build up thin pieces, so not all is lost. The new wood is almost never the same texture and color of the original so you still will have some experimental work with stains before you get a reasonable match. Keep in mind the possibility of getting veneer pieces from old furniture that is so shot it is good only for repair purposes. Richard Turner had torn up an old rosewood piano quite some time ago and I cabbaged onto some of the slivers of rosewood. Have they ever been useful on melodeons! As you nose through junk shops (as I assume we all do) be alert for things you can use.

If you have veneer problems in several places, you might consider taking a piece out of an obscure place and using it to patch the hole in a prominent place on the front. This way you are assured of a perfect wood and finish match where you most need it. You can then patch the more out-of-the-way place with wood that is not as good a match.

Fixing Bubbles

A veneer bubble can be handled so that its repair is virtually invisible. If the bubble is not very large or stretched out, Walt likes to use an old hypodermic needle to get glue in the bubble, then clamp it well. If it is too large for that treatment, you can slit the length of the bubble, using a new razor blade or X-acto knife, cutting with the grain. Carefully push down one side so that you can insert a small piece of sandpaper and clean out the other side. Do the same for the other. If the bubble shows little signs of stretching, you can then just fill the area with glue and apply pressure. If the bubble is on a panel not far from the edge, you can use large "C" clamps, with wax paper directly on the bubble, then wood blocks between the clamps and the paper. If the bubble is near the center of a large panel you must properly support the piece from beneath then press the bubble with weights such as bricks. In some cases, one slit is not enough; the bubble is too large or has become stretched so that it will not press flat. You must then do some rather delicate shaving so that when you do press the repair flat, it matches. Remember: don't make any cuts directly across the grain. Use at least a "V" cut or an oval shaped one if you must put in a patch or cross some grain. This minimizes the repair evidence.

Patching Decorated Veneers

You have a particularly difficult job if the veneer or plywood that is separating has some additional decoration on it. A common practice was that of pressing a design into the wood (rather then carving it in, for example.) Here you are simply going to have to analyze the degree of damage before you plunge in. If the damage is slight, proceed as above. If damage is extensive, you need drastic measures. I had such a situation concerning a Crown organ where a decorated front panel was badly split; the surface wood was curling and about to fall off. Here I put into practice another principle: if something is absolutely beyond saving by any *sure* means, I decide what I can do if the experiment fails, and then charge forward. In this particular case, there was no way it was to be saved normally. If I couldn't be successful by drastic surgery, I had planned to put in plain panels since I simply could not duplicate the pressed-in design. Since doing that job I now have a Sears pantograph attachment that I could have used with my router. It is not expensive so if you have a router, you may want to get one. A note of caution: the pantograph attachment does not duplicate designs in the same size as the original. It reduces them by half. Thus if I wish to duplicate exact size I am first going to have to enlarge a given design to double the finished size, then duplicate. In the case of the Crown, I think that such a procedure would have been practical. I would have had a routed rather than a pressed design, but that could have been acceptable.

In fact, however, the technique I tried worked well. I immersed the damaged panel in a pan of water until the whole thing was thoroughly soaked and the glue completely dissolved. This meant that *all* the plies had come apart. I then reassembled the under-plies, glued and clamped them securely for 24 hours. I let the decorated surface ply continue to soak. The next day I removed the main layer and put the pieces between papers and gently pressed them until they were almost dry; they were rather firm, but retained enough moisture to be a bit flexible.

I reused the bottom plies but I don't think this is really necessary. None of it will show when installed, so if you have some other plywood of the right thickness, don't hesitate to use it here. *Don't* use solid wood, though, since you might then come up with some warps after gluing the old surface back on.

While the veneer is still slightly damp, glue it to the new or renewed backing plies, using some protecton over the surface, such as waxed paper. Then use a layer of soft cloth, then the wood of your press. The layer of cloth is vital since by using it you minimize the problem of pressing out the design you are trying to save. Since the piece I was working with was only a foot or so square, I was able to cut pieces of scrap 3/4-inch wood to form a press, clamping around the perimeter with a number of large "C" clamps. Be careful to avoid uneven pressure. Also try to have the clamps spaced about midway between the center of the press and the edge (or maybe a slight bit toward the edge.) If you have access to a veneer press or book press, that is, of course, the way to go.

Use only enough pressure to be sure the veneer is flat. Too much pressure might destroy the design. Even so, the soaking process and necessary pressure will cause the design to become a bit more shallow then it was. All you can do is minimize the problem.

If there are still pieces of the veneer missing, you probably would do well to wait until the major pieces are successfully glued back in original position before attempting further repair. If you try to do both jobs in one step you may not come out with as good a match because the original veneer will shrink a bit in the drying process.

FIXING ROLLERS

Finally, check the condition of the wooden rollers on the organ. The usual organ has four rollers in little wells under the feet and, of course, two larger ones over which the pedal straps come. Frequently those foot rollers have rotted out and at times the pedal strap rollers are missing because someone electrified the organ. Each is a simple turning job on a lathe. I suggest that while you have a billet of wood in the lathe you turn several more than you expect to need. You are going to have to drill a center hole in each one and if you mess one up but have extras, it will not mean setting up the lathe again. Also, it will not be bad to have some replacements for future use. Remember also that the pedal rollers had a slight crown in the center.

You may wish to eliminate the floor rollers, even if yours are OK. (Don't throw them away, of course. Store them for possible future reinstallation.) These organs were built when most floors were bare wood or at best had good linoleum on them. Even those with rugs had hard-surface, thin pile rugs. The rollers worked well on such surfaces. Today, with shag rugs, foam backing, and the like, the organ just wouldn't roll if you tried. The rollers then simply go down into the rug leaving unsightly depressions which are hard to remove. Placing the organ flat on its feet or even on masonite or plywood panels will prevent the spot crushing of the rug.

FINISHING

With all of this out of the way you are now ready for the final wood preparation and the finishing process. There are so many books on the subject (some listed in the Bibliography) that there is no need for me to go into great detail. If you need more informaton than I give, you can easily find it. Following are practices that I have found to be practical.

Sanding

A light sanding may be all that you need. If so, use as fine a grade of sandpaper as is practical, considering what needs doing. I have often been disappointed when refinishing furniture to find that I had not really taken out the coarse scratches even though I thought I had adequately sanded with fine paper.

As I said previously, avoid power sanders. Particularly be careful of orbital sanders, widely advertised for fine finish work. If you aren't careful you wind up with little figure-eights all over the surface: some small piece of grit got caught under the pad. Some orbitals have provision for working in a straight line and just may be safer to use. Mine doesn't have this provision, so I have no experience with the other kind. A padded block of wood, or even a rubber block, is very good as a base for hand sanding. This is better than simply having a piece of paper in your hand. The latter can accentuate little dips while the hand block will tend to minimize them.

Another reason I prefer hand work to power sanders is that seldom can you use the power tool all over the case even when such tools will do a good job on the flat parts. Since the power equipment is a more efficient remover of surface wood, you usually come up with a case having distinctly different surface appearances if you mix power and hand sanding. By hand sanding you are more likely to come up with an instrument having uniform texture and color all over. Lest I be misunderstood, let me emphasize that I have power sanders and use them, but only when more than light surface sanding is required.

Using Synthetics

What about plastic wood, wood putty, and the like? Often they do very well. Be advised, though, that you can seldom stain or otherwise match color. Also, even if you do seem to match the wood with synthetics before you put on finish, the finish will quite significantly change the tone of the wood so that the almost imperceptible plastic wood repair (on the unfinished piece) suddenly stands out after being varnished. Where possible, I like to fill cracks, gouges, plugs over screws, and the like, with pieces of wood carefully chosen for similarity to the original wood, and fitted as well as possible. Be sure to pay attention to grain (coarse-fine, color, direction.) Here some of the techniques of marquetry (or inlay) might come in handy so the marquetry text in the Bibliography might be of interest.

Checking Glue Joints

A final check: look at all glue joints. Are any looking suspiciously shaky? Don't take chances. Reglue them. Is there any evidence of glue still on the surface or just below it, near newly glued joints? Get it out. If that glue is there, you just won't get a good finish job. Even if you are not staining, you will find that the glue will not darken with finish (even clear finish) as the rest of the wood around it does, and thus will really show up as a nasty light streak.

Staining

To stain or not to stain; that is the question. If your organ is made of walnut, cherry, mahogany, or other such colorful woods, don't stain it. Even if you find that the original piece had inserts of other kinds of wood, leave them natural. A walnut case is particularly likely to have pieces of walnut of such widely differing colorations that you are going to be tempted to even things up a bit. Don't, the furniture people say to me. The different shades of natural wood lend charm to the piece. Don't make the assumption that the piece is going to turn out too light; you will be astonished how much many fruitwoods darken when finished. You can get an idea by just wetting a small part of the wood; note the much darker shade it turns and the way the grain stands out. That is what you can expect from a finish. In Fig. 9-2 you can readily see the distinct darkening of tone resulting from a single coat of polyurethane varnish.

Oak is a different matter. Old oak, even when very carefully stripped with a delicate stripper, often has a rather bleached look. Around the midwest, restorers almost universally stain oak. Stain it with *what*? Astonishingly enough, almost never is an oak stain used: it looks too artificial. On the Packard, I wanted just a light toning down so I used a fruitwood stain, wiping it on and then off almost

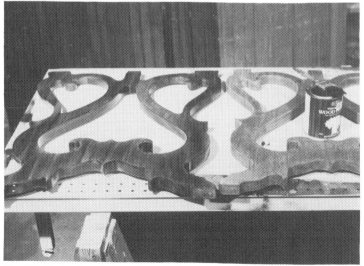

Fig. 9-2. Carhart melodeon legs; left one is finished with coat of varnish, right one is not.

immediately. If you want a darker brown, a walnut stain put on and off immediately, does a good job. I have used both.

The use of fillers poses another problem. Oak and other open-grain woods must, of course, be filled. If you use stain first, it penetrates more and will most likely take a deeper tone. However, end-grain and some other grainy portions may take too much stain, causing problems difficult to correct (though Walt says that he often gets such stuff out of end-grain with alcohol or acetone.) If you stain *after* using filler you will avoid the problems mentioned but you may have trouble getting the depth of color you want. Since there are so many variables, ranging from your taste in coloration to the varying ways given pieces of wood react to stain, your experience and that of whomever you can pump for information will have to be your guide.

A final word on stains: Choice of brand may be determined by the final finish you intend to use. While certainly not always true, some stains may work well with the finish of a given manufacturer. Particularly be careful when using water or oil stains under certain synthetic varnishes. When in the slightest doubt, be sure to get advice from someone you know has actually used the product or the combination you are considering.

Types of Finish

The type of actual finish you use will be determined by a number of factors, not the least of which is cost and facilities for finishing. Since I do have a basement that can be arranged in a manner somehow conductive to spraying, I usually stick with the tried-and-true finishes. New products such as the *Hope* and *Tesar* varieties previously referred to are very interesting. They use a type of tung oil finish which can be wiped on. Another brand is *Minwax*. All of these are listed in the Appendix with sources of supply. These products would really be the answer to the prayer of the apartment-dweller who must work in a corner of the living room or the like. While professional finishers I have talked with have some doubts about the new products (they feel that the wood doesn't get the protective coat that varnishes and lacquers give) I am a firm believer in experimentation. After all, the pros were also skeptical about the synthetic finishes when they first came out.

If you do plan to use a more tried-and-true finish, you will need some area where it is safe to brush or spray finish. If that is a basement similar to the usual ones, you need to take special precautions about such things as furnace or water-heater pilot lights. Remember that most finishes are quite flammable and can flash easily if you get too many fumes in the atmosphere. In my basement I have a window fan which runs constantly while I am using paint stripper or finishes. I also take precautions to turn down the furnace so that it doesn't come on. I work at some distance from the pilot lights and plan to work just a few minutes at a time so that I don't come close to an atmospheric saturation.

If you spray, you are also going to have to consider the problem of overspray around your work area. Cheap plastic sheets can really be your lifesaver here. I usually throw them over everything, even things that are remote from the spray area, that I certainly want protected (like my radial saw.)

Other problems raise their ugly heads. For instance, there are temperature and moisture problems. If you are fairly active in your shop you may not really be aware of the actual low temperature there. I once refinished an organ with disastrous results; the finish just didn't flow on right. I got a thermometer and found that the temperature was only 60°. Few finishes will work below 70°. Some finishes also do all sorts of bizarre things if the moisture content of the air is too high. Lacquers tend to blush (turn white) and varnishes may not dry for days (if then). Spray guns clog up as fast as you can get them cleaned out. One answer here is a moisture trap in the air-line to your gun.

Varnish or lacquer? Well, the reasons for choice are not as clear as they once were. For the home shop, lacquer used to be very good since it sets up dust-free so quickly. Now modern synthetic varnishes dry almost as fast, so that is no longer a problem. I have used *Deft*, a synthetic lacquer, and poly-urethane varnishes with equal success. Some people seem to think that touch-up is easier with *Deft* but that too is open to question.

You need to decide also whether to use gloss, semi-gloss, or satin finish. For some reason, rosewood just seems to call for gloss, as do certain other woods with strong burl patterns. I usually favor half-way; I mix satin and gloss so that I get some shine but not a garish one on oak and walnut (a trick I got from Richard). If you use a synthetic varnish with any satin content, be sure that you mix it well before using, and strain it well; the satin portion comes from an ingredient that can lump up and cause you headaches.

Fig. 9-3. My shop, set up for spraying the Packard.

Spray Finishing

Following is a rather rough idea of how I prepare my shop for spray finishing (Fig. 9-3). Each shop will have its own problems, so adapt accordingly.

First I try to get an area cleared so that I am not going to have the pieces near anything else (i.e. at least a few feet from anything). This way I can get all around each piece with the spray gun and a portable light. It would be ideal, of course, to have such a perfectly lighted shop that you have light above, around, and below the area. Seldom do hobbyists have such shops, however. Then I clean the whole place thoroughly at some time before I intend to finish. First I do a rough sweeping and vacuuming; then, by reversing my vacuum cleaner hose, I use it as a blower on everything around the spray area including the ceiling, beams, the tops of furnace pipes. After the dust has had ample time to settle I then vacuum again and use a dust rag over everything. A final touch is to put water in your spray gun and lay a fine mist over everything (*not* the pieces to be sprayed, however.) This takes the last vestiges of dust out of the air. If you are careful, you can achieve a surprisingly dust-free atmosphere for at least an hour or two.

Before moving the pieces into the spray area, go over them carefully with a tack rag. You can make such a rag by soaking a piece of muslin or cheese cloth in old varnish, but more uniform tack rags can be bought from your paint store so

I suggest you get them there; they're cheap. In order to keep my tack rag from filling up too soon I usually go over the work with two rags; one just a clean rag to get the worst dirt off, then I immediately follow with the tack rag.

While doing all of this, try to get the room temperature at least to 70°, preferably higher. Also get the temperature of the can of finish to 70°. Many amateurs forget this; we leave the can of finish in the basement where it never gets even to 60°, then wonder why it doesn't flow. Set it in a pan of hot water for a while before you plan to use it.

The techniques of spraying are well-known so I won't go into them here. Just be sure that you get the coverage you need without promoting sags. Carefully watch the piece for at least fifteen minutes after you have finished spraying in order to catch sags that might develop. The moment you see one start, wash it down with thinner immediately and spray again. What about using spray cans? That is the expensive way to buy finish since a twelve-ounce can may contain only four ounces of finish (the rest is propellant.) However, if your instrument is a small one or all you need to do is provide a light skim coat over an old finish that seems pretty good, this might be the way to go in order to save you the expense of spray equipment. The diaphragm sprayers also do a good job; you do not need a hefty tank unit to do very good furniture work. For years I have used the little unit in the picture with very dependable results.

When your first coat has dried thoroughly, carefully sand it down with wet-dry sandpaper of about 240 grit. I usually keep around some such paper that has been used, because I don't like to use a fresh hunk of even this fine a grit. You've got to start with something somewhere, though, so it is best to start with a new sheet on a flat area like the side of the case. Be very careful on corners; you can easily go through the finish. Frequently test the surface by rubbing your hand over it to see if it is properly smoothed down. As soon as it seems to be smooth, stop. Go over the piece with a soft cloth to take up most of the powdery finish then use the tack rag. You are now ready for the second coat. If you are really good at getting uniform spraying done, the second will be your final coat. If you are like I am, you often are going to have to sand down again before getting a really good final coat—at least on some sections.

Rub-Down

When the final coat has dried thoroughly (and cured for a while for some finishes) you are ready for that last ritual, the rub-down. A long while ago a furniture dealer showed me how to rub a finish with 0000 steel wool, water, and *Gold Star Furniture Polish*. I still use the method. Put some water in a small pan, dip the steel wool pad in it, then pour some furniture oil on the pad. Rub gently over the surface until you feel that it is really smooth. *Immediately* wipe it completely dry with a soft, clean cloth. If you still encounter some rough spots, use wet-dry sandpaper first, dipping it in water then putting a few drops of oil on the paper. Don't bear down or stroke fast; take it easy. Then finish up with the steel wool. I like this rub-down since it leaves an oil polish thoroughly worked into the finish.

Richard prefers to use a specially prepared cloth pad that has been saturated with oil and pumice stone. He really gets a beautiful rub-down with it. Walt likes to use steel wool thoroughly impregnated with auto paste wax. Already prepared pads of steel wool and wax are commercially available but you can make your own much cheaper. You may have your own pet methods of rub-down.

RESTORING MIRRORS

Another element of case work bears mentioning: restoring mirrors. Often an organ will have three or more mirrors in the canopy top. Frankly, resilvering is more expensive than replacing with new mirrors. I had the Packard mirror professionally resilvered because the original bevel-glass was still present and in good shape. If your mirror has chips or scratches or is apparently just a piece of flat glass with no particular distinction, you might as well go to your local glazier and have a new one cut. I suggest that you ask for plate glass mirror rather than the cheaper double-strength glass; the latter may have some waviness visible from some angles. I have seen ads for do-it-yourself resilvering but I am skeptical. The real process is both uncomfortable (because of the heat) and dangerous (because of the chemical used) so I have doubts that any home method is really practical. If the mirror isn't really bad you might be able to touch up some small spots with silver paint and get by, though it will show.

RESTORING PEDALS

Pedal restoration will complete the case. Most organ pedals will have some sort of border around them. Occasionally I see restored organs with no rim of any kind, but I suspect that the pedals had rims originally. You will commonly find that the rim is of cast iron or brass. If it is cast iron, *be careful*: those things do break easily! Your only alternative, if the rim is broken, is to have it brazed or welded. If it is brass and you are going to finish it naturally, you will want to have an expert do the work in such a manner that you can then, with a hand grinder, restore any design on the surface that has been marred. If it is cast iron you will probably paint the rim with black enamel anyway, so a bit less critical welding or brazing job will do.

If the pedals have screws on the face of the pedal rim you are in luck. These are about the easiest to put on since the thickness of any pedal pad is of no consequence. Frequently, however, the metal rim has a tab down the side which must be screwed or nailed to the edge of the wood base of the pedal. These tabs were spaced according to the thickness of the usual carpet at the turn of the century; thin, cut-pile carpets with no backing other than the jute. Seldom will you find new carpet of that type today, so you have to improvise.

Probably the easiest method for finding what you need is to go to your nearest carpet store and ask to rummage through the scraps. Look for something that looks like the old cut-pile. Frequently you will find that some of the cheaper, foam-backed carpets fill the bill. The foam, however, makes it too thick, so you will then have to peel off the foam backing before the rim will fit down far enough to be fastened. Be sure to try and get a carpet pattern that doesn't clash with the age of the organ. A Mondrian pattern just doesn't look right! On old pedals I have often found a kind of floral pattern on the pedals, so a design of that type would fit. Of course, a kind of neutral solid color works well, too.

You can really be authentic if by chance you can pick up an old carpet somewhere. I have found them very reasonably priced, especially when there is a big hole in the center or on an edge where the rug served faithfully for years by a door. Since you intend to cut it up, you can buy it for scrap. Just make sure that the pattern is such that it lends itself to being put into pads. Again, junk shops are good sources, though sometimes antique shops specializing in unrestored furniture may have some old carpet.

If you *really* want to go all out to restore pedals, try making your own pads with an initial in them. This can be done with needlepoint, but is even better with a *Speedtufting* tool's tapestry needle and the shortest pile setting. This involved a happy coincidence for me: the Packard had a decorative Gothic letter "P" on each pedal, worn beyond repair. Since the initial happens to be that of my last name, I decided to try *Speedtufting* a pair of pads, making them as close to the original as I could. I am quite pleased with the results. This little additional element could be a good means of getting someone else in the act of helping you to restore an organ if this particular skill is not your bag. I might add that the *Speedtufting* tool would also be a good means of designing distinctive organ stool covers as well as rugs to go in front of the organ. (See Fig. 21-1, Chapter 21.)

You will also find other kinds of rims. The wooden ones are quite easy to apply since many do not come down over the pedal pad. This being the case, though, you will need to be very careful in cutting the pedal pads to a perfect fit. In particular be wary of choosing rug scraps from loop pile stuff since those loops easily fray off at the side. This presents no problem if you have a rim covering part of the side, but it presents big problems otherwise. If your organ comes with the rims missing (or, lamentably, with only one metal rim left) you can use wooden rims and be well within the practice of many manufacturers. Here again, do what you can to make things look decent regardless of whether they are exactly original or not.

One final word in case you have one metal rim and really want to keep the organ authentic. In larger cities you can usually find a foundry that will be able to cast a new rim for you, using the old one as a pattern. Since the new one will probably look a bit different from the original, you probably should have two made. The cost of such casting is not cheap; but it would be worth the expense; particularly when the rim is itself intricately designed or has the name or monogram of the manufacturer on it.

INSTALLING CLOTH CUT-OUTS

The final bit of case work involves selection and installation of cloth behind the sound cut-outs on organs having such a provision. The keyslip beneath the keyboard is frequently cut out, and often on cottage organs the panels beside the book rack have cut-outs. I have restored one Packard where even the bookrack had cloth-backed cut-outs! Choosing the cloth is, most commonly, a matter of taste. The only thing to avoid is selecting cloth so dense that it might hinder the transference of sound, or so I have read when case restoration has been mentioned. In practice I doubt that the density of the cloth has that much effect. I have worked with organs with no sound cut-outs at all and I can't see that their sound was muffled.

Most commonly you will find a velvet or velveteen cloth of a solid color (red, maroon, blue, green) on the originals. On melodeons, a satin is commonly used. I would avoid using radio speaker grill cloth since its coarse weave just doesn't look like any original I have ever seen.

If you must use more than one piece of velvet or velveteen, be careful. Such cloth has a distinct nap and two pieces side-by-side may look shades different if the nap runs in different directions. For instance, cloth on a keyslip is often installed in two pieces. The same goes for the cut-outs beside the music rack. It is quite possible that you may wind up using four separate pieces of the same cloth. Be sure to look at them *in place* (temporarily thumbtacked in) before finally gluing them in. Then be sure that you do not get them reversed when you do the final installation. If you glue something in wrong, you probably have ruined the cloth. Since I have done that horrible thing, I usually buy enough cloth to allow me to replace a goof without having to buy enough to do the whole job again.

The gluing process tends to be rather tricky. The problem is that of preventing glue from seeping around the cut-out to show on the outside surface of the cloth. When that happens, you probably just have to redo the whole thing. I apply cloth with white glue, applying first a very thin line down the middle of each element of the cut-out fretwork. Then I spread it carefully with a finger. I try to keep glue at least 1/8 inch away from any edge. If it gets too close, I scrape it away with a knife blade.

Starting at one end, carefully lay the cloth on the cut-out, trying to avoid wrinkles. You can usually stretch it some or smooth things out just a wee bit if the glue hasn't been allowed to get close to the edge of the cut-out. Once the piece is on, let it alone. A very small wrinkle may not be really visible; messing around trying to get it out just may cause the glue to seep around to the front and mess up the front of the cloth. That won't help your temper one bit.

If the organ case is likely to sit in your shop for some time before being completed, you may wish to tape a protective piece of paper over the cut-outs since dust can settle on the cloth. It is hard to clean the cut-outs, so take appropriate precautions.

You will probably want to cover the entire restored case with plastic until work on other parts is completed.

CASE NOTES

Case repair

Stripping and finishing

Miscellaneous: pedal pads, cloth backing; metal parts, etc.

Chapter 10
Bellows
Restoration

As was the case with case restoration, your first decision here will be to determine how authentic you want the organ operation to be. If you wish to electrify the organ you will need to obtain a good suction unit well in advance of your restoration schedule so that you can plan exactly what is needed. The Lee Music Mfg. Co. of Venice, California makes such a unit at a reasonable price. There are three sizes of units; your choice will depend on how many sets of reeds your organ has.

ELECTRIFICATION

The following is taken from the Lee literature on installing a unit for electrification:

1. Remove the old bellows and seal up the chest slot or opening.
2. Drill a hole in the chest foundation board and attach tubing flanges.
3. Make a floor or platform inside the organ (if none exists) and set it in place.
4. Connect the unit to the chest with the flexible tubing provided.
5. Mount the switch assembly under keyboard.

Electrification is then completed.

These units can also be installed without removing the bellows. In this case the unit is placed behind or away from the organ and connected to the reservoir bellows with flexible tubing (the connection being made preferably through the main bellows safety-valve opening.)

Several very good reasons may dictate your use of such a unit. The person for whom the organ is intended may be physically unable to pump an organ; the whole bellows may be gone (though it can be reproduced as mentioned later); someone who has commissioned you to restore the organ may simply insist on having an electric unit.

Well, if you must, go to it. My own prejudices stand out here. I have never installed such a unit since I prefer the organ to be as original as possible. Some people may insist that playing an organ is hard work; they remember vividly how it was years ago, and just insist on the blower. Chances are they remember the thing when the bellows was almost shot and the organist had to pump furiously just to keep a quavery sound coming. Be assured that such is not the case with organs that have a new, tight bellows. Pumping is an easy job; the suction required, for the most part, is quite modest. The biggest problem some people have, really, is that of coordinating their feet with their hands. I can confidently say that a little practice makes perfect, but you may have trouble convincing some people. I like to put it this way: You get two for one playing an organ—aesthetics and physical education at the same time. I might add that electric units are advertised as "silent suction" units. Not so: the sound of a unit is not all that loud, but in operation the blower is definitely noticeable.

BELLOWS REMOVAL

I was lucky on the Packard; the bellows had been literally ripped out and a hole was cut in the bellows platform so that a standard vacuum cleaner hose could be jammed in. (*Don't* try it! It is noisy and just isn't remotely satisfactory!) Fortunately, those who did such a dastardly deed at least kept the bellows which then remained with the organ when it was auctioned. If you are not so fortunate, make a new one on the basis of Fig. 4-6 in Chapter 4. It is a fairly easy job for a competent woodworker.

Removing the Platform

Assuming that you have an original bellows to restore, proceed by removing the bellows platform first—*if*, of course, it is removable. On many organs (I am tempted to say most) you will find a series of counter sunk screws all around the slot that connects the interior of the main bellows with the bottom of the reed pan. (These are illustrated later in Fig. 10-13). In this case all you do is remove the screws, identify them by wrapping them in masking tape and labelling. Remove the side braces holding the fixed panel of the main bellows to the platform, and take off the platform. *Note*: Before removing those side braces be sure to identify exactly which one goes where. They look alike but be assured that they are *not* interchangeable.

If the platform is glued to the main bellows, you are in for problems. On some organs the platform is held by a combination of screws and glue. You may wish to try removing the screws, then, very cautiously, use a chisel and hammer to try separating the glue joint without splintering the wood around it.

If possible, you should get the platform off, for at least two good reasons. First, the old joint may leak air even though it seems firm. (This problem is discussed later.) The second reason is that you will have a much easier time replacing the exhauster bellows if the platform is off.

If the thing is put together so well that you would just be forced to break something to get the platform off, don't do it. The following instructions for replacing bellows can still be used, but with greater difficulty.

Removing the Cloth

There are at least three ways to get bellows cloth off reasonably intact. First, using a knife, try to lift the edge of the bellows cloth at the hinge end of one of the exhauster bellows. If it comes up when you pull on it, keep on pulling, trying to keep even pressure so that it will come loose from both edges at the same time. If it wants to be stubborn in spots, you might use a knife blade to help release it at that point. On some bellows, the glue will have deteriorated to such an extent that you can remove the whole bellows by this means.

More likely the glue is still tight at least in spots and needs heat. The best way to apply heat is by means of an old electric steam iron. I got mine at a yard sale. Above all, *don't* use a good one: it will be ruined for any other purpose. Set the iron to one of the hotter ranges, with the steam on, and apply it to to the glue seam. Hold it there until the cloth begins to stink. Then move it slowly up and down the seam. You can then easily insert a knife or chisel under the edge, raise the cloth, and pull it loose. Run the iron the same way over all seams.

You might want to run it over all the seams of a given piece of bellows (i.e. all of one exhauster) and then remove the whole thing at once. The gule will not reassert itself, apparently, once it has been heated up. While you do this job be very sure to have good ventilation because it really stinks up the joint. Be prepared for others in the vicinity to insist that you do the job outside.

Before Harlan and Walt told me of the iron technique I worked out a means of using a propane torch to do the job. It works very well although there is a great deal more danger of fire. If you use a torch for any reason, be sure to have an ample supply of water handy for emergency use. The torch still is a good means for getting into close quarters where the iron won't fit (in such cases as when your bellows platform cannot be detached; it is very cramped to get into the spot where the top of the exhausters is fastened to the fixed panel of the main bellows.) Even here Walt suggests the use of a large soldering iron. It would be slow to use, but certainly involves less danger. If you use a torch, keep it slowly passing over a seam, moving on at the moment the rubber begins to bubble. Be sure to clean out any accumulation of dust or fuzz; it flashes mighty fast.

Removing the Hinges

After removing the folding part of the exhauster, also remove the strip of bellows cloth that is glued along the top of the hinge. Here you are going to be tempted to leave things as is: the cloth will often look OK, and even the inside hinge will look OK. Why should you take off the top hinge strip? Because you need to know what's under it. Recently I almost left just such a good-looking piece but decided that I hadn't better. I found to my amazement that the cloth came off very easily (the glue was really shot) and that the wood to which it was glued was in bad shape. The exhauster panel was plywood and the plies were coming apart. If I had not removed the hinge strip I might not have known of the problem and before long I would have had the whole job to do over.

Now about that inside canvas hinge. You may find that it is really in good condition. It has always been protected and may yet be quite strong. After getting everything else off the bellows, try pulling on the hinged portion of the exhauster. Is there any sign of something coming loose? If so, take off the whole thing. But before removing the hinge, lay the hinged panel flat and carefully make a pencil mark around it on the fixed panel of the main bellows. This is done so you can get it back in exactly the same position. If you don't, it may not work properly since in operation the exhauster often just clears a nearby brace by a fraction of an inch. After carefully making the marks you need, remove the whole hinge, cutting if necessary. Clean off everything, particularly old glue.

Removing the Main Bellows Cloth

To remove the main bellows cloth, position the bellows so that you can easily get at the sides. If your organ has the springs on the outside, (Fig. 10-1) carefully remove them. Note that these springs are quite powerful. If you are not careful when you remove one leg of the spring, it might pop out with such force as to injure you. Use *both* hands, squeezing the spring together, working it out of slot or hole that may hold the free ends. Even here, be careful; you have a tiger by the tail. If you start to release the pressure on the spring to put it down, the thing will want to take off. The best procedure is to place one leg of the spring firmly on a bench top and then gradually let up. If you haven't done this before, you may think that I am being unduly elaborate. Believe me, once you let a spring get away from you, you will be much more respectful of them.

If the springs are on the inside of the main bellows (Fig. 10-2), first remove *just the sides* of the bellows. If you try to keep going around you may find that the pressure of the inside springs will cause things to come loose with disastrous consequences. So, once the sides are loose, reach inside and remove the springs, using both hands (unless you have a mighty powerful grip). All the earlier precautions hold true here also. You might have to rock the spring from side to side a bit in order to get it to come loose; usually the free ends of inside caliper-type springs have pointed ends that dig into the wood on the inside of the bellows. Occasionally they have dug in to such an extent that they are hard to extract. Once both springs are out you may wish to place a temporary wood block inside the main bellows to hold the hinged portion apart while you then remove the rest of the old bellows cloth. If there are no wooden strips nailed on top of the cloth, the electric iron technique is probably the best to use to loosen the glue since the edges are easy to get to. Keep the old cloth as a pattern.

Removing the Leather Valves

You may now remove all leather valves (there are probably four). What if they seem to be OK? Believe me, they probably aren't. After you get them off, try tearing one and see

Fig. 10-1. Typical exterior bellows spring, coil type.

how easily it comes apart. Before removing the valve you may wish to trace around it on the wood so that you can get the new one back in exactly the same place.

WOOD RESTORATION

You now have bellows ready for restoration. First examine the condition of the wood; if it is plywood and the plies seem to be separating, be sure to work glue into the plies and clamp them firmly for a day. If the screw holes where the straps fasten seem to have deteriorated wood around them, you may need to insert new wood. Those screws *must* have a good place to fasten to.

Warps can be really a problem here though a slight bit of warp may be acceptable. If the wood hinge is OK (i.e. the warp is not at the edge that fastens to the hinge) and the warp just causes a difference of, say, a half-inch at the extreme, it will probably cause you no problem. If the wood panels are of solid wood, have major cracks, and are warped so that the cracks are accentuated, you'd better replace the offending panel. Even if you are able to use clamps to pull the warped piece back and glue the cracks, chances are that it probably will split again. Since the bellows will not show, I suggest that you use plywood of the approximate thickness of the original. If the original was solid wood and you want to be as original as possible, you must glue up a panel as replacement. For this job

Fig. 10-2. Interior caliper-type bellows spring on 1891 Packard.

109

you need at least three bar clamps, a supply of "C" clamps or hand screws, plus a good joiner so that you can be assured of accurately planed edges. Be sure that you use properly seasoned wood or you will soon be right back where you started from. Are you sure you don't want to use plywood?

I find a power sander very handy when working with these panels. I follow the practice of doing a light surface sanding of all interior wood before proceeding with restoration. You will be surprised to find out how much dust and the like has accumulated on the surface of the wood. I then use a light spray coat of filler to give the wood a protective coat. This tends to seal in the surface and prevents the dusting off that can cause trouble with reeds.

Hinge Replacement

Let's assume that all hinges were bad and that the entire wooden portion of the bellows has been disassembled. Your first job will be that of replacing the interior hinge in the main bellows. The original was most likely a kind of denim or canvas (on older organs you will find, on rare occasions, leather or at least chamois). I frequently use strips of denim cut from defunct overalls. Any denim of reasonably heavy weight will do, as will other canvas. Don't use ordinary cloth since it isn't tough enough. Sand the surfaces where the hinge will be glued, using coarse sandpaper; a rough surface takes glue better. For applying the contact cement I use an oil-painting bristle brush (as shown in Fig. 6-1). Apply a liberal coat of the cement to the strip of canvas you have cut to fit. Then apply a coat of glue to the wood. Let both dry for about ten minutes, then recoat everything. After this dries you are now ready to apply the hinge to one of the pieces first; the other piece should be well out of the way. Be sure to position the hinge cloth correctly because you will not move it very easily (if at all) once the contact is pressed firmly together. You can protect the hinge from inadvertent contact with the other prepared surface while positioning the two by putting a piece of brown paper or wax paper over the exposed glue strip.

When you have both pieces approximately in location, temporarily brace them so that they will remain in place. Small tack strips across each end (like the bar of the letter "A") would do the job well. Remove the protective paper and allow the hinge to contact the other wood panel. Firmly smooth it down, making sure that all parts of the hinge are very firmly pressed to both wood panels. Try the hinge and make sure the pieces fold in the same relationship to each other that they had before you removed the old one.

If things just don't seem to work right, tear the new hinge off immediately. I know that the bond is supposed to be as strong as it ever will be but I have found that is *not* the case. You probably will ruin the cloth hinge getting it off; but it will come off much better if you don't wait even a few minutes after applying it. Figure out what you did wrong, then put on another hinge.

Valve Replacement

Most organs built before 1900 used leather valves. Obviously they worked well, often continuing to work reasonably 80 or more years. They do pose problems; they tend to curl at the sides, and they can become brittle, often even tearing loose. If you are going to keep the organ as original as possible, you will want to replace the valves with leather. Take the old valves to the nearest leather shop (or send a sample to your supplier) and try to get something very similar. A good start would be to ask for New Zealand lambskin. As you will read later, this material is also useful on pallets. You might keep in mind, however, that according to the people at the Tandy Leather Store in Kansas City the designations of specific types and qualities of leather will change. You should order not only by name but by including a sample of what you want to replace. If you have a choice, be sure to check the leather for uniform thickness and resistance to tearing.

Cut the leather to the same size as the original; probably twelve to fifteen inches long and about two and a half inches wide. Tack it exactly where the original was tacked in. You can use three regular tacks, as was originally done, or you can use a staple gun. For security I use the staple gun with three staples across each end plus an additional staple just below the two outer ones. This tends to keep the edges from curling. (Fig. 10-3).

Be sure to lay the valve in place so that it has no wrinkles. If it is too loose it will not seal properly. Of course you should place the soft side of the leather toward the valve holes. In time the valve will take a kind of set that causes it to seal very thoroughly with only slight vacuum. Do not stretch the leather in place over the valve holes. This will cause the valve to vibrate in use, producing an annoying sound. Moderation's the word: not too loose, not too tight, just right.

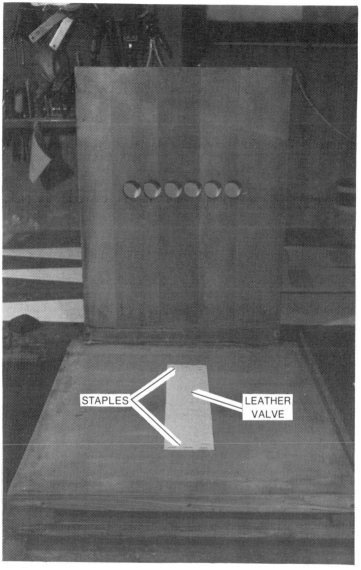

Fig. 10-3. New inside valve installed.

You may wish to change materials as previously suggested and use the heavy grade bellows cloth. In addition you may wish to add a little idea used on the 1908 piano organ. (See Chapter 20 for details.) When you use bellows cloth be sure to put the *rubber* side of the cloth toward the valve holes.

CLOTH RESTORATION

You must apply the valves on the main bellows before working on the exhausters since they go inside the exhausters. If you are starting from scratch and have no scrap bellows cloth available, you may wish at this time to lay out your whole bellows requirements on the cloth you bought so that you can have the scrap pieces you need for valves. A piece of bellows cloth of standard width (three feet) and about seven feet long is sufficient for the usual organ. While some people seem to prefer a lightweight cloth, I prefer the heavyweight variety. It works quite well and I don't think makes that much difference in pumping. It has the added advantage that it minimizes the flapping sound one can hear from a bellows being pumped heavily. Try to get cloth of about sixteen to twenty ounce weight per yard. I might also add that the lighter weight cloth tends to curl on the edges where glue is applied. Not so with the heavier. If you prefer the lighter weight, however, it will do a good job and will last probably as long as the heavy cloth.

Laying Out the Cloth

Try to arrange a bench so that you can spread the cloth out fully. Obviously you can spread it on the floor, but that can get awkward to work on. In laying out the bellows, make careful use of your own measurements of the wood on the bellows, as well as measurements taken from the old cloth. You will find that the old stuff has stretched so that it will be difficult to use for anything but general ideas. Be very careful that you lay out the bellows so that they will fit properly. For instance, do not make the mistake of assuming that the side of each pump bellows is symmetrical on either side of a centerline. My experience has been that frequently they are not symmetrical, though John's experience has been the opposite.

The best thing for you to do is plan to make a paper pattern, then fit it to the bellows wood in exact position, taping it on. You can then make sure it will fit and that the bellows will fold with the cloth as cut. Even better would be the use of scrap cloth of some kind as a pattern. Mistakes in cutting bellows cloth can easily occur and boy do they hurt. I strongly suggest that you make patterns in pencil, double checking each measurement. (Being left-handed, I am always trying to read a yardstick upside down, with sometimes disastrous results like cutting six inches instead of nine!)

When planning, be sure to allow the exact amount needed for gluing to the edge of the bellows. Some original bellows included a generous amount of overlap though most often they were glued only to the edges. Modern glues are sufficiently good that overlap is not necessary. Overlap would be a bit of insurance, though; if you want the extra be sure to allow cloth for it.

The bellows cloth comes with about a quarter inch or so of rubber lapping over the cloth at the edge. I trim that off first before starting to lay the pattern out.

Marking the Cloth

The main bellows will usually open about six or seven inches when fully extended. Add to that the thickness of the wood on the moving wood part of the bellows (usually from 1/2 inch to 3/4 inch) and the width glued to the fixed part of the main bellows on the other side (about 1 inch.) Thus in order to establish a centerline, take half of the bellows' open dimension (say, it's 7 inches, so half would be 3 1/2 inches) plus 5/8 inch for the edge on the moving wood. This equals 4 1/8 inches. Mark this distance all along the total length of the bellows cloth parallel to one edge. This is your centerline. Mark 3 1/2 inches on the other side of the centerline, then 1 inch on the other side of that, for the fixed part of the main bellows, and draw lines the full length of the cloth. This gives you the outside edges of the main bellows cloth. Then draw the taper to fit you bellows. Follow a similar plan in laying out each of the exhauster bellows cloth. A full set of bellows cloths, cut, glue applied, ready to put on, is shown in Fig. 10-4.

When you lay out a bellows in this manner, be sure to indicate exactly where the bellows cloth will be glued to the various edges. These lines will then be your guide for applying glue. If your organ included some pieces of cardboard inside the bellows (called *folders*—they keep the bellows from flapping and help them fold right) lay out indications exactly where they will fit (see Fig. 10-4). Some later organs included folders only in the exhausters, some had none whatever. The folders can be made from any cardboard you have which is about the same weight as the original. I have a supply of old file-dividers (not file folders—they are too light) which do very well. Cut your cardboard to match the size of the originals and be sure to pre-fold them on the exact centerline of the bellows.

Applying the Glue

Here again is where I use the 1/2 inch brush to apply glue. Lay out the exhausters first for applying cement. If you are

BELLOWS CLOTH

MARKS FOR FOLDERS

Fig. 10-4. New bellows cloth cut, with contact cement applied. Cloth is ready to install.

going to do the whole bellows job in one day, you can apply glue to all the bellows pieces at once since contact retains its effectiveness for hours after it dries. Just keep dust from it. I assume that you are going to use contact cement so I will proceed to describe that method. (I will shortly go into the method favored by John and Harlan, using white glue, and I'll detail a modification of my method as favored by Walt, too). I'm sure you get the impression that this is an area where each restorer develops his own pet methods. You will develop your own, too.

When applying contact cement to the areas you have marked out on bellows cloth, work fairly quickly, not worrying about trying to be too meticulous either about smoothing out the glue or keeping inside the lines. Of course, don't slop the stuff around or allow glue to build up in any area. Also cover the areas where the folders will go if you plan to use them. Then do the same to the parts of the wooden bellows where the cloth is to be glued. Also coat the mating surface of the folders. *Immediately* after you finish this job on one piece (taking not much more than five minutes) dip your brush in a small jar of lacquer thinner and wipe the brush clean. You may need to dip the brush three for four times. If you don't do this you are going to wind up with a ruined brush in short order.

115

HINGED
PART
OF EXHAUSTERS

Fig. 10-5. Exhausters ready for new cloth.

After about ten minutes, give everything a second coat of glue and again clean the brush. While waiting for this to dry you can prepare some strips of brown paper or wax paper about a foot or so wide and two feet long for use as protectors over the contact cement to keep one glued area from grabbing another before you are ready. A standard test for maximum efficiency of contact cement is to touch it with a piece of brown paper. If the contact is ready, it won't stick to the paper but it certainly will stick to other dry contact cement.

When you are ready for application, first apply the folders to the previously marked-off spots on the inside of the bellows. Be sure that the fold you put into the cardboard matches the centerline of the bellows. Smooth them down firmly and use a small rubber mallet all over the folder for insurance. Now apply the cloth to the exhausters. Which one you start with makes no difference.

Installing the Cloth

The bellows should be lying on a worktable with the exhausters up, hinged part away from you (Fig. 10-5). If your bellows platform is not removable, you will just have to work on the thing in reverse, hinged portion of the exhauster toward you. Place a piece of scrap wood inside the exhauster so that it props the movable side open at an angle *greater* than it will be open when the bellows is fully installed. Take the pieces of

116

protective paper and lay them over the three exposed strips of prepared glue areas on the main bellows, as shown in Fig. 10-6. This keeps accidents from happening while you attach the bellows cloth to the top panel.

Be sure you know exactly which edge of the bellows cloth goes to the moving panel and which goes to the side of the main bellows; this is especially important if the exhauster cloth is not completely symmetrical. After determining which edge goes to the panel, pick the bellows cloth up by that edge, holding it at the two top corner spots. You should have a mark on the cloth indicating where the corners are and where the center is. Make sure that you are holding the bellows straight but do *not* stretch it from corner to corner. Touch it to both corners just firmly enough that it will hold. Then grasp the edge of the bellows near the center and position it. If you are in luck, you now have the cloth properly positioned on the front edge. You might find that you prefer to position the bellows at the center and one edge first, working outward to each edge from the center. Here also, be sure not to stretch the cloth more than absolutely necessary; if you do, it will throw off your side measurements. I might add that if you do get outside the lines or if the cloth doesn't go on exactly as planned, don't worry about it. Some trimming is almost always necessary since the bellows cloth will stretch some in spite of your best intentions.

Fig. 10-6. Cloth partially applied to exhauster, protective paper in place.

CLOTH CUT SO
IT CAN BE BENT

Fig. 10-7. Exhauster closed, prior to mating glued bottom surfaces.

With the protective paper still in place, now apply the cloth down the sides, still on the exhauster panel. With scissors, cut a slit of about 1/2 inch on the exact corner mark on the two *bottom* corners of the exhauster. This is done because you must be able to bend the cloth at right angles when you attach it to the main bellows. (You can see the cut in Fig. 10-7). Now comes the ticklish part. Holding up the exhauster with one hand, reach under the free bottom edge of the partially-applied bellows and remove the block that so far has held up the movable panel of the exhauster. Compress the exhauster, carefully helping the bellows to fold inward in the manner it should when operating. Be sure that while compressing the exhauster the protective paper doesn't slip. When fully compressed, adjust the bottom of the exhauster so that the still-free bottom edge of the cloth is in approximate position directly over the glued area below it (Fig. 10-7).

When you know for sure that all is in position, *carefully* pull the front piece of protective paper from under a corner of the exhauster. Pull with one hand while holding up the free end of the bellows cloth. When you know that the corner is properly in registration above where it goes, carefully press the cloth to the glued surface of the wood. Pull the rest of the paper from the front and press the front edge in place. Now do the same for the inside edge of the exhauster (the one toward the center of the main bellows). If you need to, you can insert your hand from the other side inside the exhauster and guide the cloth with both hands so that it fits the area you marked off for it. Then do the final side. You will need now to clean an area at the hinge end of the exhauster so that you can apply more contact to about two inches on the top of the hinge. If you haven't installed bellows cloth on the outside of the hinge, do that now before folding over the end of the sides. Finally the tail end of the sides is folded over and securely glued to form a good seal at the hinge. It is important that all in this area be well glued as it is a common source of leaks. Figure 10-8 shows a completed exhauster.

Really go over each inch of the contact area to make sure that the glue is secure. I use the back end of a prybar to get to difficult areas. (Fig. 10-9). When I can, I use the small rubber mallet to pound down on the seams to make sure I have good contact. The last thing to do is to put a tack exactly at the corner where you cut the bellows cloth so that it could be spread to attach to the main bellows panel. Put the tack at the inside juncture of the cut (just in front of the head of the prybar in Fig. 10-9, though the tack was not yet in when the picture was taken). This promotes a better seal in a weak area where leaks are common. Do the same as above for the other exhauster. If you wish you can now install the valves on the outside of the exhausters, but you just may wish to wait until the main bellows is completed. The reason for waiting is that there is a means of testing the inside valves of the main

Fig. 10-8. One finished exhauster; next one in process.

Fig. 10-9. Miniature prybar in position for rubbing down edge of bellows cloth.

bellows if the exhauster valves are not on. They can then be installed later. Again, check the piano organ bellows section in Chapter 20 when you do plan to put the valves on, for a possible useful improvement.

MAIN BELLOWS INSTALLATION

By now you have the worst of the installation completed, and are ready for installing the main bellows. Before getting to that, check the inside where the springs go, if yours uses inside springs, to make sure that the pads all are OK and in place. They are necessary to keep the springs from knocking against the wood under heavy pumping. If you need to replace them, use felt-type weatherstripping, securely cemented (Fig. 10-10).

The large piece of bellows cloth goes on the main bellows fairly easily. First, raise the bellows to its normal full opening by using a temporary wood block. Walt prefers a more accurate method and temporarily tacks the panels open with a piece of scrap wood at either end. Then, as you did with the exhausters, determine the exact center of the bellows top panel and the center of the top of the bellows cloth. Both the wood and the cloth should be prepared with glue as was done with the exhausters. Carefully position the bellows cloth at the middle of the top piece, work out to the corners without stretching or allowing wrinkles on the actual glue surface. Do the same for the bottom edge of the front. It should look somewhat like the one in Fig. 10-11. The slight wrinkling shown disappeared when the springs were installed, which is the next job.

Installing the Springs

Install the first one by checking exactly where the original prongs of the spring went, then put the spring in. Do so by picking up the spring and compressing it on a workbench. Hold it closed with both hands. If you bought new springs, they came held closed by a ring like a "C" that clipped over the closed ends of the spring. You can put that ring on and then, after getting the spring in place, carefully remove the ring. Try it first, though, to make sure you can get it off properly.

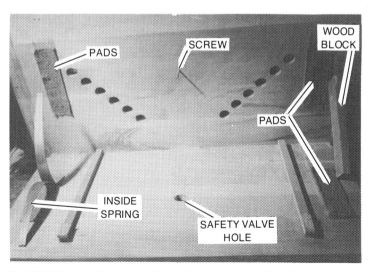

Fig. 10-10. Main bellows ready for cloth, showing position of spring, pads, and the screw that operates the safety valve.

You may find it easier just to hold the spring closed as you maneuver it into place. You may need a dropcord light source here so that you can see what you are doing. When the spring is in, test it for security by wiggling it back and forth a bit. This seats it in its original holes. If the riveted end of the caliper-type spring seems to rest very close to the wood so that it would tend to hit whenever the bellows is compressed, try reversing the spring or putting it in on the other side. The riveted end should rest somewhat midway between the panels of the main bellows.

Before installing the sides of the main bellows be sure that you mark the location of any holes for screws holding the side braces. After you put on the bellows cloth, you may have difficulty determining where the braces go unless you have so marked screw hole locations. You can now glue on the sides of the main bellows just as you did the exhausters.

Walt's Variation

Walt uses a slightly different method of installing bellows with some advantages over my method and, as you guessed, some disadvantages. First he just tears or cuts a strip of bellows cloth the required length and as wide as the widest part needed. With the panel propped open the required distance, (or nailed temporarily), he then attaches the front two edges *only* with contact cement. When that is on properly, he then folds the side panel back along the tapered side and marks on it exactly where it is to fasten to the wood. He then applies contact to the mating areas and when it is dry, fastens them, trimming to fit afterward. This method is better for assuring you do not make a mistake in measuring and in compensating for possible stretching. It is not as easy to apply the glue to the sides as the means I use.

John and Harlan's Variation

John and Harlan have for years successfully used white glue in the same manner that the old hot glues were used when the organs were built (and is still used at the Smithsonian where the original methods and materials must be used as much as possible, I understand.) This method has the distinct advantage of using a glue that allows the cloth to be moved around a bit after it has been applied to the bellows wood. The cloth is prepared the same way as in Walt's variation, tearing a strip the maximum width needed, cutting it the proper length. Then the exact center of the bellows cloth strip is found and marked, as is the center of the front edge of the top panel.

122

You will need to have available a supply of strips of wood approximately 1/4 inch thick and of a width equal to the edge thickness of the bellows panel. Put a block of wood inside the exhauster to hold the panel open and apply white glue liberally to the wood edge at the front; also apply some to the mating portion of the cloth. Apply the cloth to the edge of the panel then nail the wood strip over the bellows cloth, securely holding it to the wood edge. Do the same for the bottom edge. Now do the same for the sides, not worrying about trimming until the strips are all securely nailed in. Trimming then is easy, though you should wait several hours before trimming anything. The principle is the same for main bellows and exhausters. Be sure to use a tack in the corner of the exhausters as earlier mentioned.

This method is certainly a good one and may be more forgiving of possible mistakes, though I don't feel it gives quite as good a seal as contact does. I see no reason, however, why the technique of using contact cement to plug small leaks could not be used as well with bellows applied initially with other glues.

Installing the Safety Valve

The final element to go on the bellows is the safety valve. This is a necessary item since someone pumping the bellows up too tight might literally suck the bellows apart. (Dear little monsters just *love* to romp on organ pedals!) The safety valve opens when the main bellows has been drawn in to within about an inch of its total possible travel. All valves exhibit the same principle: They have some means of pushing the valve open if the two panels of the main bellows are sucked in too close. One method, shown in Fig. 10-10, simply uses a large screw attached to the inside front of the bellows in such a location that it will protrude through a hole in the rear panel if the bellows is pumped too much. The screw head then pushes open a little block of wood that is faced with leather and hinged at the top. This little block usually has a small spring running from the bellows to the block to keep it in place until it is forced out.

Another method has everything outside. A block of wood faced with leather or chamois, covers the valve opening, but protruding from its center is a piece of wood (or a screw) that will hit the opposite side if the bellows is pumped too much. You will find safety valves either on the rear of the bellows or on the front between the exhausters as is the case with the piano organ (Fig. 10-12).

Fig. 10-11. Main bellows cloth partially applied.

PLATFORM RESTORATION

The bellows platform is a large piece of wood that goes on top of the bellows with an opening through which vacuum is drawn (Fig. 10-13). The reed pan sits directly on top of it on the felt seals. This piece is quite important, so check it very carefully. It cannot be warped or cracked; it must be fastened

Fig. 10-12. Typical safety valve (from piano organ.)

Fig. 10-13. Bellows platform of Packard.

completely airtight to the bellows and must provide a perfect mate to the bottom of the reed pan so that it can be completely airtight also. You will find a number of construction techniques that builders used to minimize problems here. The photo of the Packard bellows platform shows that the builder used a number of pieces of wood to minimize warping of a single piece. In addition, he deliberately left spaces between some pieces to allow room for swelling and shrinking. In order to make the platform airtight, one builder covered the spaces with bellows cloth. When I tried to take off the old cloth I found it stuck so thoroughly that I would have had to use a power sander to remove the stuff. There were some weak spots in the cloth over the cracks, so it needed repair. I decided to sand the area thoroughly, coat the original strips with contact cement, then cover the cracks with furnace duct tape. It has worked quite well, with no problems.

Other means of building the platform are not as thoughtful as this one and you may have problems with cracks and warping. For instance the platform of the piano organ had a slight warp (who said plywood won't warp?) Before deciding that you must junk the whole platform and make a new one, try the reed pan on for size. It may be that as the platform slowly warped over the years, the reed pan took a slight warp with it. Such seems to be the case with the piano organ. In that case, you are home free. If the warp is of a very slight degree (about 1/8 inch or so) you might be able to compensate with slightly thicker seals at one side. If the bellows platform is slightly flexible, you might be lucky enough to have the screws holding the reed pan to the platform effectively pull the warp out and allow a good seal. Your exact choice of what to do will, of course, depend on your individual situation. Your guide should be based on what you know you will have to do if your first choice won't work. If a problem that remains will require a complete disassembly to correct it, you might better take a bit more time and make some more adjustments rather than take a risk. I would be cautious about modifying anything that you cannot put back as original; for example don't try to curve the bottom of the reed pan to fit a warped platform. If it doesn't work you are in real trouble.

After making sure you can live with the major condition of the platform, check the screw holes where the screws holding the reed pan go in. If they are at all suspicious you might try a treatment suggested to me by John. He places a few flat toothpicks around the inside edge of an enlarged hole, gluing them in with white glue. Then when the screws are inserted they are able to take a firm bit in the bellows platform, thus insuring a good seal.

SEALS RESTORATION

Now the seals. Here you must decide what condition the original seals are in. Frequently you will find that builders used ordinary blotting paper as seals. Generally the original seals are so compressed that is it doubtful they will perform their job very well. You can replace them with other pieces of blotting paper obtained from your local office supply. My preference is to use strips of felt, though others suggest thin gasket cork obtainable from an auto supply house. To prepare for seals, clean off the originals and sand slightly.

Next is an important step: Be sure to mark where the screw holes are so you can find the holes after they are covered up with the new seal. If you use felt, you must take an awl and punch through the seal *before* you attach the reed pan to the platform. If you don't, you will find to your grief that the screws do not just go through the felt: they grab it, causing it to twist and causing the seal to be broken. To reduce this problem you can pre-punch the seals using a paper punch, but lately I have found that properly punching with an awl works well.

The best way to mark the holes is to make marks *outside* the area covered by the felt, pointing in to where the hole is.

126

Then after the seal glue has dried thoroughly (don't do it before the glue is set—the seal will pull loose) you can take the awl and start probing gently in the area where the hole is below the felt. Then you can punch through when you have located the hole. It really works well. Walt also prefers to stick each screw into a block of beeswax before inserting it in its location; he finds that the wax minimizes the problem of grabbing the felt.

Finally, apply new seals also to the top of the opening of the bellows itself where it is screw-fastened to the bottom of the bellows platform. The same techniques and materials apply here as they do to the seals on the platform. Once the seals are dry and holes punched, securely fasten the bellows to the platform. Now add the side braces, making sure that you have the right brace in the right location, the proper length screw for the right hole. This could be a problem since two different lengths of screw were often used on those braces; getting the longer screw in where the short one belongs could result in a hole on the other side of the bellows board that you don't want. You are now ready to test the bellows.

TESTING THE BELLOWS

To test you must first seal the slot temporarily. A very good way to do this is to use a three-inch wide strip of furnace duct tape, available at any hardware. It is a very tough tape with a good adhesive. Put a strip of it over the full length of the slot and securely smooth it down around the edges. Put the bellows in such a position that at least one exhauster can move freely and the main bellows can collapse inward without rubbing on anything (like the floor). Then take hold of the top of one exhauster and pump until the main bellows is completely closed and the safety valve opens. Stop pumping and measure the time the bellows takes to completely open. A good bellows will hold vacuum for up to a minute and a half (the piano organ did, for example.) Other restorers are not so demanding as I am in this regard. One author of an early book on organs suggested that fifteen seconds is a sufficient time. I still prefer that it work for at least a minute, and find it quite possible to achieve this goal. If it holds for less time, you need to look for leaks.

Finding Leaks

This is the only situation that makes me sometimes wish I smoked. The best way to find a leak is to pump the bellows fully exhausted then blow smoke around various seams to find where the smoke is evidently being drawn in. Not being a devotee of the weed, I must listen for the sound of air being sucked in and then try to find the openings. Here one property of contact cement is very helpful. Once I find a suspected pinhole opening (it doesn't take much of an opening to cause a sizeable leak) I then coat the suspected spot with contact and immediately pump the bellows up. This will cause glue to be sucked into the hole. If I know I got the right spot, I then coat it again and leave everything to dry for a while. You might find more than one leak and may have to perform this ritual several times. The second hand on your watch should tell you quickly if you are making headway.

One source of problems, as mentioned earlier, could be a bellows platform that is not removable. The one I worked on had a severe leak somewhere even though the bellows itself seemed tight. I was able to trace the leaks to numerous very small holes in the original glue holding the platform to the bellows frame. Not wanting to knock the whole thing apart, I tried the contact cement trick, pumping the bellows up several times just after giving the suspected areas coatings of contact; the leaks stopped.

Installing the Pedal Straps

Now you should attach the pedal straps to the exhausters in preparation for final installation of the bellows. You will find that the straps are usually held by a small block of wood and two screws. Be sure to cut the strap long enough; I usually allow about three feet per exhauster so that there will be enough. Punch holes through the pedal straps so that the screws will go through the webbing and into the top of the exhauster. Note that the strap goes *behind* the block and then extends over the *top* of the block. After the bellows is installed in the case, the strap will then go over a pulley and down to the pedals.

Just a word about sources of supply for pedal straps. For years I have been using a two-inch wide webbing I obtained at a local hardware. It is also commonly available at farm stores. The only problem is that recently it has taken a horrendous jump in price. I suggest that you get the material sold for pedal straps from the suppliers listed in the Appendix.

Before actually fastening the strap to the exhauster, check the condition of the screw holes. If the holes are enlarged or if the wood is deteriorated around them, be sure to do secure repairs. Those screws must hold considerable pressure so be sure you can tighten them as much as possible.

You will be tempted to avoid all above problems by simply moving the location of the screw block. Be careful. The pedal strap must go straight from the exhauster to the pulley. If it doesn't, the strap will be continually sliding off the pulley, much to the disgust of the organist. A very slight alteration up or down might not cause trouble, but be careful of too much change in location. With the straps installed you are now ready for installing the completed bellows in the case.

FINAL BELLOWS INSTALLATION

Installation is probably as easy a job as you will have. Simply place the bellows in position with the bellows platform resting on the side braces. You may wish to use an awl as a screw-hole locator. Once one screw is in place, the others on either side are usually easy to put in.

If the pedals have not been installed, you must install them now. Lay the organ over on its back (or side if it doesn't have handles on), protected from the floor with an old quilt or the like. Installation of the pedals usually involves no more than four flat-head screws. Before going farther you should put a protective strip of something over the bent ends of the pedal hinges. These consist of a kind of large staple that is clinched on the bottom of the pedal platform. If not covered, they can hook into the pile of a modern rug and really do damage whenever the organ is moved. I usually put a strip of that furnace duct tape over the bottom of the pedal platform, and make it secure with a staple gun. With a tack hammer you might want to tap the staples you just put in to make sure none of them is sticking out.

Decide exactly where the pedals should come to rest when the straps are fastened. This will usually be at a point where they are parallel to the edge of the side brace that supports the pedal platform, though not always. In any event, be sure to leave some travel at the top; don't tie the pedal up as high as it will go. I usually try to leave about 1/2 inch. The straps are held to the inside top of the pedal by a wood block much like that holding the strap to the exhauster. Here you will have to forget your dignity and lie down on the floor (unless you have the case on its side or on a workbench). Hold the strap in position behind the pedal in such a position that the pedal rests where you want it to. Put the block of wood where it will go and mark where the screws go through the strap. Be sure that the strap is still running over the pulley where it should. Leave at least a couple of inches of pedal strap extending below the

Fig. 10-14. Completed bellows installed in Packard.

block just in case you have positioned the pedal too high and must lower things a bit. Install the block, securely fastening the screws. If you have an organ that uses a block with only one screw, I suggest that you make a new block using two screws; a single one can work itself out, much to your disgust. Figure 10-14 shows the Packard with the bellows installed, pedal straps just visible. Pedal straps can be anchored just about anywhere on the originals; you will notice that the Packard straps anchor near the outside edges of each pedal. Others will be more centered or anchored at the inside edges. Note that the Packard had different pedal pads when this photo was taken than those that were later installed.

Place your organ back upright and check to determine that both pedals come to rest exactly side-by-side. If not, adjust them appropriately. Be sure that your final adjustments are taken with the pedal springs installed. These usually are caliper-type springs of less pressure than the main bellows springs, their prongs fitting into a spot at the top of the exhauster on one side and into the inside front of the case or a strip of wood inside on the other. If each exhauster isn't held in its proper place when at rest, you cannot adjust the pedals precisely.

John has had difficulties with the pedal pulleys squeeking, so he routinely drills a small hole in the center of the pulley roller and puts oil in it to halt the squeak. Since oil can attract

130

dirt, you may wish to consider using graphite or silicone spray for the same job.

With this job done cover things up, set the case back, and get ready for some action—organ action, that is.

BELLOWS NOTES

Chapter 11
Action
Disassembly

Ordinarily the organ *action* consists of all that sits on top of the reed pan. The usual major units are the stopboard, keyboard, octave coupler, pitmans, vox humana, swells, mutes, and reeds. Disassembly will proceed in that order.

Before beginning, be sure to check very thoroughly the operation of the stopboard and associated linkages. If all seems well, needing only some cleaning, repadding, and adjusting, you are in luck. More likely, you will find items missing or, worse yet, improperly hooked up. Look for evidence of some hamfisted "repairs": hunks of wire substituted for wooden connectors between stop action rods and associated mutes and swells, or leaky mutes taped, nailed, or even glued shut. I could go on. The point is that you should be suspicious of anything that doesn't look just right.

I know that sounds about like the dilemma of the student who thinks dictionaries are ridiculous: if he could spell the word in the first place he wouldn't need to look it up. In this case, however, you really *can* decide that something is wrong with an organ action and figure out the correction even if you haven't a good model in front of you. If you get well acquainted with the principles of organ operation and check carefully the pictures in this book, you ought to be able to do a better job than you think of figuring out what is wrong with a defective action. And you'll do so even though I can't begin, in a book of this size, to show the wide variety of mechanisms that were devised during the heyday of the reed organ.

In case you do find something that seems wrong, try to get it repaired before you disassemble any further. You can probably make a good guess at the effectiveness of your repair. Also, before disassembly, be quite sure that you have very clear drawings or pictures of which connecting rod goes where at the sides (or at the rear in such organs as the Cornish) of the action. Here you are going to be very tempted to feel sure that you will remember just where that part went; after all, it isn't exactly like any other. Famous last words. I agree that you can probably fit things back, eventually; but I hope you like puzzles. Even simple mechanisms for which the operation is so clear when viewed as originally assembled, become infuriatingly difficult when all pieces are apart. Figures 11-1 and 11-2 show the connections at both sides of a 1914 Windsor with four ranks of reeds. In cases such as this, where the side connections consist of strips of wood, you might also label each side connector to record which side it belongs on. Here Harlan prefers a dot system; a single dot of paint on the first connector to be removed, and a corresponding one on the side of the action; two dots on the next, and so on. This produces a permanent code for the order of the parts regardless of how many times you have to take them apart. I have had the experience where the rods on either side were not the same length but were so close that it took a lot of time just to juggle them around trying to get the action working properly. The fact that often the action travel is critical to within 1/16 inch means that very slight differences in connector dimensions are of very real significance. Labeling them as you take them off saves a lot of grief.

THE STOPBOARD

As mentioned earlier, stopboards really perform a simple function: as you pull out one of the stopboard's stops, it activates the swell, mute, octave coupler, or vox humana to which it is in some way connected. The joker consists of getting quite familiar with that "some way" in which it is connected. Almost every brand of organ has its own ingenious linkages. The Packard has an extremely easy system to work with. All that is needed for removal of the stopboard is the extraction of two screws at each side, easily reached behind the vertical portion of the stopboard, and the removal of the control stick going to the vox humana. The horizontal rod part of the linkage terminates in 90° angles in such a manner that it easily contacts the rods going to the mutes, etc., yet is not

Fig. 11-1. Side of action of 17-stop Windsor.

actually hooked or screw-fastened to them. When the stopboard is free it is very simple to lift the whole stopboard up and set it aside. Figure 4-2 in Chapter 4 showed the Packard action with stopboard on, and Fig. 11-3 shows it with stopboard off.

A more common method involves the use of wooden slats about 1/8″ thick with slots at one or both ends as with the Windsor shown in Fig. 11-1 and 11-2. These must be disconnected before the action can be lifted off. The first thing to do is to slide the connector off the end of the rod that can be seen in the photos at the upper end of each connector. Then the bottom end can be removed by twisting the connector in such a way that it slides off the bent wire that holds it to the mute or swell. Some will be held at the bottom end by small screws (as one is on the Windsor.)

Note that these wood connectors are subject to cracks; as you remove them you should repair them by filling the cracks with glue and clamping them with masking tape. You will sometimes find that wood will be gone from the upper end of the slot so that nothing holds. You will have to replace that wood. Since the exact dimension of that slot is rather critical, you will probably have to do some adjusting to it with a very small rat-tail file to get the proper length of travel of the mute associated with that stop.

I strongly suggest that you have a fairly large box available; tape all linkages together, properly labeled, and put

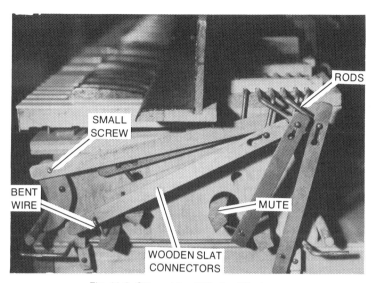

Fig. 11-2. Other side of 17-stop Windsor.

them in the box along with whatever smaller boxes or cans you use for the screws and the like that come off with the linkages. Keeping all these together can really be a timesaver. Nothing is more infuriating than having to spend an hour or more looking for that coffee-can of parts you were "just sure" was on the other end of the workbench somewhere under that pile of clean-up rags.

Fig. 11-3. Packard action with stopboard removed.

THE KEYBOARD

Before removing the keyboard check to see if all keys are reasonably level. If not, spot which ones are high or low and specifically make note of the number of each key (numbering from either end.) The problem may be a defective pitman or pad under the key, or problems with the spring on a pallet beneath things. In any event, if you know before removal of the keyboard where the problem is you can then correct it better than if you wait until reassembly. More about this later. Just be sure at this time that your scribbled notes are decipherable (that's my problem) and that they are accurate enough for you to find the culprit some time later.

The keyboard is usually held at the ends and center. There will usually be two flat-head countersunk screws at either end, easy to locate. Most often there is also a hidden screw near the center of the keyboard. To get at it you must remove the wooden keeper that fits in the slot behind each key. You will need a small screwdriver to take out the five or six screws holding it. Then remove a few center keys until you find the hidden screw. Remove it and try to lift the keyboard off. If it still seems to stick at the ends, it might be because of the pin that sometimes provides exact registration for the keyboard frame. It is a small wood or metal dowel fastened permanently to either the frame itself or to the side wood support. Ordinarily the frame just lifts out, but sometimes that pin gets corroded or crudded up and sticks. In this case insert a thin chisel or sturdy knife between the frame and the side mount and *gently* pry up. On most organs there is also an easily seen bent wire rod brace at the front of the key frame; this is easily removed. If things don't come loose yet with all of these items checked, start looking for other fasteners such as nails, other screws, or even a misguided glue job that someone decided on when the original screws may have loosened up. Just work very cautiously. Too much pressure on parts here can result in disastrous breakage.

Once you have removed the keyboard, replace the keys in the center, put in the rear wooden keeper with its screw, and wrap the whole keyboard along its length with a strip of sturdy masking tape. The tape is precaution: without it you might damage keys if you turn the keyboard over and cause the keys to fall out of their normal position. You could bend some pins or break the wood at the end of a key. Now cover with plastic and set aside for the time being.

THE OCTAVE COUPLER

What you remove next depends on the accessibility of the screws holding the octave coupler to the center of the action. If you can get a small screwdriver in to the screws, fine. Remove the screws and lift off the coupler. You may have to wiggle things around a bit, but it will come off. If you find that the cloth hinges of the coupler itself are about to come loose from the square wooden strip they are attached to, be sure to fasten the parts together with masking tape so that the pieces are kept together *in the exact position they occupied originally.* If you put the hinges back but don't get the coupler parts in exact registration, your coupler simply will not work properly, if at all. Now set the coupler aside.

THE PITMANS

The wooden guide strip for the pitmans may, however, extend out so that you cannot get to the coupler until the pitmans are removed. Figure 11-4 shows the Cornish with the pitmans, guide strip, and octave coupler still installed. If the pitman guide strip is intact, with pitmans all seemingly OK, you might try to remove it and the pitmans at the same time. Put a strip of tape down both sides of the pitmans, as in Fig. 1-5 and then remove the pitmans, strip and all, by removing the

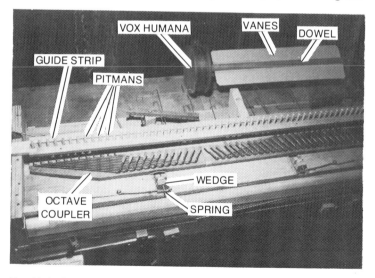

Fig. 11-4. Cornish action with keyboard removed; pitmans, guide strip, and octave coupler are still in place.

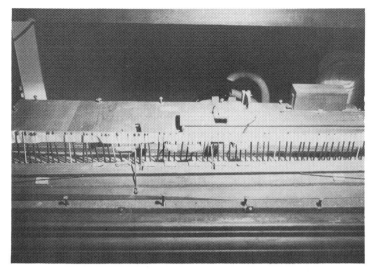

Fig. 11-5. Pitmans of New England organ covered with tape and ready for removal.

small screws or nails at either end, and the small screw or nail at the center. (Note: there is no guide strip in Fig. 11-5 because the New England organ did not have one.) Before removing the strip be sure to indicate which end of the guide strip goes where when you reassemble; the strip and pitmans look symmetrical at either end but really aren't.

While doing all of this be very careful to keep the action reasonably level. Above all, don't turn it upside down. If the pitmans fall out you are in trouble. Don't be tempted just to put the pitmans all in a box since they all look alike. True, you can just stick them back in and the organ will work, but you will have a snaggle-toothed keyboard. If many of the pitmans are badly damaged by mice, or are broken, then just put them all in a box and resign yourself to the time-consuming job of leveling a keyboard.

THE VOX HUMANA

Vox humana removal is next. This is usually a circular box at the rear of the action with peculiar cardboard vanes extending from a dowel running from the side of the box (See Figs. 11-4 and 11-6). You have already removed the control strip from the stopboard so all you need to do now is to remove the three screws that hold the mechanism to the floor of the reed pan. Do *not* attempt to take anything apart any further.

The thing is rather delicate inside and you are in trouble if things get jammed. Do not try to take off even the dowel in which the vox humana vanes are inserted. I know that it comes off rather easily—it just pulls off the wire shaft of the inside rotating mechanism— but I have found that in pushing the dowel back on you can jam things inside. If you don't absolutely have to remove the dowel or get inside the box for repairs, don't. Some organs have a different vox humana, more properly called a tremulo, in a small box at the rear of the reed pan. Figure 11-7 shows the one on Turner's Prince. Removal of one or two screws releases the box which can then be set aside. Be sure that the spring mechanism inside it is securely fastened so that you don't mistakenly lose part of it.

THE SWELLS

Next remove the swells. They are the strips of wood about three or four inches wide running the full length of the action in front of each set of reeds (or in front of each pair of sets in case the organ has more than two sets.) Figure 11-6 showed the swells still in place. Before removing them check the condition of the springs that keep them shut. These springs are made of either spring brass or music wire and are so bent that they act much like an auto torsion bar. Even though the spring may seem to be in good shape, be suspicious of it if it has more than

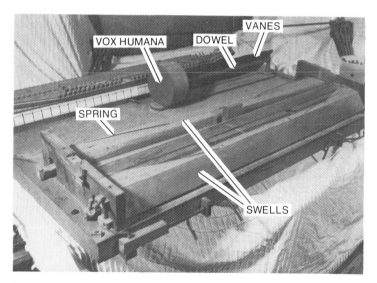

Fig. 11-6. Unrestored Packard action showing swell shutters. The vox humana is the circular structure and with its extension vanes at the rear.

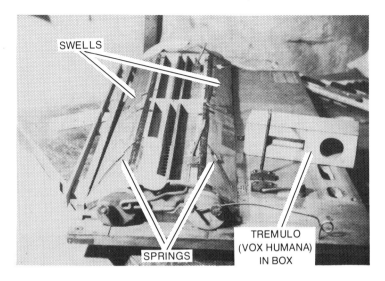

Fig. 11-7. 1875 Prince showing removed tremulo box at right and activating mechanism.

surface rust. Also try to make sure that the spring is of original length and is anchored in original position. Often, years ago, a spring broke and rather than replace it, an owner would just bend another end on the spring and force it into a new location. That may or may not work properly. Look for other small holes in locations near the present spring mounting to see where it might have been attached originally. If there is more than one spring hole evident, try to determine which one seems to be original and circle it. It will probably be the one farthest away from the end of the bobtailed spring.

Test the operation of the swell. Does it work well on its hinges and does the spring cause the swell to return to position firmly? Also be sure that all springs are present. Most often you will find two such springs on each swell. The action will work with only one operable, but it might not seal properly or might not force the other parts of the lever action to which it is connected to return to their proper positions. Figure 11-7 shows the two springs and their positions. This configuration is characteristic of both front and back swells.

These springs do not have a great deal of tension on them so they are not as dangerous as the main bellows springs, but they can be troublesome. You will find that the portion of the spring that is forced into the wood is sharpened. When you pull it out it will snap immediately about 90° away from you. If your

141

finger is in the wrong place you can get stuck. I usually pry the spring up about 1/4 inch with a screwdriver then use long-nose pliers to pull it the rest of the way out.

If the swells are in good shape, and the springs also in good condition, you may not need to remove the springs at all. Often the swells are attached to a wood strip that slides in slots in the support brace at either end of the action. You may need to remove only about three screws at the far edge of that strip (accessible after you have removed the octave couplers) and the whole strip and swell will slide out. If you don't have to take out the springs, don't. This way you keep the springs where they belong. They can get lost very easily if taken off.

THE MUTES

The mutes are next. They are triangular strips of wood that fit closely in front of the reed cells. They are held by two or three brass hinges and usually have a spring similar to those on the swells. A long mute (usually treble side) may have two. The Packard (shown in Fig. 2-3 Chapter 2) had one spring on each mute. Remove the spring from the mute, leaving it in the top of the reed cell if the springs seem to be OK. Then take out the little screws holding the hinges to the mute. These little screws can be real headaches: I usually take an old knife blade and attempt to clean the slots thoroughly before even trying to take them out. For some reason, these screws are often corroded. There have been times when I have just had to pry them out then replace damaged wood before putting back new screws. Put all mutes together, preferably taped in a bundle, then set aside in a good storage place. Keep even those that are obviously too badly damaged by vermin or moisture; you will need them as patterns. If there are small parts about to fall off the mutes (like the dowels at the end for connection to the stopboard) be sure to keep them, preferably taped in place. Don't be surprised to find these mutes, normally hidden from view, badly damaged by mice. Inside the swells was a good location for mice to build nests and the mute wood and leather covering apparently tasted good. See the extensive mouse damage in Fig. 11-8. A question you are going to have to deal with is that of when to replace such wood.

THE REEDS

For reed removal you will need a reed hook or reasonable facsimile thereof. These are available new, if your organ

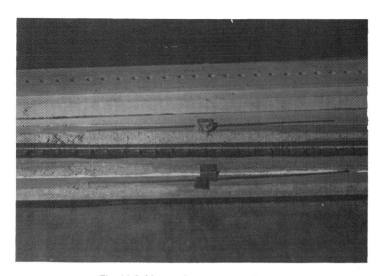

Fig. 11-8. Mouse damage on mutes.

Fig. 11-9. Reed hook mounted on New England organ.

doesn't have one with it, so you really don't need to make one. If you just must have an immediate substitute I suggest that you make yours from a paint-can opener which already has a hook at the end. Bend the hook a bit more until it makes an angle fully 90° and then grind it a bit on the edges so that it fits snugly in the slot at the end of the heel of the reed. The paint-can opener makes a very good puller for the melodeon reeds and early upright organ reeds which have only a small projection at the heel or just the projection of the rivet on which to pull. The opener-puller will look much like the original that came with the New England organ (Fig. 11-9).

Reeds are just inserted in slots in the reed cells when organs are built, so they should just slide out when you pull directly out with the hook. They very often don't slide out easily, though. At times a brass reed will corrode to the point that it sticks to the wood at the side of the cell; the wood may have gotten wet and swelled; or some ham-fisted person may have forced the wrong reed in a cell too small for it. If you get all the reeds out with no more than a little occasional wiggling, count your blessings. If things look fairly good, you can prepare for your ordeal by just laying a strip of 3/4 inch or so masking tape in front of the reed cells all along the full length (sticky side up.) Leave six inches or so extending beyond each end. Then when you remove a reed, you will place it on the

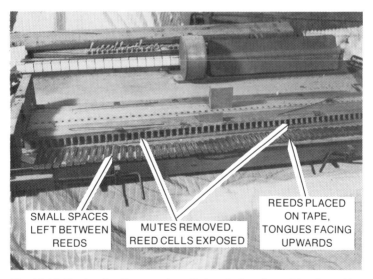

Fig. 11-10. Packard action, reeds pulled and placed on strip of masking tape.

Fig. 11-11. Same reeds rolled and labeled.

masking tape, reed tongue *up* (Fig. 11-11). You will probably find that each reed will have its note designation (C#, G, etc.) stamped on the heel. I suggest that you don't rely on those designations to tell where a given reed goes. In the first place, you may be surprised to find out how long it will take you to sort them out if you just dump them in a box. Also, not all ranks of reeds progress from bass by half-steps to the highest treble; one set of reeds in the bass is often a duplicate of the octave above it. Even worse, some organs have a celeste rank of reeds which is tuned slightly sharp of the rest of the organ. Get those mixed in with other reeds and you have a *real* puzzle to solve. Also you may find that someone has replaced some reeds with those taken from other instruments. These may have been retuned to fit, say C natural even though they may be marked C#. The tape roll, properly marked, is your safest bet.

This doesn't mean that you should just go to rolling the bundle. You probably should place a loose piece of paper on *top* of the upper dozen or so of treble reeds as a precaution against damaging the delicate tongues. *Do not use sticky tape of any kind.* Getting it off could in itself damage the tongues. When the protective strip is on, roll those reeds. Before you roll, however, carefully check the reeds for evident damage— cracks around the rivets, broken tongues, etc. If there is much damage, you need to find out for sure what you can do about it.

Now for actually pulling the reeds. First and foremost, as the label on the New England organ (Fig. 6-2) cautioned, *don't*—repeat—*don't* insert the reed hook beyond the slot or projection at the back of the reed which is designed as the means for pulling. If you catch the free end of the reed with the hook, you've had it. A problem in pulling reeds is that of having the reed come out rather suddenly. This can happen even if you are trying to be careful. A reed may stick; but when it finally does come after you exert more pull, it flies out. To guard against this I always use both hands, one positioned to prevent sudden releases.

If you use the usual reed hook, put a finger through the loop. I use my right hand for this function. My left thumb and forefinger grasp the hook very near the end of the cell so that if the reed releases suddenly, my left hand can prevent things from flying out. I brace the left hand on the floor of the reed pan just in front of the reed cell. Also be sure that you pull straight out. If you check your reed cells you will find that the reed slots are slightly above the reed pan. If you keep the hook low you will be pulling slightly down and that could cause problems.

If the reed doesn't come you have another problem. *Don't* apply much pressure in any direction except directly out. If you aren't careful you can easily break the rather fragile separations between reed cells. To break the reed loose if it is stuck, you might try grasping the reed by the end of the frame with a pair of long-nosed pliers. *Gently* work it sideways until it breaks loose. You might try pulling with the reed hook at the same time you are rocking it with pliers. Another caution: If you remove the reeds on both sides of the stuck one in order to allow a bit of moving room, it might help; but this also increases the danger of your breaking the cell separation.

There is one other thing to try: A long X-acto blade slid beneath the reed, or even for a short distance beside it, might break things loose. The danger is, of course, that of cutting too far or in the wrong direction. Your own ingenuity will have to come into play here as you try other means for getting a reed loose.

Sooner or later I have managed to get almost all reeds out without damage to anything and so will you. There just might be the rare instance when nothing works. Then you must just take a deep breath and pry things far enough to risk breaking a reed cell. All is not lost if you do. Just be sure that if pieces come out you *immediately* put them in a safe place. I have a

146

Fig. 11-12. Stripped action of Windsor, showing double set of reed cells.

can handy just for that purpose. Then when the reed is out, *immediately* put the pieces back with glue in exactly the same spot they came from. When they are in, I run a miniature screwdriver blade or a very fine file down the reed slot to make sure that no glue has accumulated there. (See Chapter 14 for ordering new reeds if that becomes necessary. Chapter 17 deals with repairing and tuning existing reeds.) Figure 11-12 shows a stripped set of reed cells for a Windsor. By now the base of the action is quite light and easy to work with.

THE PALLETS

Last to be removed are the pallets under the reed pan. Figure 11-13 shows an unusual set of pallets (New England organ), where an extra set exists for a back rank of reeds. The pallets are connected end-to-end. If you run across something like this, make sure you know just how it works and how it will go back. More likely you will find just a single row of pallets like that shown in Fig. 11-14.

Before removing any pallets, number them for accurate replacement. This step may not be absolutely necessary since you probably are going to replace all the leathers, but I have found it to be a good precaution. Remove the pallets, one at a time, lifting off the spring and moving it sideways enough to allow removal of the pallet. Unless there is something wrong with the wood strip the pallet springs are fastened in or unless

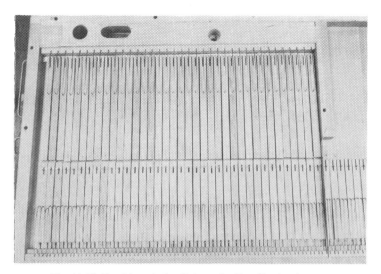

Fig. 11-13. Double set of pallets under New England organ.

the springs are bad, there is no reason to remove the springs. Place all pallets in a box and set aside. If your organ is an old one and the springs are made of spring brass, don't be surprised if some break as you lift out the pallets. This probably is nothing you can prevent and it is best that you find the weak ones now. They are not difficult to reproduce from music wire. If you have many to replace, they can be bought

Fig. 11-14. Normal (single) set of pallets.

148

new. If the spring block does need work, pull all springs with pliers and store them in a box. No need to indicate which goes where unless yours has some unique features I have never seen.

Finally, strip off the felt that is in front of the reed cells. It is usually quite ratty. The best way to strip it is, of course, to lift up one end and carefully pull the whole thing off. You will not usually be so lucky since the felt is frequently quite deteriorated. In such cases carefully run a sharp 3/4 inch wood chisel down the shallow slot the felt fits in and scrape the felt out. Be *very* careful not to let the chisel slip. If you hit a reed-cell separation with even the slightest pressure you will probably break it. *Always* work at right angles to the reed cells, *never* toward them, at least with the chisel. If you have a pesky piece of felt located right by the cell, you may have to use a knife blade to get the last remains. When this is done you have completed stripping the action.

ACTION DISASSEMBLY NOTES

Chapter 12
Reed Pan and
Cell Restoration

Begin restoration of the reed pan and reed cells by checking for cracks and loose glue joints. Very often you will find cracks in the pan similar to the one in the piano organ action illustrated in Fig. 12-1. These cracks come simply from the shrinking of wood and they must be filled. There is no way you can clamp them back so that they will hold. If the crack is just a hairline, impossible to get anything in, you will do OK with glue thoroughly rubbed in from both sides. In other cases you will need to fill with something more substantial.

I find that a strip of veneer is an ideal sliver to get in the usual crack. First, fill the crack with glue and then work in a sliver of the veneer, trying to get it through to the other side. After all has dried, trim the top and bottom flush with the reed pan and sand lightly. Check for small pinholes still remaining at either end of the crack. Fill in as appropriate. Walt prefers to cover the crack with thin bellows cloth or linen about 1 inch wide, even after the crack has been filled, because what has once cracked can do it again.

CLEANING THE REED PAN

After getting major cracks and glue joints repaired, clean the reed pan very carefully. Particularly make sure that you get all dirt out of the reed cells. Unless the organ has been exceptionally well taken care of you will find that generations of insects have found the reed cells made to order for their

CRACK

Fig. 12-1. Crack in reed pan.

nests. I first try to blow the cells out using a vacuum cleaner with hose reversed. This does a lot of cleaning, but many of those nests are stubborn. You must then inspect each cell to determine that all is indeed cleaned out. If not, go to it with whatever you need to reach the sticky stuff. Do the same for the holes through which the pitmans go. In organs having more than 61 notes, you will also find small additional openings into the cells of the very highest notes. These holes serve a very important function: They relieve the pressure of vacuum on the small delicate reeds which need much less vacuum to sound than do the lower notes. If you leave one of these holes plugged, you can ruin the reed the first time you play that note.

CHECKING THE REED CELLS FOR CRACKS

At this time check very thoroughly the condition of each reed cell. If there is the slightest evidence that there is any crack between cells, by all means get the cell repaired. If left, the crack will allow air to bleed into an adjacent cell causing it to sound when its key is not depressed. Repairing many such cells at this stage is not impossible (though it is time-consuming) but your temper will have a hard time (or you with it) if you must remove the whole works later in order to correct the cyphers. Check also the glue joints between the reed cells and the reed pan. Here you can run into serious problems. I have been told by a restorer (some time ago) that he just won't bother with an organ having unglued reed cells. The Packard had that sticky (or unsticky?) problem and I can testify that it is solvable. 'Tain't easy, though.

Check the degree of separation; is the lack of glue true of just a few of the cells or all of them? If just a few are loose, you will want to try to run some glue in the open crack and just seal things as best you can. If the problem is more general, you need to arrange to raise the cells off the board just enough so that you can get some fine sandpaper under them. To hold the cells up, cut some scrap soft pine so that it has a taper that can fit into a reed cell. Make several of them. Then gently, *by hand only*, force the tapered block into the reed cell just enough to raise an area off the reed pan. Do the same for at least a couple of others areas down the line of reed cells. If you can get the finest sandpaper between the cells and the pan you are OK. Don't go higher. Figure 12-2 shows such tapered blocks in place with white glue already applied. Once the blocks are all in place, and the areas cleaned are ready for glue, arrange some blocks of wood nearby so you can get them quickly along with a supply of parallel clamps.

White glue is applied by using a coping saw blade with the pin cut off one end. This gives you a very thin but tough instrument to use in forcing glue into the narrow crack. Once you start inserting glue under the reed cells, proceed as rapidly as possible. When all is in, place a scrap of wood under the reed pan, directly under the glued area, then clamp everything as shown in Fig. 12-3. There is no substitute here for the large handscrews. (Yes, I know that the wood-threaded

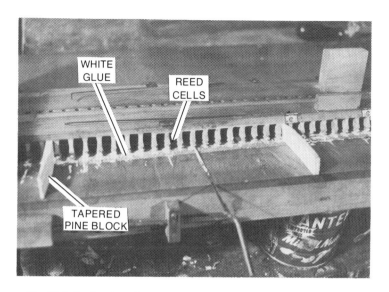

Fig. 12-2. Packard reed pan in process of being reglued to reed cells.

hand screws in the photo are antiques in themselves, but they work beautifully!) Clamp only firmly enough to get the reed cells properly seated back on the reed pan. Too much pressure here can break the reed cells. This would result in disaster.

Fig. 12-3. Packard reed pan and reed cells in clamps.

154

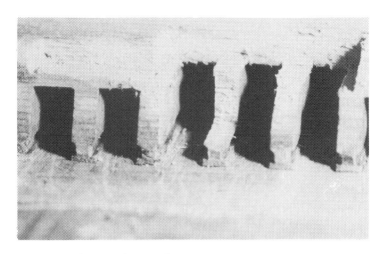

Fig. 12-4. Damaged reed cells cut back in preparation for new wood.

CHECKING FOR VERMIN DAMAGE

Another common problem is that of the reed cell that has been damaged by vermin. Here you will have to trim back and fit blocks in to replace the damaged wood as shown in Figs. 12-4 and 12-5. Note that in the last picture the replaced blocks have been only roughly trimmed to shape. The only critical places are the slots where the reed slides in and the face where the mute must seal; the latter must be exactly parallel with all

SLOT FOR REED

FACE WHERE MUTE MUST SEAL

Fig. 12-5. Wood back in, partially fitted.

of those on either side of it. If the opening isn't the exact size of those around it (above the reed slot, that is) there is no problem. In this case the openings of the reed cells were square so it was easy to fit the block in and make it appear more like the original. In other organs the openings are rounded. You can easily shape them after the blocks are glued in by using a small motor tool if you wish.

The process of trimming the front of the blocks can be a bit of a problem since you will be using wood rasps and sandpaper blocks to be sure that the face of the repaired reed cell is perfectly flush with the rest of the cells. This must be very carefully done, since the mute will not seal the cells and you'll get sound when you don't want it. Work your rasp or sanding block in short strokes, particularly taking care not to hit nearby cells; as mentioned earlier, they break easily. Also make frequent use of a straightedge so that you don't take off too much. Things can be built back with thin slivers of wood (like veneer) but that is time-consuming.

FINAL, OVERALL CHECKING

After all repairs have been completed, including crack-repair of the reed pan and the wood frame surrounding the edge of the reed pan, do a thorough check of the whole area. Using a light from beneath, look for hairline cracks between cells, either at the junction of the reed pan and the cells, or between cells higher up. Also, with light from outside the cell, look for any obstructions in the slots where the reeds will fit. These obstructions can be little pieces of glue or small wood chips that fell into the cells, particularly if you had to do extensive regluing or repairing. I have used very small jewlers screwdrivers as chisels to get things out of that small slot.

You may have to devise other tools. Walt likes to use two hacksaw blades taped together to clean out such slots. You can also use the end of a coping saw blade after cutting off the pin and grinding down the teeth, then sharpening the end. It becomes a long chisel. Use your ingenuity. A penlight small enough to insert inside the cell would be a good thing for further checks. If I seem to be unduly cranky here it is for good reason. I remember with pain the times I have had to take apart what I thought was a completed organ to find those doggone cyphers.

Once the reed pan and cell-block have been restored, give everything a once-over lightly with fine sandpaper and then spray with a light coat of wood filler. Here a spray can is

156

mighty handy. When you sand you will note how powdery the surface of the old wood is. By using a quick coat of sealer you prevent further deterioration and, more important, prevent little grains of stuff getting into the reeds later. After the filler has dried, sand lightly again and dust off. Installation will be covered in Chapter 14. Set the action base aside and get out the pallets.

REED PAN RESTORATION NOTES

Chapter 13
Pallet Restoration

Now get out the box of pallets and check the leather on all of them. It just might be that the organ has been fortunate enough never to have been subject to excessive moisture, dryness, or vermin. In that case you may be able just to treat the leather and proceed. John often uses the familiar *Neatsfoot Oil* to soften old leathers that are otherwise good. You should carefully clean all the pallets before giving any treatment. The oil will otherwise tend to imbed some of the dirt. Another product, *Silicone Solution For Organ Leather And Fabric*, is made primarily for pipe organs. It waterproofs leather, also making it more flexible in low temperature. It is available from Durst Organ Supply Company. Be sure to check every pallet before deciding to give this treatment. Of course, if just a couple or so pallets need work, you need not redo the whole bunch. If, however, the leathers of very many seem stiff even though all there, better plan to replace the lot. If the pallet doesn't seal its opening very thoroughly, you can do nothing to make the organ play right or hold vacuum as it should.

STRIPPING THE LEATHER

Assuming you are going to have to do the complete re-leather job, strip off the old leather. Be sure to take note of exactly where the old leather was glued on since you must put the new leather in exactly the same place. Most pallets have the leather stop at the edge of the front guide-pin slot. One pallet that I restored didn't—and I had assumed that it did. The leather needed to extend at least a quarter of an inch *beyond* the slot: I had a job to do over.

Strip off the old leather and felt. The stuff might just come off by hand with no difficulty. Some, however, are better glued than others, and need a knife as an aid to removal.

Lay a sheet of sandpaper (about 60 grit) on the bench and after removing felt and leather, sand the pallet to remove lumps of glue and felt. While you should get the majority of this off, particularly the lumps, don't worry if a bit of the glue and felt is visible. If things are reasonably flat that's as far as you need to go. Put the pallets back in the box for safekeeping. If you have some pallets too badly damaged for salvage, or if some are missing, now is the time to make new ones. Be sure that the slots are accurately copied both front and back so that the guide pins will fit right.

Most organs have just a simple layer of felt between the pallet and the leather. The Cornish, however, had an interesting wrinkle. As you may know, the pitmans cause a dent in the leather and felt of the pallet. Since not all keys are played the same amount, after some time the key most used will become a bit lower than those near it. The Cornish makers solved this problem by inserting an oblong piece of wood in the felt right where the pitman makes contact (Fig. 13-1). Then the

Fig. 13-1. Cornish pallets, with just the leather removed to show small, wood, oblong inserts in felt.

leather was glued over it. This feature need not be kept on your organ but it is a curious gimmick and certainly does its job. I decided to cut individual pieces of felt for the pallets so that I could replace the wood pieces as original. If you go this route, however, be prepared to take more time. Time's the name of the game, though, with this hobby anyway.

I always restore pallets in the original manner—felt and leather—and the rest of this section will deal with that method. There is a 1/8 inch thick neoprene sponge designed for the job, available from some suppliers. Since I am not convinced that such sponge material is as good at sealing the valves, I prefer to stick to the felt and leather. You may wish to check the new material, though.

MAKING A HOLDING JIG

To use my method, first make up a jig to hold the pallets. This is a warp-free 1 inch by 8 inch plank about three feet long. It should have a piece of wood nailed securely to one end and side so that the edge is above the surface of the board about 1/4 inch. Put all the pallets on the jig, bottom side up, with all pallets facing the same way; that is, if the pallet has a taper to indicate the part going toward the front of the organ, place all tapered ends the same way. Some pallets may be identical front and back so you may have no problem with them except that the depression on the top for the pallet spring may not be in the right place if you reverse it. This is no great problem since you can easily make a new hole for the spring.

Get another scrap piece of wood about 1/4 inch thick, an inch or so wide, and about eight inches long. This will be a stop piece at one end. Now start two brads, of about 3/4 inch length, into the flat side of the stop. Push the stop against the open end of the row of pallets and compress the whole row firmly against the stop at the other end of the jig. This leaves only one end of the pallets without some stop against them but I haven't found one to be necessary. Just be sure that they are all snugly pushed up against the stop along the length of the jig, as in Fig. 13-2.

MARKING THE PALLETS

Now mark on the pallets exactly where the felt and leather are to go, using the measurements you made before stripping off the old felt and leather. Make a mark the full length of the pallets on both ends where the new material will go. The marks usually will be about five inches apart. Cut a piece of felt exactly the width of the original and about an inch longer than the block of pallets. Do the same with the leather. *Note:* If you do not have a piece of leather the proper length but have one from which you can get two pieces of the right width, you can use the techniques here but in two batches, half of the pallets at a time.

Have available a flat piece of plywood or the like about five or six inches wide and at least as long as the block of pallets you are recovering. Also have about three bricks nearby. You are now ready to apply the felt and leather.

APPLYING FELT AND LEATHER

Probably several types of glue would work in the process, but I find white glue the easiest to use. Also, I like to use the smallest squeeze bottle (about two ounce or less). One bottle will be sufficient for the average pallet job. Keep in mind that you do not need to have the felt or leather thoroughly glued from edge to edge; in fact, glue seeping out the edge of a pallet can be a source of trouble since it tends to cause the felt or leather to get stiff at the edges where it should be flexible.

When you strip the old leather off you will see that the original material was applied with some sort of jig that applied five or six dots of glue to each pallet. You can approximate this by putting similar dots on each pallet with the glue bottle. However, you will find that trying to get uniform dots gets

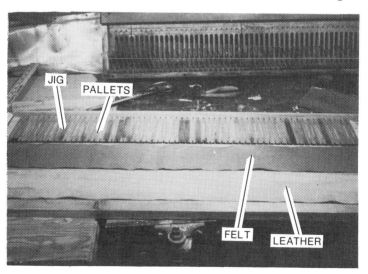

Fig. 13-2. Pallets in jig, ready for application of new felt.

Fig. 13-3. Glue applied to pallets, ready for felt.

difficult; it is also a slow job. I have found it better to use a uniformly thick line of glue down the middle of each pallet (Fig. 13-3). Your stickiest problem will be that of starting the line without leaving a glob of glue. Don't hesitate to clean things off if you get too much glue on. Do try, however, to use all deliberate speed. White glue starts to set within a few minutes, though it is not as fast as contact or model cement.

As soon as each pallet has a line of glue on it, carefully lay on the felt, smoothing out any wrinkles. Now put the same line of glue on the back of the felt, using the slots in front and back of each pallet as guides for application. If you have difficulty keeping in line from slot to slot, you might find a piece of heavy cardboard useful as a quick guide. You may have to clean it off a couple of times or so to keep excess glue from coming off it to parts of the felt where you don't want glue. Now put the leather on, *soft side up*, and, as with the felt, smooth it out. Then lay the board on top of the leather and put the three bricks on it for weight (Fig. 13-4). Let the whole thing dry for a day.

CUTTING PALLETS APART

To cut the pallets apart, use a *new* single-edged razor blade for each pallet job. In fact, you may need to have more than one available (they're cheap). Remove the bricks and board and take the line of pallets out of the jig. Turn them over with the leather down. If the jig is made of soft pine, you can

163

cut directly on it. Otherwise you may wish to put a pad of newspapers under the pallets so that you don't dull the razor blade. Holding the blade firmly between thumb and forefinger, insert it at the front between two pallets being sure that the *heel* of the blade (the part of the blade nearest you) is *below* the top edge of the pallet (Fig. 13-5). The reason for this position is that the heel of the blade tends to dig into the pallet if it is not just barely above the felt. Make a firm cut front to back, pulling the blade toward you. The pallet should be cleanly cut through both felt and leather with one firm stroke. If it doesn't come apart easily, carefully put the razor blade down *flat* in the area where something seems to be still holding, and slide the blade forward (opposite the direction of the original cut) for about 1/4 inch or so. This should complete the cut. Do not attempt to pull the pallet away from the one next to it if something is still attached. Be sure all is completely cut loose. If you pull or tear it you can cause a defect in one or both pallets involved. This will result in turn, in a poor seal later.

My most common problem usually comes at the very beginning of the cut; why I don't really know. You may find it advantageous to make a *forward* cut right at the first and then come back with the full cut. That has worked for me.

Fig. 13-4. Leather applied, board placed on top, and bricks placed on board for weight.

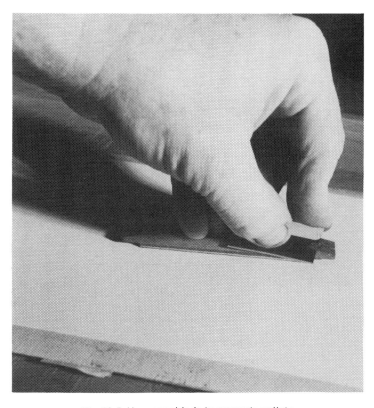

Fig. 13-5. Use razor blade to separate pallets.

Before putting the completed pallet in a storage box, examine it for little slivers of felt or leather still hanging on the side. If you find any, carefully place the pallet on the jig, leather side down; and with the blade flat and flush against the side of the pallet, trim the slivers off. *Don't* angle the blade in. You may cause a gouge in the side. You may find some problem pallets where for some unknown reason your razor hung up and caused either a tear or a gouge in the side of the leather. You probably have enough scraps of leather and felt to do these over. Since the pallet seals at the very edge, often only 1/8 inch or so from the opening, any lessening of this seal area brings the risk of leaks. Don't take chances on a cypher. Be sure that the leather is firm and straight at all edges of the pallet.

PALLET NOTES

Chapter 14
Mutes,
Swell, Coupler, and
Pitman Restoration

Now to the restoration of mutes, swells, octave couplers, and pitmans.

RESTORING THE MUTES

You have some deciding to do concerning the mutes. It may be that the wood is OK, the leather seals OK, the hinges and connections OK. If so, just lightly sand the surface of the leather to soften it and then set the mutes aside for a while.

Often, though, the leather is in bad shape either from vermin or moisture, with the wood badly chewed or warped (See Fig. 11-8, Chapter 11). In this case the damage is not sufficient to affect the operation of the mute and, in normal operation of the organ, the damage is not visible. It is always there, of course, when someone must check the reeds. If you don't like the looks of the chewed areas then you must either patch the wood or make new wooden mutes. Use clear, straight-grained pine or basswood and duplicate the cross section of the mute with a tilt-arbor table saw or radial saw.

If the original wood is acceptable, but the original leather needs replacing, peel it off. If it won't peel, carefully cut it off, being sure not to dig into the wood. Sand the surface of the mute. I find that ordinary chamois skin, available at any auto supply store, makes a good substitute for the original doeskin that was on the mute. The only problem with chamois is that it does stretch and crawl so you will have some trimming to do in spite of your attempts to cut the chamois to fit. Unlike the seals on the pallets, this glue seal must be good from edge to edge. Just try to avoid letting the glue seep from the edges to the face of the mute. If it does, you may have to reface the mute since the leather must remain soft and pliable (Fig. 14-1).

INSTALLING THE REEDS

You can, of course, install reeds after mutes and other elements are on, but it is best to get them in now since nothing is in the way. It is particularly necessary that you do so now if you had work to do on the reed cells. Quite often after cells have been repaired the reeds do not go back in properly in spite of your careful precautions, so you must be prepared to work on the reed slots. Believe me, you will not want the mutes in the way when you do this. Also, check the reeds very carefully for damaged ones. If you need to buy any you must send to the supplier either the reed from an octave above (when replacing a bass reed) or an octave below (when a treble reed is to be replaced) so that the supplier can then match it in tone and pitch.

Assuming that you now have all reeds present, you need to clean them and check for damage or misalignment. Some reeds are not really very dirty and what discoloration is present is in no way a problem. You may need only to wipe them with a soft cloth and install. *Note*: Be *very* careful in

Fig. 14-1. Refaced mutes—chamois over the wood.

cleaning reeds, particularly the small treble reeds. If you wipe the reed with anything, *always* wipe one way only, from the heel toward the free end of the tonque. Be very careful not to let anything catch the tongue and do unhappy things with it. If the reeds need more cleaning, the best brass cleaner you can find is— no joke—*Lysol Toilet Bowl Cleaner.* Warning : The stuff is potent and murder on hands. Use rubber gloves. Soak the reed in the cleaner, carefully rub with 0000 steel wool (again, one way) then very thoroughly rinse in water and dry. If the reeds need tuning or adjusting in any way, that is the subject for the next chapter so jump there if it is your immediate problem. For now we will assume that the reeds are OK and simply need installation. Incidentally, there is good reason for installing the reeds before you install the newly-surfaced pallets. In spite of everything, you are going to dislodge some small bits of stuff when you insert the reeds. By leaving the pallets off, excess junk simply drops through. If the pallets are on first, you risk having some small bits lodge around the edges of a pallet and cause a cypher. If you install reeds, mutes, then pallets in that order, you effectively seal the reeds in and minimize the chance for dust and the like to get in.

Unroll the bundle of reeds and lay them out just behind the reed cells where they go. Clean them one at a time so that you don't get them mixed up. I know that this can be time-consuming but it saves a lot of confusion. After cleaning, carefully push the toe of the reed in the slots of the cell where the reed goes and gently push it the rest of the way. It should go in with enough friction to hold it securely. If it seems to stick, move the heel from side to side, no more than 1/16 inch. If things still don't go, take the reed hook and put it at the end of the reed and push firmly straight in. If things *still* don't go, remove the reed and check to make sure that you have the right reed (see stamped designation on the heel) and then check the slot to see if there is some obstruction (like a spot of glue.) Check the reed against those beside it to determine if years ago someone might have inserted a "foreign" reed from another organ which works but has very slightly different dimensions.

If the cell itself seems to have swelled too tightly and you know that it has not just picked up excessive dampness from your workshop, you might have to run a small file in the groove to remove a minute amount of wood. Just be very careful not to remove too much. It's much easier to go in again than it is to add something if the reed rattles around. After installing the reed you can test some of the treble and mid-range reeds by blowing gently in the cell through a plastic straw. If the reed sounds, you are in business. This will not always work, particularly with bass reeds, but it is a quick check that sometimes helps. You will have to experiment with the amount of air pressure you need to use to cause the reed to speak. You may need to close off the front of the cell to make the larger reeds sound.

INSTALLING THE MUTES

Install the mutes next. If the hinges and all associated with them were OK, installation is just a matter of putting them back. If the small screws were hard to remove, you would be better off to get new ones. If the wood around the screw holes is questionable, you can fit in new wood or use slightly larger screws. Be careful not to use much longer screws since they might split the reed cell or extend down into the reed cell.

Next install the springs. If the originals are OK just use long-nose pliers to twist the hinge clockwise (as you face the spring) and insert the bent end of the spring in the original location. You can usually grasp the spring near the bend and thus get at least half way in before letting it go. You can then force it the rest of the way with the pliers or by gently tapping with a tack hammer.

Frequently you will need to make new springs. Your local model airplane supplier is your best source of materials. Either take with you a sample of the wire you need to replace or use a little wire gauge like the one shown in the tool picture, Fig. 6-1. Ask for the appropriate size of wire. Very slight differences in size probably will be of no consequence. You can usually match the size quite closely since model stores carry quite a variety for use as model plane landing gears. Bend the spring wire to approximate the original, making sure that the bend on one end is about 90° away from the other, counterclockwise from you as you face the end of the spring. Then when you twist it back to insert it in the mute it exerts a constant pressure to keep the mute closed.

INSTALLING THE PALLETS

Now turn the assembly over and install the pallets. First, of course, lay them out in order according to your previous number system. In some cases there is a thin strip of felt glued to the reed pan behind the rear guide pins. If you haven't replaced that, do so now. It's a simple job. As you install the pallets, give each a final once-over to make sure that no foreign matter is clinging to that soft surface of the leather. Install them in order, making sure that the pallet spring end goes in the same location near the middle of the pallet that it came out of. Finally, lift up the front and back of the pallet so as to make sure that it does not stick in any way on the guide pins. Some organs have a wooden keeper that is fastened at the end of the pallets to prevent them from lifting up too far. That keeper is installed last.

RESTORING THE SWELLS

You will usually need to replace both the bottom felt edging on the swells and also the cloth hinges. I have found a convenient hinge can be made from the bias tape or seam binding sold in any dry-goods store. After cleaning off the old hinge (making sure you have marked exactly the relationship between the swell and the fixed portion it is fastened to), sand the surface where the new hinge goes. Now cut a thin strip of felt for the bottom of the swell and glue it on. White glue is OK here.

Treat the hinge area with contact cement as you did with the bellows cloth. Hinges are installed in a variety of ways, but usually the swell was attached first with two or three small pieces of hinge material just to get things in proper registration, then a single piece of hinge cloth was run the full length of the swell. After gluing the bias tape on, give the whole thing another coat of the cement. It is a flexible cement and the additional coat will be just good insurance. After the hinge has dried thoroughly (oh, about an hour) you can then insert the hinged anchor panel in the horizontal slot in the end pieces just above the reed cells and screw it in place. The torsion springs are replaced next, just as they were with the mutes. Do this for the swells on both front and back.

RESTORING THE OCTAVE COUPLERS

The octave coupler is next, and here you can run into all sorts of snags. Cleaning the thing is only a start, but even this chore can take time. Make sure that you know *exactly* where the two halves of the coupler hinge, just in case the moving portion is about to fall off the strip it is fastened to (a common condition). If you make marks to indicate where the parts fit, be sure to make them clear enough that light sanding or the like will not destroy them and that the installation of the new hinge will not obscure them.

Cleaning The Coupler

Begin cleaning by using a small screwdriver or round toothpick to clean the dirt out of the parallel shafts of the coupler (Fig. 14-2). This process can be frustrating since clumps of fuzz will insist on getting lodged beneath the rods and will seemingly defy your efforts to dislodge them. After a while you'll get them all. A quick source of air is quite helpful here; I usually just blow on the thing and usually succeed in getting a faceful of dirt. Frequently flip the shafts over to help dirt to come out. When most of it seems to be removed, you can begin using 0 grade steel wool to polish the shafts. You may also wish to run strips of fine sandpaper under the shafts to clean the wood surface beneath.

Repairing Damaged Couplers

Couplers that are damaged pose real problems. The most common will involve damaged or missing bearings at either end of a given shaft. In Fig. 14-2 you will notice that the bearings are simply small pieces of wood held by a small screw (not visible in the picture). I have found that most often it is impossible to remove that screw without having something break; the screw or the wood. If you just have to

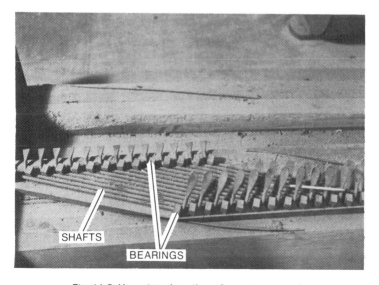

Fig. 14-2. Unrestored section of an octave coupler.

remove the screw, go to it. You will probably have to replace the bearing. If all seems solid—maybe even too much so since nothing moves—try soaking the bearings in a silicone spray like WD40. Things may work loose then.

Other types of bearings use a small "U"-shaped piece of metal that has pointed ends like a staple. The ends are forced through the wood base of the coupler and bent over. These inevitably break if you try to remove them. Since they often have small pieces of felt to cushion the metal bearing, you may think that you need to remove the metal to be able to better replace the felt that may be gone. It's best not to do so; try to clean the area and, with a jeweler's screwdriver, carefully work a new felt piece in. A new metal bearing can also be fabricated and installed to replace a rotted one. I have used medium-hard aluminum or brass for this part. As a sidelight, I keep an eye out for bendable brass, copper, and aluminum for jobs such as this. A well-stocked junk box really comes in handy.

Replacing The Hinges

In all probability you will have to replace the hinges. Here again I use bias or seam tape. You probably will not be able to get the hinge back exactly like the original since it evidently was installed before the coupler rods were put on. You can get close. First note exactly how the original was put on, making a drawing (with dimensions) if necessary. Put the strips on with contact cement at either end of the hinged portion and position it on the strip that will be fastened to the action. Apply contact to the strip and then cut a piece of cloth for the lengthwise portion. Apply contact to the wood and to the hinge-cloth. Apply the cloth and carefully smooth it down. I usually add another coat of contact. Do this for both hinged portions of the coupler.

After all the hinges are dry, use an awl to punch through the screw openings that have been covered up by the rehinging process. Next give the whole works a good spraying with silicone spray, working each one of the coupler rods to make sure that all operate smoothly. You are ready to install the coupler.

Installing The Octave Coupler

First make sure that the activating mechanism that raises and lowers the coupler table is in good shape and ready to install. In the usual type of organ, it is a bent rod, having a "U" shape bend in it where it goes directly under the coupler table. There will be two such rods, one under each side of the coupler. When the rod is activated by having a stop pulled, the "U" portion raises up and elevates the coupler table the amount needed to cause the little arms of the coupler to rest on the pitman collars. Be sure, in reinstalling the rods, that the "U" shaped portion is facing toward the *front* of the organ. When installing the small metal or wood bearings that hold the actuating rod to the action under the coupler, be sure that any necessary felt or cloth pads are included.

The "U" rod is by no means the only way to operate the octave coupler. Another method can be seen in Fig. 11-4, Chapter 11. Here a small wedge-shaped block (seen at the front of the coupler) slides in a shallow groove so that when the stop is pulled, the wedge is pulled toward the coupler causing it to rise. At the front of the wedge can be seen the straight piece of spring wire that is loosely fastened at the front through a screw eye. When the stop is pushed back in, this spring pulls the wedge out from under the coupler allowing it to drop out of action. There are many other schemes for accomplishing the simple task of raising and lowering the octave couplers. Now that you have an idea of what is needed, you should have little difficulty figuring out how yours works if it is different.

After the actuating mechanism is in and tested, install the octave coupler, making absolutely sure that the screws go exactly in the same location they came from. A shift of a very small fraction of an inch here can make the coupler useless.

INSTALLING THE PITMANS

Now reinstall the pitmans. If they were all OK, the guide strip OK, and all held together with tape, just carefully insert the pitmans in the proper holes and see to it that the guide strip is properly anchored both at the ends and at the usual spot in the center.

Making New Pitmans

If you have damaged pitmans they must be repaired or replaced. If they are missing, try to find a dowel of the appropriate diameter from your local lumber yard. Frequently, however, you will find that the pitmans are not of a standard size. Here you can either drill out the action to take a slightly larger dowel (*don't*), try to use a smaller diameter (and run the risk of having things rattle around too much), or size a dowel to proper diameter. Obviously I prefer the latter. If you don't have one, buy a good-quality drill of the exact diameter of the dowel you need (I once had to buy one that was 11/64 inch). Using a drill press, make a precise hole in a piece of 1/16 inch steel or thicker. Mount the steel in a vise and proceed to cut a new pitman from a dowel the nearest size larger. Cut it about 1/2 inch longer than its final length since you are going to damage at least one end a bit. Drive the dowel through the die you just made and sand the dowel, finishing by cutting to proper length.

Making Octave Coupler Collars

The above is all you need to do for pitmans that do not have an octave coupler collar on them. For the latter, you need to make a new collar, too. Sometimes the old broken pitman may have a good collar on it and you can carefully drive out the old dowel and reuse the collar. If not, you must manufacture some. If you need only a few you can cut them by hand. Put a large dowel of the appropriate size (probably about 1/2 inch) in a vise and saw off a piece about 1/4 inch thick (the exact thickness is not important.) If you need to make a whole set, and if you cut by power saw, you will have to use some sort of a jig since the saw blade will throw the things all over the shop, breaking most of them in the process. Figure 14-3 shows a simple holder that can be made by drilling into the end-grain of a piece of wood with a drill the same size of the dowel to be chopped up. The distance drilled in should be the exact thickness of the desired collar cut. Trim the piece on two sides so that the recessed portion can be set against the rip fence of a radial saw, and the end of a 1/2 inch dowel can be inserted in it. Since I use only the radial saw I do not know how this might work on a table saw. You may have to come up with your own jig.

To use the jig, clamp securely to the rip fence of the saw so that the blade will just clear the face of the jig. Put the dowel in the jig and slowly pull the blade through. If you go fast, the saw will kick the dowel piece out of the jig. It is best *not* to pull the saw all the way through: When you return the saw it is liable to kick the piece out. Pull the saw through to a hair before finishing the cut then return the blade. You can then remove the dowel and easily break off the cut piece. Cut quite a few more pieces than you think you will need since you might ruin some in the process of drilling the center hole.

Use any means familiar to you to find the exact center of the dowel, and center punch or center drill it. While you might

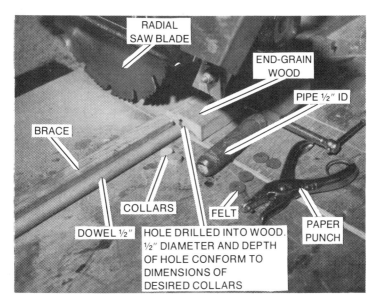

Fig. 14-3. A jig for making coupler collars, along with pipe-punch and paper punch for making felts for top of coupler collar.

luck out with a hand drill and fervent prayers, you probably will need to devise some sort of vise to hold the dowel for center drilling in a drill press. I used a "C" clamp to hold the dowel slice for center drilling. The "C" clamp is in turn clamped to the drill press table.

If you have at least one good pitman with collar from the original set you can use it as a guide in positioning the coupler collar on the new pitman. Apply some white glue in the approximate position on the pitman shaft and slide the collar on. Set it aside to dry.

Your task is much more complicated if something has damaged all of the pitmans beyond measurement. Since there is just no standard pitman length, you must determine it experimentally. Here you might give thanks for the discoloration on the front of the keys on the usual keyboard: It can be your indication concerning how far up the pitman raised the key above the front of the keyslip. To determine this distance you may have to install the action temporarily on the previously-installed bellows. No need to put in all the screws—just put in enough to hold things reasonably in position. One in each corner will suffice. If the keyboard is usable as is, install it on top of the action. Remove the rear keeper from the

176

keyboard and fasten it to the center support (you'll have to remove a key or two.) Now put in the keyslip on the front of the organ case.

You will see that without the pitmans in, the tops of the keys are almost touching the top edge of the keyslip. Lift up one key until the discoloration line near the bottom of the key front is even with the top of the front piece. (This will be about 1/4 inch from the bottom of the key front.) This is how high the pitman should lift the key. You can experiment with a piece of dowel inserted in the action under one key until you have found the proper length. Then cut a whole set to match. A further check is, of course, the dip of the key; it should be on the order of 3/8 inch. After you have this little chore finished, remove the keyboard from the action but leave the action temporarily in position for some early testing as soon as the pitmans are ready.

Determining where the collar should go on a pitman is a bit easier even if you don't have a sample. Slide a collar on a proper-length pitman (no glue yet) and also put on a circle of felt (described below) the same diameter as the collar. Flip the action rods of the coupler back so that you can insert the pitman in any hole communicating with the pallet below. (Any one, that is, that will need a pitman with a collar on it.) With the coupler table resting in the off position adjust the collar until the short arm of the coupler rests on top of the felt but does not depress the pitman at all, just barely touching it. This is the proper location of the collar. Mark it carefully then glue it on. This pitman can then be used as a jig for the easy setting of the other couplers.

Now for making felts for the top of the coupler collars. You can, of course, cut them out by hand if you need just a few. If you need a set, again you need some kind of jig or die. Such dies can be purchased from Brookstone Tools (see materials source in the Appendix) in various diameters. If you will need only a few sets, you can make an acceptable die by grinding down a six-inch piece of 1/2 inch ID pipe, and grinding on the outside so that the inside diameter of the pipe becomes the diameter of the die. See Fig. 14-3. Using it is simple: Get a scrap piece of soft wood, put the felt on the wood, and hammer the die on top of the felt. It will cut a neat 1/2 inch circle. You may find that the edge dulls a bit before you complete a set, so be prepared to resharpen a time or two. A good paper punch will do the job of punching the centerhole for inserting over the pitman shaft.

When all is done, install all pitmans making sure that the arms of the couplers rest on top of the collars at least 1/16 inch away from the vertical shaft. If the arm touches the shaft when the coupler is at rest, you will find problems when the coupler is activated. In use the platform will be raised half an inch or so; that causes the arm of the coupler to move forward just a bit, hence the need for clearance. If the clearance is not there, the arm will bind on the pitman and cause the note to stick once the key is depressed. This will depress *you* even more. Full adjustment of the operation of the octave coupler will come later.

TRYING THINGS OUT

Right now you may wish to try things out to see if the pallets and reeds are working. Even though the action is not fully screwed down, if you have those four corners anchored you can pump the bellows and see if anything sounds. Nothing should sound if nothing is pushing the pitmans down. If all is well so far, gently push a pitman down maybe 1/8 inch while you pump. You should hear a beautiful tone—the first sound your organ may have made in many a year. Do *not* push the pitman down more since you can cause the pitman to push the pallet off its guide pins. By this means you can tell if you have pallet leakage or cyphers before you have gone to the trouble of anchoring the keyboard and everything on the action base. If you have troubles, go over the steps you have taken and try to find the culprit. More of troubleshooting will come later, in Chapters 17 and 19.

MUTES, SWELLS, COUPLER, AND PITMAN NOTES

Chapter 15
Keyboard
Restoration

You are now ready to restore the keyboard. Number each key, indicating which end you start from. Remove the rear keeper, properly storing the screws that hold it in. Lift off all the keys and store them in a box after numbering them for replacement. You are now looking at a really cruddy keyboard frame. For some reason, these things seem to attract—and keep—all kinds of dust and dirt.

REPAIRING THE FRAME

Strip off the padding that is between the two rows of guide pins in front of the keyboard. Before taking a chisel to the padding, check for some tacks buried in the padding at least at each end if not in between. The padding usually comes off easily with just some slight encouragement from a one inch chisel. Then remove the thin felt strip behind the rear row of guide pins. Blow off the worst of the remaining dust. Using coarse sandpaper, clean off the remaining fuzz between the front guide pins. Using finer sandpaper, go over the rest of the frame. You may wish at this point to use fine sandpaper or 0 steel wool to clean up all the guide pins. They usually have some rust on them, but seldom are they really damaged.

After completely cleaning things, examine the frame very carefully for questionable glue joints, missing wood, or warps. If glue has weakened so far that it allowed the frame to get out of shape, be sure to glue and clamp the frame in a perfect square; otherwise you can expect keys to stick, or to refuse to mate with the pitmans or the octave couplers. Check each guide pin for security: If it seems about to come out, remove it and glue it back in. If wood is badly damaged on the frame, particularly the strips holding the guide pins, you have some difficult decisions to make. I would suggest that you go through some time-consuming attempts at piecing things together so that you can keep the original guide pins in their original location. If you *must* replace the pins, be sure to make an exact, full-size paper pattern of the location of the pins. Do not depend on measurements alone to do the job.

When the frame and pins are all OK, replace the small strip of felt behind the guide pins at the rear. The padding between the front pins can be replaced from standard felt weatherstripping available at any hardware or variety store. Glue the strips down with white glue, tacking at each end as was done originally to prevent problems should an end come loose. (See Fig. 2-2 in Chapter 2).

REPAIRING THE KEYS

Look very carefully at all the keys to see if anything has been pencilled on the raw wood behind the ivories or black keys, as was mentioned earlier. After checking and copying down anything found, lightly sand with sandpaper all the exposed wood without markings. For those pieces that do have markings, just go over them with a damp cloth. When they are dry, lightly coat with wood filler or the like to preserve the markings. If there is damage at the rear of the key where the guide pin is inserted, repair it now. Be sure that the guide pin fits rather snugly in the bottom hole and that the top hole is sufficient to allow for normal up-and-down action movement. If the original has worn enough to allow for lateral movement, you may need to replace some wood and redrill.

The Felt Guide-Pin Openings

Also check the condition of the felt in the guide-pin openings in the bottom of the front of each key. This gets considerable wear and very commonly needs replacing. You can sharpen an old narrow screwdriver and use it as a chisel for cleaning out the old felt. Measure the distance to the bottom of the opening then cut pieces of felt a bit more than double that length and of the same width as the opening. To install the felt you can either apply glue to the felt itself or to the wood by using a sliver of wood or a screwdriver to get it in.

I prefer the latter since that means I can handle the felt better. You do, however, have more trouble with glue seepage inside.

Anyway you do it, fold the felt around a screwdriver that is the width of the opening and insert. Take a minute to press alternately on both sides of the opening to seat the felt. After the glue has dried for a couple of hours, be sure to go back and run that screwdriver up the opening again to make sure that there is plenty of clearance. I usually put the key on the frame experimentally to make sure that there is no binding on that front guide pin. Do this job after about two hours since you can easily remove the felt if something is wrong. If you wait until the glue has completely set you may have problems if the felt is too tight on the pin.

Warps

Check also for warped keys. At times I have found a key that seems OK near the front but for some reason has warped wood at the rear. This causes obvious binding problems. If the warp is slight, you might try soaking the key in water overnight (just the back part—be careful not to get the ivories wet; they may come off.) Then clamp it for a week in such a manner that you slightly reverse the twist. When you remove the clamps watch the key for a few days to make sure that it is back in normal position. Failing in that, you may have to sand off wood in one location and glue a small sliver in another to make things match. This may also require redrilling of the rear guide pin holes.

The Ivories

Your next problem is, or course, the ivories and black notes. The ivories can be polished fairly easily with 0000 steel wool. Don't forget to polish the small vertical part in front of the key. If you have just a few cracked or chipped keys, contact your local piano tuner or music store to find out if you can get any old replacement ivories or pieces he has taken off. If so, take your keys to him and try to match the color of yours. Check also for thickness; you can sand a slightly thick piece to match. Working carefully you can trim a broken piece so that another old ivory can be fitted to match fairly well, though the crack will show. If you can get a full replacement piece that, of course, is certainly preferable.

If the ivories are just too far gone to repair, you must then remove the old and replace the works. The suppliers listed in the Appendix have new ones available but the problem is that they are of plastic and are thicker than the old ones. This does not bar their use, but it does raise another problem that we will discuss later. It is sufficient here to say that if you install ivories thicker than the originals you will have to make some adustments relative to the stopboard or the associated side parts to compensate for the new ivories.

To remove old ivories, get out the trusty old iron you used to remove bellows cloth. Using a low heat, heat the ivory until you can get an old paring knife under the ivory. (Have the key clamped in a vise so that you can use both hands.) As was the case with the removal of bellows cloth, work in a well-ventilated area. You might even wear a mask if you are sensitive to acrid odors. Since the old celluloid can catch fire very easily, have a squirt bottle of water handy. After a while you will get the ivories all off. What about cutting them off with a knife? It just won't work. You will frequently find yourself cutting into the wood of the key, or worse, you may find big cracks opening down the key. Use the iron, stink and all.

It is highly unlikely that any new ivories will exactly match the size of your keys so you will have to trim them to shape. I suggest that you mount the new ivory with white glue, taping the ivory on with masking tape; then, after the glue is dry, trim the key. A hand grinder is handy here. A belt sander may also speed things up a bit but if you do use one, be very careful not to sand too far.

The Black Keys

Black keys are not as much a problem unless you happen to have an organ with genuine ebony keys (I have heard of such) and some are missing. You can get ebony from suppliers such as Craftsman Wood Service but since even ebony wood has a variety of distinct colorations you will have difficulty matching the rest of your keys. More likely you will have black keys just painted with enamel. If you lack a few of these, you can make them easily from pine or basswood.

The whole set of black keys, most likely, will show signs of wear so you may wish to renew all of them. Here you can use the keyboard frame as a convenient holder for the black keys. Clean them with paint thinner, mount them in reverse on the frame (Fig. 15-1), and put protective paper over the white keys, which are still in normal position. Spray the black keys with gloss black enamel using a convenient spray can. Don't worry if the black gets on other parts of the key. You may see where your keyboard was originally painted with the black part

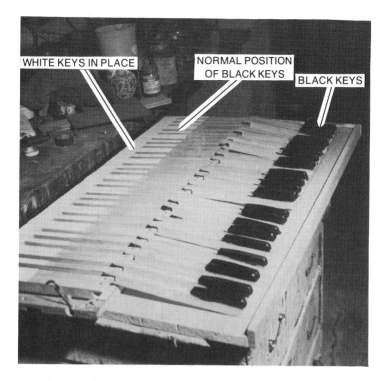

WHITE KEYS IN PLACE

NORMAL POSITION OF BLACK KEYS

BLACK KEYS

Fig. 15-1. Black keys reversed in keyboard frame for spraying.

alreay glued to the raw wood and the black spilled over on it. No problem. Have a good hand-light ready so that you can check to make sure all keys are properly sprayed and that no paint-runs developed.

The Felt Pad

Next replace the felt pad on the bottom of the key where the pitman strikes. Before stripping off the old felt, measure exactly where it fits on the key. Cut strips of felt the same width as the key and then cut one-inch pieces from it. After the bottom of the key is cleaned, glue back the new felt. When this dries, check the small dowel pieces on screws that are located also on the bottom of the middle half of the keys. These are the strikers that contact the upper arms of the octave coupler. At this point don't try to adjust them even though they appear to be uneven. Later, if you find that a given key doesn't seem to activate its associated coupler, it might be that this little dowel should be screwed down to where it contacts the coupler better or, if it seems to hinder the operation of the key, screwed up a bit higher (Fig. 15-2).

MOUNTING KEYS AND KEYBOARD

Before mounting the keys back in the keyboard frame make sure that all guide pins have been cleaned of rust and dirt, and that they have been sprayed with silicone spray. Put the keys back on, including the keeper at the rear. Test the

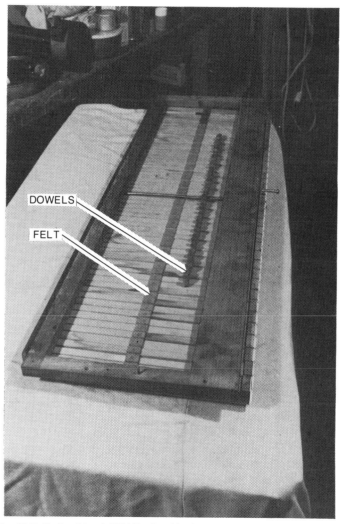

Fig. 15-2. Underside of 1891 Packard keyboard showing felt where pitman strikes and adjustable dowels for octave coupler mechanism.

free operation of each key by lifting it up maybe half an inch and dropping it. If there is any binding whatever, correct it now.

Mount the keyboard frame on top of the action, being sure that all pitmans are operating freely and striking the bottom of the key in the proper spot. You should have no difficulty determining where the frame screws to its side-mount. You will have to remove the rear keeper from the keys and remove some center keys in order to fasten that center screw. Replace the keys and keeper. Also fasten in the bent rod that acts to hold the center of the front of the keyboard frame to the reed pan. If all has gone well, the keys should be reasonably level and each key should move very easily.

LEVELING THE KEYS

All does not always go well, however. A common problem is that of keys not being level. Either someone in the past has been fiddling with the pitmans, or the key itself has shrunk, or something has happened to the felt pad the pitman strikes. It takes only a very slight change in something to cause keys to be out of alignment. If a given pitman is obviously too long, you will just have to remove it and take off a small bit. If it is a pitman without a coupler collar it will simply lift out of the pitman guide strip. If the offender is a pitman with a collar you must remove the whole keyboard and then take off the pitman guide strip just below the keyboard. I usually have been able to avoid doing that. With the key removed you can probably make some adjustments to the top of the pitman without taking off the guide strip. I avoid that chore since getting the thing back on over the pitmans can be more of a headache than you might think.

When taking anything off the top of a pitman *don't* take off much; if you remember your geometry, you know that the pitman works closer to the pivot point of the key and thus the removal of only 1/32 inch on the pitman will make over 1/16 inch difference at the front of the key. If the problem is a low key or two, you can solve that by using a paper punch on cardboard (such as an old cereal box) and then gluing the punched piece to the top of the low pitman. Do one at a time, let it dry, then check. If this is not practical you also could glue another layer of felt to the bottom of the key and achieve the same effect.

A problem you will face is that of keeping the keys in proper alignment with the rear keeper out; yet the keeper

Fig. 15-3. Steel bar laid across rear of keys to keep them aligned while keeper is out.

must be out or you can't remove a key to work on the pitman. If you have something heavy to lay across the rear of the keys right by the guide pin this will keep things in line, yet be easy to remove for access to a given key (Fig. 15-3). It is also the easiest way to get the keys in alignment for reinstallation of the keeper.

Harlan sometimes gets just one key out for height adjustment by pulling out the guide pin at the back and therefore not having to remove the keeper. The key then can be taken out and adjusted. When putting it back, be sure that the guide pin is securely seated or the key will stick later.

Don't be surprised if leveling the keyboard perfectly proves to be a frustrating task. You will probably settle for getting things fairly close. When you reach that point, the action is reasonably complete and you are ready to start the stop—the stopboard, that is.

KEYBOARD NOTES

Chapter 16
Stopboard
Restoration

Before disassembling anything on the stopboard, be sure that you make a careful record of what goes where—preferably with pictures. The linkages go every which way and you certainly should not try to remember the connections. First make a careful diagram of the front, indicating the exact designations of the stop faces. If all faces are intact and appear to be in original locations, you are in luck. The fact that all are there, however, is no guarantee that they are in correct position. These things had a habit of coming unglued, so if some had fallen off, they could have been replaced incorrectly. I have also seen organs where a stop face from another organ had quite obviously been glued on (the style of the text was markedly different from that of the rest.) In such cases be sure to take note of what the designation is because it might be correct or it might not. Check to make sure that the faces still glued on are firm. If they will come out when a thin knife blade is inserted under the edge, take them out and store them in an envelop.

DISASSEMBLY

There were jillions of stopboard action linkages, or so it seems. It is really impossible to describe them all, even if I thought I knew what they were. This section will attempt to describe the restoration of the style that was apparently the most common; it is to be found on a number of organs of different manufacturers. If your organ has a different

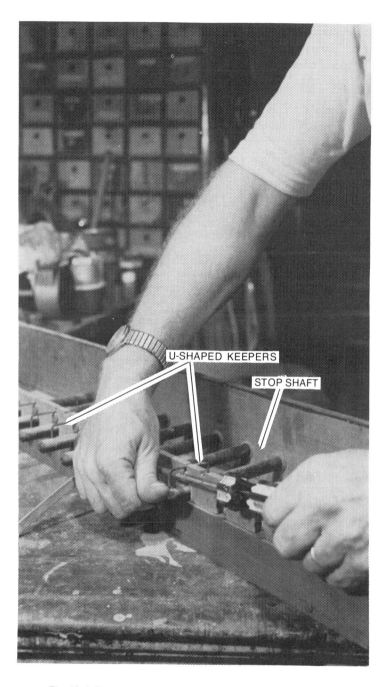

U-SHAPED KEEPERS

STOP SHAFT

Fig. 16-1. Removing ''U''-shaped keeper on rear of stop shaft.

mechanism, I think you can extrapolate from this. Be sure to make proper notes concerning yours on the pages provided at the end of the chapter.

The Stops

The stops are removed by first taking off the "U"-shaped keeper that straddles the brace at the rear of the stopboard. Put a large screwdriver through the back of the "U" with the tip on the end of a stop farther down the line. Pry up until the wire begins to loosen. Do the same for the front of the "U" on the other side of the brace (Fig 16-1). By alternately prying up front and back you can easily remove the keeper.

Now remove the pivoting fork that goes from the slot in the bottom of the stop shaft to the rods on the floor of the stopboard. Do *not* try to force the pin out by pressing it with pliers: you can crush the side of the stop shaft. The best way to proceed is to use long-nose pliers. With the point of the pliers on the floor of the stop assembly, grip the protruding part of the pin with the wire-cutting part of the pliers. Obviously, you should grip only hard enough to hold the pin. Pry sideways until the pin comes out (Fig. 16-2). Remove the pivoting wood fork, noting exactly how it went in. There will be an angle cut at the top front of the fork. You can now withdraw the stop from the front of the stopboard.

Caution: Keep the fork with this stop. The pins are probably identical with others used in the stopboard, but there are small differences in the forks. Tape the fork to the stop it goes on. Also, if the stop face is gone or you have removed it, put a piece of masking tape on the stop pull somewhere and number it so that you can put it back in the right hole. Be sure to indicate which side you started numbering from. Put all stops, each with its fork taped to it, in a box. You may find that the vox humana stop has a spring mechanism attached to it to hold it out. Carefully check how the spring is installed before removing it. Keep the spring with the stop. The majority of vox humana pulls, however, do not have either a spring or a fork.

The Action Rods

You will now have to decide whether to remove the action rods from the floor of the stopboard. Most often they are really dirty, so you will have to clean them before deciding further. Here a small wire brush comes in handy, as well as various toothbrushes, knives, and small screwdrivers. If, after cleaning, you find that the rods are OK, the blocks holding

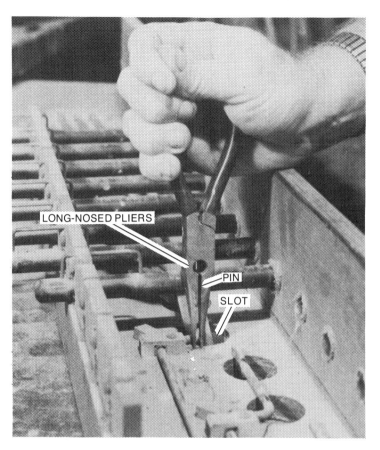

Fig. 16-2. Removing the pin that is holding the pull fork in the slot.

them are OK, and the padding is OK, you may wish to leave well enough alone. If there is damage, or if water has gotten in and the rods are badly rusted, you must remove them. Again, be sure that when you remove each piece you make some chart or diagram as to which goes where. I make a diagram of where the wood blocks and wood bearings go, then when I remove each one I put a piece of masking tape on it and number according to the diagram.

When you have the rods from a given side out, tape them together as in Fig. 16-3. You will notice that in the picture the bearings associated with a particular rod have been taped to the rod to keep them together.

Finally, remove the felt strip under the front of the stopboard and the felts in the stop holes. You are going to be tempted to leave the latter in, but if you plan to refinish the stopboard, you need to get them out. It is almost impossible to avoid getting enamel on them. This completes normal disassembly of the stopboard.

RESTORATION

If the turned pulls on the end of the stop shafts are missing or badly damaged, you will have to order new ones. Here is another distressing fact of life: each organ seemingly used a

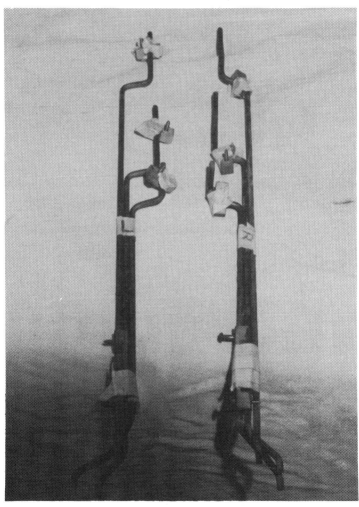

Fig. 16-3. Stopboard actuating rods from base of stopboard, bundled and labeled.

slightly different design of pull. It's not really true, but it certainly seems so. There are many diameters, angles from the vertical at the face, cross sections, etc. on each. Your chance of replacing one or two just like the others in your set is virtually nil. If there is no way for you to repair the damaged one, you will have to reconcile yourself to the replacement of the whole set. The pulls are not really expensive and can be bought from suppliers listed in the Appendix.

The Pulls

The replacement job for pulls can be a ticklish one, though. First you must take off the old ones. Try twisting them in hopes that the glue is bad and they will just slide off the dowel they fit over. It probably won't work, but at least you tried. John suggests that the best way to get them off is to soak them in boiling water; the old glue softens easily that way. I wish I had known that trick a while back. If this fails, you must then cut them off with a coping saw. (Keep the old pulls—you never know when they will come in handy.)

If the pulls were broken off or if you had to cut them off, now comes the tricky job of drilling out the dowel from the pull shaft. Don't trust yourself to do it free-hand. The drill will inevitably skid around some and you will wind up with an off-center dowel hole. I use a drill-press stand for my quarter-inch drill and set up a hand-screw clamp for the shaft-holder. I might mention that you need not drill the same size hole as was originally used. Wait until you have the new pulls and get a dowel the same size as the pull hole. This may or may not be the same as the original.

The last time I installed new pulls I had the problem of finding out that the new pulls had a hole slightly larger than 1/4 inch. Not wanting to size something down for a whole set (seventeen in this case!) I decided to use a Richard Turner trick. After getting the dowel in the new hole in the shaft, I glued a small scrap of cloth to the dowel and forced the pull over it. It works fine. (Try it on chair rungs sometime.) You may have to work it several times before the cloth seats in properly; it tends to scoot ahead of the pull as you push it on, instead of going inside. If you rotate the pull as you push (!) that will sometimes help to work the cloth in properly.

The above is all you need to do if your pull has a face that is perpendicular to the keyboard. If your organ has a slanted pull, be careful. You can easily wind up with an uneven row of stop pulls. Before installing the pull, make a holder for the pull out of a piece of scrap wood that will just fit in the slot at the bottom of the pull shaft (where the fork normally goes.) Put this in a vise and then put the shaft on top. Install the pull knob, making absolutely sure that it is perfectly vertical.

As a final precaution, you might put all the pulls in the stopboard, temporarily inserting the "U"-shaped keepers so that you can check alignment before the white glue has thoroughly set. Make minor adjustments to any that seem out of line. Allow to dry before putting away. Also, while you are at it, check the sides of the pull shafts for cracks around the slot. Repair with white glue and masking tape. *Don't* put the new stop faces in now. Again, you might get them slightly askew. This comes last.

The Badge

Renewal of the stopboard frame begins with any wood or glue-joint that needs repair. When that is done you can ponder the best means of renewing the badge on the front of the stopboard. This is a matter that is frightening to many people. I have seen many restored organs with blank stopboards: the restorer just washed things off and, with it all, washed off the manufacturing identity of the organ. Other organs show evidence of careful case work but the stopboard shows no work whatever. The result is an incomplete-looking job. If you are willing to take the time, and have a steady hand, there is a method by which you can do an amazingly accurate job of restoring even an almost gone badge. Occasionally I hear that some decals are available for some brands of organ. I have yet to find one that I need. Only a very few are available and there were several hundred brands of organs made. So much for your chances here. The following method might be your salvation.

Most likely your disassembled board will look something like the Packard board shown in Fig. 16-4 (before stop felts had been removed). What doesn't show well in the picture is that the gold of the decal is by no means as good as it seems. It is cracked and flaking off. As you can see, the black enamel background is almost gone from the flat portion of the board and is bad on the rest.

To start restoration, first sand the black area, particularly feathering in the chipped parts. Be careful *not* to sand very close to the gold decal of the badge; the gold can flake off very easily. When you have things sanded as well as you can, even though you can still feel some edges of the chipped enamel,

Fig. 16-4. Unrestored Packard stopboard.

brush wood primer on the bare areas using a small high-quality water color brush. Don't use cheap brushes; they keep losing bristles at the most inopportune times. When the primer has dried, sand with fine sandpaper until you can feel no edges where there were chips. If you need to, use another layer of primer, thinned a bit. Now comes a routine that is quick to describe, but will take time.

Mix black enamel with thinner, at least 50-50, and carefully go over the whole board where you have primed. After this first coat you will go over all the black—the areas where black is still good as well as the bad areas. This way you get a uniform background. Use the watercolor brush and carefully brush things out.(Yes, I know that the primer shows through—it will continue to do so for two or three coats.)

After the first coat of black has dried, use a *very* small sable lettering brush (one with just very few hairs in it), and begin to restore the lettering with gold lacquer. This can become a very touchy job, particularly for those Old English capitals that have very fine lines. Note that if you go out of the boundary of the letter you can use a small cloth or even your finger to wipe the gold off and start over. You will frequently have to close up the bottle of gold and shake it since the pigment will not stay in suspension long. I usually shake the bottle then use what is in the cap to dip into. If it still shows where you went out of the lines, don't worry. When the gold has dried, you can then go back with the thin black and outline the letter.

Keep up this routine for as many as ten or more coats of black and gold, alternating. If, after several coats, you still see some of the chipped edges of the original damaged areas showing, sand down again before putting on another coat. The reason for the thinned enamel routine is twofold: One, you can avoid leaving brushmarks, and two, any slight spill-over from gold to black or the reverse can easily be covered with the next go-round. If you are persistent, and don't rush, you can wind up with an amazingly well-restored stopboard. When all has thoroughly dried, say in a week, you can put a spray coat of clear over everything so that the gold is protected. Many of the original stopboards seem to have had a black satin finish so if you wish you can use a satin clear spray to accomplish all in one swoop.

But what if the badge is just so far gone that the touch-up routine won't work? If you can even guess which letters went where, you are still in business. Such was the situation with the Cornish organ I restored a while back. I discussed the matter with James McKenzie, the son of a friend of mine, who happens to be an engraver for a local jewelry store. He measured the badge of the stopboard and made a paper pattern, including indications of what style of lettering the original used, exact dimensions of each letter, and the relationship of the whole to the top and bottom of the board. Then I stripped the whole board, finished it with three spray coats of black enamel, and rubbed it down. James then re-lettered it. The result was the beautiful job shown in Fig. 16-5.

A final plea: Don't decide that all of this is too much hassle. You need to retain the identity of the organ if at all possible, and the badge is often the only such identification on it. If you can't renew the badge just now, please leave it at least as is so that you or someone else can have the opportunity of doing the job later.

REASSEMBLY

Now comes reassembly. First, install the felts in the pull holes. If you can obtain thick felt, just cut it to fit and insert the felt, seam down. Be sure to push a stop through to make sure that all fits; it also insures that the felt is forced snugly against the sides of the holes. If you must use standard felt, double it

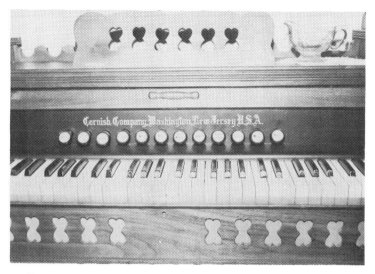

Fig. 16-5. Restored Cornish stopboard with reproduced music rack.

and you will find it satisfactory, though more difficult to use. Be sure to fold and glue the inside of the fold rather than using two pieces. In the latter case the raw edges would show.

Do the same for the bottom edge of the horizontal part of the stopboard, the part that sits on the back of the keys. Turn the stopboard over and measure the felt needed. If you have thick felt, just put glue on the board, not getting closer than 1/4 inch to the front edge, and install the felt. Cut it about the same width as the strip you removed. Be sure not to extend the felt in front of the stopboard more than 1/8 inch; it can interfere with the operation of the keys. Use tacks or a staple gun at each end and at about five points in between. Don't get very close to the front tapered edge of the stopboard with the staple gun; you could wind up having staples go through the top of the board.

The Rods

Check the condition of the rods that go on the base of the stopboard. Usually you will find them with only surface rust; a good sanding will put them in shape. Renew all the felt pads on the various little blocks of wood associated with bearings and blocks that limit the travel of the rods. Reinstall the rods and check with your drawings or photos to make sure that they are in original locations. You may wish to spray all with silicone to insure future smooth operation.

The Stop Pulls

Check your stop pulls to make sure that they are all ready for installation. I usually find a small crack somewhere that forces me to do quick repairs and wait another day, fuming that I missed it the first time. Also check the felt that is sometimes to be found in the slot of the activating fork that pivots in the slot on the pull shaft. If it shows wear, replace it. This is important since a slight difference in the distance the rod goes up in that fork can cause problems in adjusting the operation of some mutes.

The Pull Shafts

Insert each pull shaft in its proper hole. Then insert the fork in the slot, *top bevel toward the front* of the shaft. Now try to get the pin through the hole in the side of the shaft, into the proper hole in the fork, and then on through the other side of the slot. Since this is a friction fit, everything is snug. Don't try to enlarge the holes to make it easier to install the fork. You might have to rotate the shaft 90° to do this, so you can hold the fork where you can see it better and the pin will then go straight down. Before you push the pin fully through, I suggest that you make sure that you can get the fork back in position on the rods. There are slight differences in dimensions between organs using this system, and some have enough leeway to allow the rod to rotate while others don't. If the latter is the case with yours, you must just resign yourself to working with that pesky pin from the side, the fork hanging down and often falling out. Be particularly wary of putting too much pressure on the pin or any other part; you can break the side of the pull shaft or the fork. Getting that pin in the proper small hole in the fork can be a real pain. Since it is a friction fit in the side of the pull, it is often difficult to know if you have it in the hole or not. If you keep forcing the pin you can make a new hole in the fork—which then won't work right—or you can split things. When you think the pin is started properly, be sure to move the fork on the pin some to make sure. If anything binds, check it. Once the pin is in and the fork properly positioned, replace the "U" wire keeper at the rear and test the stop for ease of draw. You may have to raise the "U" a bit if it seems to drag.

The Stop Faces

New stop faces can now be installed, if necessary, since all stops are installed in proper alignment. Be sure that you have the designations concerning which stop goes where. If you know what belongs on your organ or you have an old ad that shows the stops, you are in business. I assume that you have ordered them some time ago and have the proper set on hand. If you don't know what goes where, be sure to consult the chart on stops (it's coming up next) before ordering or installing anything. Even if you have a full set, the stops might not have been well installed. If you took them off, check below and make sure they really do go back where you took them off from.

Stop Face Designations. One of the most frustrating aspects of restoring an organ is determining what replacement stop face goes on which stop. Frequently organs have had all the faces fall off and, through the years, they have gotten lost. Fortunately for you, the suppliers listed in the back have available a fairly complete stock of replacement faces—*if* you can decide what you need. Life is going to be much easier for you when you realize that there are several stop face designations that in reality apply to the same function. If you can't find exactly the face your organ had, I am sure that you can substitute another that means the same thing. There are in reality only a very few functions for the stops to perform, so I will list them by the function that describes what actually happens: e.g., the front bass mute (this mute controls the bottom third or so of reeds in the front rank of a standard organ) is listed as a function. Beside it are all the names of stops that perform that function. "SS" behind a given face designation means that it is a "soft stop." This indicates that the stop opens only slightly the same mute that another stop opens fully. Here goes:

FUNCTION	STOP NAME
Front Bass Mute	Diapason
	Dulciana (SS of Diapason)
	Stop Diapason (SS of Diapason)
	Dolce (SS of Diapason)
	Diapason Bass
	Dulcet (SS of Diapason)
	Dulcet Bass (SS of Diapason)
Rear Bass Mute	Bourdon
	Principal
	Viola (SS of Principal though at times is a full stop name.)

FUNCTION	STOP NAME
	Violina (SS of Viola when Viola is a full stop.)
Front Treble Mute	Cremona Melodia (SS of Cremona) Flute
Rear Treble Mute	Echo Celeste (SS of Echo or some-times a full stop name.) Celestina (SS of Celeste when Celeste is a full stop.)
Front Swell Shutter	Diapason Forte (always goes with Principal Forte)
Back Swell Shutter	Principal Forte (always goes with Diapason Forte)
Any Swell or Both Together	Expression Forte

There are other designations for use with other ranks of reeds or for use in the standard two-rank organ as well. They are as follows:

FUNCTION	STOP NAME
Bass Mutes (front or back)	Viol d'Gamba Gamba Echo Horn Trumpet Choral
Either Treble Mute	Celestina Violinetta
Couplers	Treble Coupler Bass Coupler

Another possible help is for you to know that all of the following stops are bass reeds: Diapason, Principal, Clarionet, and Bourdon. The treble reeds are: Melodia, Celeste, Flute, and Cornet.[1]

Following are some typical line-ups of stop designations for organs you are likely to encounter. You may find that yours can use the same. Designations read from left to right as you face the stopboard.

LAKESIDE: Bass Coupler; Principal; Diapason Bass; Dulcet; Diapason Forte; Vox Humana; Principal Forte; Echo Horn; Melodia; Celeste; Treble Coupler.

WINDSOR (four ranks of reeds, Action E.): Bass Coupler; Bourdon; Cornet Echo; Principal; Viola; Diapason; Dulciana; Principal Forte; Vox Humana; Diapason Forte; Cremona; Melodia; Cornet; Celeste; Flute; Clarionet; Treble Coupler.

STANDARD WINDSOR(Two ranks, eleven stops, action D.): Bass Coupler; Diapason; Dulciana; Principal; Diapason Forte; Vox Humana; Principal Forte; Celeste; Cremona; Melodia; Treble Coupler.

PRINCE(early upright from 1875) See Fig. 1-3. Function are listed, as well as names: Diapason Treble (rear treble mutes); Principal Treble (front treble mutes); Harmoni (controls vibrato, possibly not an original stop face); Divided Swell (rear treble shutter); Principal Bass (front bass mute); Diapason Bass (rear bass mute.)

PACKARD(1891, the organ described earlier in this text) Functions are listed here, as well as names: Bass Coupler; Viola (4 ft., front bass mute); Violina (4 ft SS of Viola.); Diapason (8 ft., rear bass mute); Dulcet Bass (8 ft., SS of Diapason); Vox Humana; Dulcet Treble (SS of Melodia); Melodia, (rear treble mute); Celestina, (SS of Celeste); Celeste, (front treble mute); Treble Coupler.

Some years ago the Schaff Piano Supply Co., in response to demand from reed organ repairmen, compiled the following list of stops for a few organs with differing numbers of stops:

SET OF FIFTEEN: Base Coupler; Aolian; Treble Coupler, Viola; Vox Humana; Sub Bass; Melodia; Diapason; Flute; Echo Horn; Cello; Celestina; Dulciana; Clarinet; Bassoon.

SET OF FOURTEEN: Bass Coupler; Treble Coupler; Tremolo; Bourdon; Celeste; Principal; Melodia; Cello; Clarinet; Diapason; Dulcet; Flute; Forte; Horn.

SET OF ELEVEN: Bass Coupler; Treble Coupler; Vox Humana; Melodia; Forte; Diapason; Viola; Dolce; Dulciana; Celeste; Aoline.

SET OF TEN: Bass Coupler; Treble Coupler; Celeste; Principal; Medodia; Diapason; Dulcet; Forte; Diapason-Forte; Echo Horn.

SET OF TEN FOR CHICAGO COTTAGE ORGAN: Bass Coupler; Diapason; Echo; Piano; Vox Humana; Forte; Celeste; Dulcet; Melodia; Treble Coupler.

Note that only the last of these sets seems to be in the order in which the stops appear on the actual organ. The others, however, could probably be figured out by the process of elimination; thus if you had no idea of what the Aoline was for a set of eleven, get the rest of them in right and put Aoline on what's left!

If this sounds anything but scientific, I assure you that the original choices for stop designations were not very scientific either. Don't be surprised to find all sorts of information that contradicts what I have listed here. Most of those I indicate I know to be correct since I have restored organs with stops so designated, assuming of course that they were on right when I got the organ. Someone years ago could have put some on in the wrong place without my permission. I also know that I have seen organs with designations I thought to be exclusively bass but used for treble ranks of reeds. Some Estey organs used the same designations in both treble and bass.

All of which I hope is a real comfort to you: If you get something in the wrong place, who's to know? When it comes to stops, when you are stopped, don't stop. Or something.

Stop Face Installation. I find contact cement, applied with a tube, the best for securing stop faces. Put some cement on the center back of the stop face, making sure that it does not come anywhere near the edge of the face. I usually cover about half the diameter. Then press it, *still wet*, to the center of the stop pull and hold it there for about a minute, making sure that the text of the face is perfectly level with the bottom edge of the stopboard. When it seems to hold satisfactorily, go on to the next one. Keep an eye on recently installed faces for a while since they could slip or come out. You are OK after about ten minutes.

A problem is likely to be that new stop faces are slightly smaller than the openings in your pulls. Since there is a distinct variation in the inside diameter of various pulls, the manufacturers apparently have settled on 7/8 inch as the standard for new faces. Most pulls, however, are one inch ID so that poses problems. You will have to hold the face exactly in the center of the pull long enough for it to dry thoroughly or it will gradually sag down. If yours does this, you can move it back up if you catch it right away. Why don't I use the trick of applying contact to both pull and face, let it dry, and then apply? Simply because I don't trust my ability to get things absolutely right the first time. By applying the contact wet you have a little while to do adjustments.

OVERALL INSTALLATION

You must now decide if you can install the stopboard on the action before the whole shebang is put in the case. The first problem concerns the case pieces that are installed right next to the keyboard. Some of these have screws that must be installed right next to the keyboard. Some of these have screws that must be installed *under* the horizontal portion of the stopboard. Obviously in this situation the stopboard cannot be installed until after the action, including keyboard, has been installed in the case. If those pieces can be installed after all else is in, you could fasten the stopboard to the action now. This has advantages in that you can work on the side linkages much more easily, making adjustments with everything open and easy to get to. This is particularly advantageous when you must do some rather minute adjustments to the slots in the wooden connection pieces some organs use (Figs. 11-1 and 11-2).

At times you will find that the addition of a small scrap of felt will make all the difference in the operation of a given linkage. However, the whole action and stopboard is heavy and bulky, making final installation difficult if not impossible, particularly for one person working alone. Various top pieces or braces on the main case may also dictate the procedure you use. Just make sure that you check out all problems before deciding which route to take.

In any event, you are now ready to install the action. If you have previously checked out the basic operation of the pallets as suggested, and have found no problems, you may be able to skip the next sections and go to the chapters on final installation and adjustment.

Notes for Chapter 16

1. THE REED ORGAN. How to Give it Proper Care. Reprint of Sears and Roebuck pamphlet by Vestal Press, Vestal, N.Y.

Chapter 17
Reeds
and Tuning

Earlier in this book I treated the routine problems of pulling, storing, cleaning, and reinserting reeds. If you have no problems other than those, you can skip this chapter. But, unhappily, some of you may have an organ with reeds missing. Or, happily, you may have some spares which, unhappily, are not in tune. Or you may find that the reeds seem OK but just don't sound. Now is the time to try some repairs and tuning techniques.

If the reed doesn't sound, even though it appears OK, look at the reed with a light behind it. Assuming that there is no foreign matter in it (really it doesn't take much to cause troubles especially for the treble reeds) you might find that somehow the tongue of the reed is touching the side of its frame. This is particularly a problem with reeds that have only one rivet holding the tongue.

MISPLACED TONGUES

For reeds from about the middle of the keyboard down through the bass side, you can insert a small screwdriver by the side of the tongue and *gently* pry it toward the center (Fig. 17-1). Look at the reed again against a light until you see an even clearance all around. Walt prefers to use an artist's palette knife for this job since it is made of very thin but tough metal. If the tongue of the reed seems to move suspiciously freely, you have a loose rivet. Use the pry tool on the other side (if you went too far on the first try) and, with less pressure,

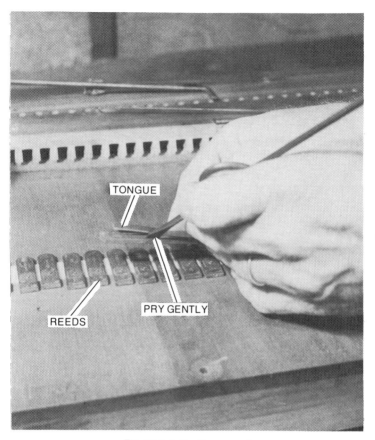

Fig. 17-1. Adjusting a reed.

very slightly move the tongue back. Try the tongue by gently pressing it straight down into the frame. When you have it clearing both sides, place the reed on a firm surface and lightly tap the rivet with a tack hammer. Tap *once* then try the reed to see if it is OK. If things aren't right yet, do it again. Careful with that hammer: too much tapping and you can split the reed—and your poise.

You can move the tongues of treble reeds the same way but because they are more delicate, you must use even greater caution. You will find, however, that you will have less problem with treble reeds than with bass; they don't have as much mass to move and are therefore less liable to vibrate out of kilter. If you just must move the treble reed some, use a very thin knife blade or palette knife as the lever, and work as delicately as you know how; above all, don't rush things.

CRACKS

What if the reed shows small cracks, around the rivet, that are evidently the reason it has come loose? Here is where I follow procedures designed for situations that can't be made worse. The reed, as is, is just shot. If you do something to make it worse, nothing is lost. If you do luck out and do something that works, hooray.

First move the reed to where it seems adequately centered in the frame. Then use a soldering gun to flow a drop of solder around the rivet, making sure that it has been properly cleaned first. Don't use any more solder than absolutely necessary and *don't* let solder flow down the tongue of the reed. This trick has worked for me about half of the few times I have tried it. It is particularly successful when there are a few cracks which are just barely starting.

TUNING

Now for tuning. Here I strongly recommend Robert Gellerman's book, *The American Reed Organ.* The book has a lot of other miscellany about organs too—you'll like it. While Mr. Gellerman doesn't give many details about other facets of organ restoration (hence my decision to go ahead with writing this book) he really does an excellent job of describing the tuning process. I had found a way of my own before Mr. Gellerman's book came out—and I will shortly describe it to you—but I have no intention of stealing Bob's thunder. In particular I am intrigued by the electronic tuning aid he describes on page 90. I haven't gotten around to building one yet, but I intend to.

There are only two reasons for you to get into the tuning business: a reed or two has changed pitch causing dissonant chords, or someone has inserted reeds from a set not tuned exactly like the rest of yours. Here the problem is simply that of bringing the offending reed into exact pitch an octave above or below the other reeds in that particular rank. Or, you may wish to tune a whole set to A440 since so many of the organs made before 1900 were tuned to a higher (A452) or lower (A435) pitch. Be warned: tuning a whole set is a *job*.

A preliminary caution check: Are you sure that the reed needs tuning? Reeds can get put into the wrong cells and cause some real squalls. Is the reed heavily corroded or covered with dirt? Cleaning may do wonders for its pitch.

Before you start any tuning, be sure that you have an ear for very fine tonal and beat-note distinctions. All piano and organ tuning is based on the tuner's ability to hear the very slight harmonic beats that characteristically accompany the simultaneous sounding of two notes. If you wish to test your ear, find the nearest piano that you know is in perfect tune and strike various two-note combinations, listening for beat notes. Thus, from middle C down to the G below (an interval of a fourth) you should hear about four-and-a-half beats in five seconds. Middle C to the F below (an interval of a fifth) should produce about three beats in five seconds. Also, get hold of an A440 tuning fork, tap it lightly on something, and set the shaft of the fork on the piano. You will hear the tone very clearly. Strike A; there should be no beat note at all if the piano is in tune. Then try various other single notes in combination with the fork. You should be able to detect varying frequencies of beat notes. If you find that you just can't hear those intervals or the beat notes, don't risk lousing up a reed. Leave it as is until you can replace it or send it (with the correct octave above or below it) to a reed source who can tune it for you.

So you think you can hear enough to tune a reed or two. OK:

Principle One: Scraping at the *base* of the tongue (just ahead of the rivet where the main flexing of the tongue takes place) *lowers* the pitch.

Principle Two: Scraping at the *end* of the tongue *raises* the pitch. *Exception:* don't mess around with the reeds of the top treble octave. You seldom use them in practice anyway, so let them be, even if they are not in exact tune. I'm sure the professionals can do something with them, but you will find, to your horror, that those thin tongues very quickly curl up and die if you scrape them even the slightest bit too much. I know.

Sharp or Flat?

Your first job is that of determining if the bad note is sharp or flat. Make sure that only the mute associated with the rank of reeds you are dealing with is open. If an associated rank is also sounding, even very slightly, you can't possibly tune anything.

Principle Three: When you slowly reduce the air supply to a given reed it will vibrate a bit slower, thus becoming lower in pitch. This is a very important factor in your becoming aware of whether the reed is just slightly below or above its target pitch. The best way to reduce the air supply is to slowly let up on the key, but you can also do it by slowly closing the mute or even by putting your hand over the opening to the reed cell, if you have easy access to it.

Find the out-of-tune note and sound it along with the octave above it. Then, while maintaining an even pressure of air, slowly let up on the offending key. If the beat notes get faster, the note is flat and you must file the end of the tongue very slightly to raise the pitch. If the beat note gets slower, the note is sharp and you must file the base of the tongue.

Tuning Procedures

There was a tool once made for scraping the base of the reed to lower pitch without removing the reed from the cell. That certainly would speed up some tuning jobs. The tools seem to be in short supply, however, so you will have to improvise.

Remove the reed carefully. Have available a piece of cardboard (cut from a file folder will do) about $2 \times 2''$. Gently insert it under the tongue of the reed and push it back to where it naturally stops. Don't push back so far that it starts to force the reed tongue up, though. This cardboard will keep the tongue firm while you work on it. You can use a very small file or knife blade to remove metal from the tongue. Take off *very* little, and then try the reed, particularly with smaller reeds. Here even a scratch can make a measurable difference. Further, remember that the heat of your hand can cause slight pitch changes. If you can restrain yourself, let the reed sit for a minute or two in the cell after scraping it and before testing it.

I suggest that if you have several notes to tune you start with the lowest note. Here there is less change in pitch for the removal of a given amount of metal so you are less likely to go too far. When you get close to zero beat, go very cautiously. When you get near one beat per two or three seconds, consider leaving things for a while and do the rest. You can always go back and do slight touch-ups later. If you do overshoot you can, of course, go back the other way. In so doing, however, you are liable to change the whole voicing of the reed even though you may finally reach the proper pitch.

Raising pitch is much the same as lowering except that in taking material off the tongue you should be sure to use the file or scraper one way only—from a point a little back of the tip, scraping off toward the tip. When you have all notes in acceptable pitch, sit back and congratulate yourself.

An important observation: Don't be too disturbed if you felt you had all octaves of a given note in zero beat but when you listen in actual playing conditions you sensitive ear jokers may feel that slight differences in pitch have developed from treble to bass. That is just the nature of the beast. As you may well understand, the large bass notes take a lot of air to sound and the more air they get, the longer the swing the reed makes. The result is a slightly lower pitch because of the inertia of the heavy end of the reed. On the other hand, the small reeds need less air to sound; they are quite light, and they may vibrate faster under heavy pumping. The result is a slightly sharper pitch. There is only one ideal condition of vacuum in the main chamber that will keep all reeds in perfect pitch, a condition very seldom reached and not sustained for long when it is reached. If perfection of pitch is your fanaticism, get a Moog synthesizer.

TUNING ALL THE REEDS

Now for you nuts who just must tune a whole set of organ reeds—all 122 or more of them! Go to your local library or music store and borrow a piano tuning book; there are several on the market. Read the process of setting temperament. You will read of such things as "setting the bearings" and the like. I used an older text called *Piano Tuning And Allied Arts* which I borrowed from Walt Butler's music store. In it is a chart listing 49 steps for setting a perfect piano temper. The same procedure and beat-note identifications can be used on the reed organ. If you use the same book you will need to get a tuning fork for middle C for use in setting your first octave. For those not acquainted with the process, it is a detailed method of literally tuning each note very slightly out of tune from a perfect scale in any one key so that it can be played in other keys as well. If you research the history of music you will find that early music was written for a limited range of keys since a keyboard instrument tuned perfectly to a given key would sound out of tune in others. The discovery of temperament tuning opened up the range of possible keys considerably.

You will notice in the instructions a precise list of steps called a "chain" to follow; do so exactly, observing all the beat-note test points as you go along. After you have completed tuning one full octave from C to C′ you can then do the rest of the reeds by tuning them in unison with the corresponding notes in the completed octave. Once you get the hang of things it will go faster, but don't try to rush. Particularly for those of you who have never done this before, better plan to take several days to do the job. I once read that tuning an organ is easier than tuning a piano since you deal with a continuous tone. That may be true, but in tuning an organ you can't just back off on the tuning hammer and try again. You can ruin a reed very easily if you don't get things right almost the first time around.

A further plug for Mr. Gellerman's book: he has tuning chains developed specifically for reed organs not only for A 440 but for A 435 and A 452 as well. He also developed a simplified chain of only twenty steps using intervals of only octaves and fifths. It would pay you to get the book for this feature alone. I wish I had had it a few years ago.

Caution: Be careful of ranks of reeds labeled Celeste or Voix Celeste. Sometimes they were originally tuned a couple of beats or so sharp compared to other ranks, and they should be left that way.

Let's say you have an organ with a good set of reeds tuned to A452 and would like all nearer to A 440, but exact concert pitch is not necessary. A cheap and not completely accurate way to tune them would be to move each reed up one slot, thus lowering the pitch of the whole organ by a half-step. Be sure you do so for all sets of reeds in the organ or you will get dissonances! That will mean that no reed will be in the bottom bass slot and you will have one left over at the top. It will also mean that you will have one or two places where you will have to do some work on the reed cells to get a reed to fit. The opposite would be true if you wanted to change A435 to a generally higher pitch. In both cases you can get the organ near enough to A440 that instruments like trumpets and guitars can easily be tuned to match it without sounding odd.

A final word about voicing: This is really a technical problem involving not only tuning but shaping the tongue so that it gives a different quality of tone. You will notice that certain reeds are flat at the end (giving a fairly loud tone) while others have a curve at the tip end of the tongue (giving a more mellow tone.) I won't say the amateur can't properly voice a reed (Walt insists it can be done—he has) but I must confess to being too chicken to try it. In selected instances you might find it necessary to do so, but I hope you don't make more problems for yourself than you solve.

Tuning is the ultimate task in organ restoring: if you can do this you can probably do anything associated with a reed organ. The stakes are mighty high, though, if you goof something up; so I hope you don't attempt tuning unless absolute necessity dictates it. Experiment with the wood; wood can be replaced fairly easily. But treat those reeds with the utmost respect because they are not easy to come by.

REEDS AND TUNING NOTES

Chapter 18
Vibrato

The vox humana stop is simply a means of getting some sort of wavering to the organ tone (vibrato) in a manner reminiscent of the human voice (hence the name vox humana, voice of the human). The most common type of vox humana is a mechanism on the rear of the reed pan which flutters the air as it is drawn through the rear bank of treble reeds. It consists of a lightweight windmill inside a round box. It is positioned over a hole in the reed pan so that when an opening in the top of the box is uncovered, air is drawn through the box causing the wheel to turn. The wheel is connected to a dowel outside which has two pieces of cardboard in it, in slots 180° apart. When these vanes are turning, they cause the air to fluctuate. (See Fig. 11-4 and 11-5, Chapter 11.)

If you can possibly avoid it, don't take the air box apart or remove the dowel. Getting things back can be a pain. The most common problem you will have is simply that the cardboard vanes may be broken or chewed up. Try to use a very thin knife blade to clean out the slot so that you can replace the cardboard. I have used old file-dividers for replacement here. Whatever you use, try to get something with a fairly slick finish and of a thickness approximating the original. Cut the cardboard to size and glue in the slots. After the glue has dried, balance the whole thing by cutting off minute pieces of the corners of the vanes. The whole thing must operate with very slight air pressure, so if the vanes are not in balance you will not get proper operation. Also spray the bearing points of the thing with silicone spray. Do *not* use any kind of oil; it causes wood to swell and attracts dust.

Replace the seal under the vox humana and mount the whole thing securely on the reed pan. You will note a small wooden shaft pivoting on the side of the round air box. This has a piece of 1/16 inch wire sticking out one end and felt or leather on the other. In one position the felt contacts the shaft of the vane and acts as a brake. This is the control arm to which the stopboard pull is attached. The wire end goes through two holes in a piece of leather that is glued (at the other end) to the top of the air box on the other side of the hole in top. It is so arranged that when the brake is contacting the shaft, the wire draws the leather tightly down over the hole, cutting off any air supply to the windmill inside. When the stop is pulled out, the wire moves forward, uncovering the box opening and releasing the brake. Air is drawn in, the windmill rotates, the vanes flutter the air to the reeds, and the fluttering sound results. (See Fig. 4-3, Chapter 4).

Your choice of material for covering the air opening is a bit of a problem since it must be quite flexible, yet airtight. Harlan uses bonded vinyl cloth available from any fabric store. I have used chamois but must double it directly over the opening since a single thickness of chamois will leak air. You might experiment with various types of single-surface leather that is more airtight yet flexible enough to stretch over the hole without distorting the mechanism associated with the stop.

Another type of vibrato often found on organs made before, say, 1890 is seen in the photo of Turner's Prince action in Fig. 11-7, Chapter 11. This is a really heavy tremulo and works either on the full organ or on specific sections of the reeds as chosen by baffles installed under the reed pan. To be perfectly frank, it is much too heavy a vibrato for my taste. It reminds me of some church choir sopranos I have heard who never seem to find a note to light on. Anyway, under the reed pan is a channel that allows the air to be drawn unto the tremulo from a hole on top of the reed pan. The mallet-like round piece covers it in the photo. When this is opened, air is drawn into the box from beneath, causing the hinged piece of padded wood covering the other opening to shut (it normally rests slightly open.) However, there is a weighted spring wire on top of it which rebounds after the wood has snapped shut, causing the wood valve to open again and the cycle is repeated. The amount of weight on the spring and the tension of the wire control the frequency of the vibration.

A method used on an early Packard was a real fooler. There was a vox humana stop, but no gadget on the back for it to control. I got the organ completed and still couldn't understand what the vibrato was supposed to be or do. When I tried to play the organ, I found that the vibrato stop opens both front and back treble reeds and lo—there was a very pleasing vibrato. The back set of reeds was tuned about three cycles or so per second higher than the front, creating a beat note. Darn clever those Packard builders. I guess they abandoned the method since that meant that the two sets of reeds could be used together only when a tremulo was wanted, and one set could not be used together with the bass reeds at all since the two would be out of tune. The mechanical tremulo allowed more stop combinations with a given number or reeds, but frankly is not as good a vibrato.

Vox humanas have a way of disappearing from organs in poor shape. If you suspect that your organ once had one, seal up the openings where it went (including screw holes) but don't permanently put new wood in them. I once found a spare vox humana that fit an organ I had without one! You never know.

VOX HUMANA NOTES

Chapter 19

Final Assembly and Troubleshooting

Now is the time to run those final checks before putting the whole thing together. First, don't do as I do and rush through. Taking it all apart again can be exasperating.

THE BELLOWS

Run another check of the ability of the bellows to hold vacuum. I know you did that when it was completed, but do it again, this time as it is installed in the case. Seams have a way of opening up. If you still have that strip of furnace tape over the slot in the bellows platform, check it to make sure it is firmly sealed. Pump up the bellows until the safety valve opens. The bellows should still hold for at least a minute, preferably longer. If so, take off the furnace tape and throw it away—now. You don't want to forget and leave it in! If something seems to be leaking, go through the routine in the bellows chapter and find the problem.

THE REED PAN

Check the felt seals around the perimeter of the reed pan seat. Are holes punched through each screw location? Any screw holes in the wood apparently enlarged and need repair? Use the toothpick technique. Harlan has used small strips of wire solder inserted with a screw to help tighten things up.

Rummage through your storage boxes and find all the screws that hold the reed pan to the platform. Be sure you have cleaned out the slots in the heads and that all washers are present. Some organs use only flat washers, easily replaced, while others use some interesting tapered washers that exactly match the inside taper of a flat-head screw. Those may be hard to duplicate if some are missing. They do prevent the screw from biting too far into the edge of the reed pan.

Now comes the moment of truth: If you didn't believe me when I said to label even each screw, you are probably scratching all over to find the screws you were just sure you could remember went where. Fortunately, you can usually buy new ones to replace the old if you come up missing some. An added note: If some of the old screws seem questionable, don't pitch them. They might be handmade (from the early organs and melodeons.) Note the frequently off-center slots and very blunt ends of some oldies.

Check the reed pan very carefully for any new cracks that may have opened, and take appropriate measures if you find any. This is going to be your chronic problem unless your house is properly humidified.

Before setting in the action, assemble everything (if you haven't already) and check very carefully to determine that all keys work completely smoothly. Nothing should bind, rub, or even threaten to hang up. Use silicone spray or graphite liberally.

THE STOPS AND SHAFTS

This is also the time to check the operation of the stops and connecting shafts. Particularly check the stops that are the "soft stops" of another stop. These are tricky: If they don't open enough, you get no sound at all or at best an out-of-tune wheeze. If they open too far, you get no different tone from that produced from the full stop. While final adjustment may have to wait until you have things installed in the case, you can do a rough check here to see if things seem to be right.

THE OCTAVE COUPLER

Also very carefully check the operation of the octave coupler. When the couplers are not activated, the coupler tables should be out of the way of any other operation of the organ. The arms of the coupler rods should rest on top of the pitman collars without in any way binding. When the coupler pull is drawn out the associated coupler table should raise up about 1/2 inch or so and the pull should stay out without difficulty.

Test each key which activates a pitman having a coupler collar on it. Does the coupler arm in any way touch the pitman when the coupler table is raised? If so, you will note that it will cause the pitman to bind and stay down. It might be that the table is rising too far and a very slight adjustment of the connecting elements will lower it enough to prevent binding yet still fully operate as a coupler. Also check the operation of the small screw-adjusted dowels on the bottoms of the center keys which activate the front arms of the coupler rods. Does each key-dowel strike the arm properly and cause a corresponding response from the note an octave above (or below) it? You may have to adjust those dowels a bit to get uniform action from each key. An early set of instructions for adjusting such a coupler is to be seen in Fig. 19-1. With inventor Wilcox glaring at you, you can't go wrong.

THE ACTION

How you install the action will depend on the construction of the case of your organ and your preferences. Be sure to determine how those cheek pieces by the keyboard are fastened in. Since there is a variety in means of attachment, you often must put them in *before* the stopboard is installed. Others can be installed last. Since screw holes in the bottom edge of the action are not visible when it is in position, you should make marks indicating exactly where those holes are, with corresponding marks to indicate where holes are on the platform. That way you can line up such marks and minimize

Fig. 19-1. Wilcox octave coupler instructions.

the adjusting necessary after the reed pan is placed on the seals. Too much scooting around can cause the seals to leak.

If you are working with an organ that has a non-removable top to the main case, you must insert things either from the front or back. Your biggest hang-up (literally) will be the actuating rods for the knee swells in the front. If they are not easily removable (usually they are not) you probably will have to lift the action in from the front, over the cross-piece of the case just under the keyboard. You can do it yourself but if you are installing the whole action at one time, it will be murder on your back; plan to have help. Be careful of those knee-swell rods; they can strike that cross-piece and leave a nasty scar on the new finish.

Harlan prefers to install the action one piece at a time even though he has completely assembled it outside of the case for checking, as previously described. He sets the reed pan on, minus stopboard and keyboard, holding it at first only at the corners. Screws are tightened down just enough to enable the action to hold a bit of vacuum long enough for testing the pallets by pushing down a pitman with a finger. If something haywire shows up on the finger test, the action can be removed for checking much more easily than if everything else were mounted. Once the pallets check out and reeds seem OK, he then installs the keyboard, checks it, then installs the stopboard and makes more checks.

Once you have the action apparently positioned on the bellows platform, use an awl to locate a screw hole through the rear of the reed pan. I usually start at one corner, install a screw fairly well in, but not tight, and then go to the other corner and do the same. You can then insert the rest of the screws that go in from the top. Don't forget those screws down by the action at the sides. They are somewhat hidden and will be a bit difficult to put in. Then put an old quilt on the floor in front of the case and, while lying on your back, install the flat-head screws from the bottom of the platform up into the rim of the reed pan.

You may now start tightening. I prefer to work as if it were the head of an auto engine: working from one side to another and one corner to the other, tightening down at one corner a bit (not doing the final tightening), then the opposite, then alternating screws from each side, and so on.

After all the screws are fairly well seated, go over the whole lot and really seat them in. What if one doesn't grab? Well, you should have anticipated that earlier and repaired the enlarged hole by adding wood, inserting a dowel by pre-drilling and cutting the dowel to fit (Walt's preference), or inserting toothpicks as John prefers. If you are now installing the whole thing and unexpectedly find one screw that won't hold, you have to take stop-gap measures or remove the whole action and do things over. If the problem screw is a front one and you have only a 3/4 inch portion of the platform to go through, you may be able to insert a toothpick or two up in the hole (with glue), then the screw, and make it hold. Also try inserting a strip of fine wire solder as Harlan suggests. Just make sure that things are firm. If you can't tighten a screw down very firmly you are probably going to have a leak at that point. If the problem can't be solved by the above methods, you will have to remove the action and work on those screw holes.

Even after getting everything tight you will want to go over all the screws after a few days to snug them up a bit. The felt and the wood will give a bit after the initial tigthening. If the stopboard is not on, install it now, making sure that all linkages are correct and that they work exactly as they did when you bench-tested the full assembly.

THE KNEE SWELLS

Next install the knee swells. Note that for most organs, the knee-swell arms fold inward when not in use. The bracket and single screw that usually hold the knee-swell pedal to the bottom of the bellows platform are quite simple and should pose no problems. Make sure there is a washer between the swell and the platform to prevent possible dragging during operation (Fig. 19-2).

TRYOUT AND TROUBLESHOOTING

Don't put the rest of the case together yet. We hope you are all done at this point, but let's try things out. Pump up the bellows until the safety valve opens, then time things again. Expect the time to have dropped in half or a little more. That's normal. If you do better, you are genius. Remember, you now have many other seals that must hold: Not only the felt along the action, but every pallet, the vox humana valve, all four bellows valves, and sometimes much more. Each can be expected to leak a few molecules of air under the best of conditions.

If you hear any note sounding, even very slightly, you have troubles. Try opening the stops associated with each mute, one at a time, and pump things up, not touching a note. Is there any

Fig. 19-2. A knee swell.

sound? If so, try to find out which note sounded and write it down. Also record which mute controls that rank of reeds.

If nothing sounds but the bellows doesn't seem to hold, go through the same process you used to test the bellows. This time, however, suspect the seals around the edge of the pan. Look carefully for evidence that something has gotten under the seal as you were installing the action; or look for a wrinkled seal. Sometimes you can correct things just by loosening screws and using a screwdriver or knife to reposition the offending seal. Frankly, there have been times when I have had to remove the whole action and rework the distorted seal.

If you have severe leakage, along with some groaning from several notes, it might be that for some reason the stopboard is binding and pressing down on the back of the keys, causing very slight leakages from several pallets. This is a common problem if you have installed new plastic ivories since they are thicker than the originals. To check this, loosen the screws that hold the stopboard to its mounting, wiggle it a bit to let it move up, and see if that helps matters. If so, just insert some shims under the stopboard until you can anchor it down without further problems. You will usually have enough leeway to do so without linkage difficulties.

Now check each rank of notes to make sure that each reed is sounding. Don't be surprised if some don't, even if you checked them earlier and they were OK. In the top octave in particular, a piece of dust virtually too small to see can prevent the reed from speaking. Open the appropriate stops to give you access to the particular rank of reeds (using a block of wood or screwdriver handle to hold up the swells), and remove the reed. Look for small particles wedged by the tongue. Carefully clean it, blow out any dust, then check the reed cell and surrounding area for more dirt. If necessary, carefully use a vacuum cleaner to clean the area again if it shows an accumulation of dust. Replace the reed and test again.

I'd be here all day describing all the possible things you could find that could cause you trouble. However, by now you should know the organ fairly well. Don't hesitate to formulate your own sleuthing methods and cures.

Once all works properly, install the remaining case parts such as the lid (did you put felt on the sides and small pads under the edge that contacts the top of the keyslip?) If you wish, you may remove the brass lock and attempt to get it working if you haven't already done so. I have found that antique dealers frequently have supplies of old keys so you can probably find one that will fit your lock if you look diligently enough. It would help if you have the lock with you.

You now have an organ that is by no means just a decoration. Its tone is just as pleasing today as it was a century or more ago, its gentle voice as soothing to us as to the listeners then. Have fun.

FINAL ASSEMBLY NOTES

Chapter 20
The
Piano-Cased Organ

We are accustomed, in the twentieth century, to feel that only our age is hung up on being fashionable, and that yesterday's things rapidly become outdated. The Victorian age was not really that much different.

DEVELOPMENT OF THE PIANO-ORGAN

Reed organs had been around since before the Civil War, and by the middle of the 1880s that parlor fixture was beginning to look old-fashioned. One very real threat to its dominance was the piano; it certainly was not a new invention, but before that time it was considered to be the property only of the rich or the serious musician. As general affluence began to spread, pianos began to be popular—especially the upright "parlor grand" piano style that so many of us learned our scales on.

There were two real problems, however, to the rapid acceptance of pianos by those accustomed to organs. First, the technique for playing a piano is very different: The player just can't hold a key down and fish for the next note as he can with an organ (a minor aside—you will find an organ easier to play than a piano.) Probably more important, the price of pianos was very much higher. When pianos were selling for $200 and $300,organs could be purchased for as little as $19.95.Check the reproduction Sears and Wards catalogues that are widely published today, and see those low prices.

Still, people wanted the fashionable look. It reminds me of the little girl in the late '40s who pleaded with her dad to put, at the very least, a TV antenna on the roof so that it would at least *look* like they owned a TV! In the same way, enterprising manufacturers decided to put organs in piano cases, and sold them for much lower than the going prices for pianos. The Beckwith featured in this section of the book sold in 1908 for $68. (See Fig. 5-1 Chapter 5). Even today it is fun to have people look at it close-up and be completely fooled. When they touch a note and nothing sounds, they have funny looks on their faces—but nothing like what they have when I open the lid to show that there is nothing there. Then when I pump a pedal and the organ tone flows forth, their astonishment is complete. More fun.

Quite some time ago I found this lovely piece of deception at an antique dealer's auction and couldn't resist it (Fig. 1-5, Chapter 1). In the following restoration discussion I will try to avoid duplicating advice from earlier parts of the book as much as possible though there may be times when some duplication will be necessary to avoid having you do too much leafing back and forth. Bear with me.

OPERATION

A must for you is that of determining exactly how things work. You will note that one of the selling points of the piano-organ is that it has fewer gadgets to pull, push, squeeze, or what-have-you. Yet the buyer certainly wanted such stock organ necessities as swells and octave couplers. Be sure you know how everything operates.

If you have the original book with your instrument, you are fortunate indeed; otherwise you have to hunt. I was fortunate in finding the ad for my instrument in the Sears catalogue. The ad speaks of the various operations of the organ. Nowhere on the organ are there even stop labels to say what does which. If you look closely you will see three small brass stops hiding in the decoration on the edge of the portion just above the keyboard. There are no designations whatever of which organ functions they are supposed to perform. Each does in fact control a mute but by 1908 the buyer, supposedly, no longer needed a label for the stop that sounded like it belonged to a pipe-organ. One simply pulled whichever stop gave the sound he wanted—and hang the identification.

In order for you to be able to observe what happens, remove the front panel just above the pedals. Pivoting from a single screw in the underside of the bellows platform is a stop that holds the panel in. Swing the stop to one side, grasp the small knob near the top center of the panel, and pull forward. It will tilt out to where you can lift it out. It is held in at the bottom by some pegs in the bottom cross-piece of the case; they are easy to lift off. Set the panel aside in a safe place. You will see something like what is shown in Fig. 20-1. Remove both the upper and lower back panels being careful in lifting since the glue may be shot and things can come apart (this one did.) You will see there something like what is shown in Fig. 20-2. Next remove the upper front panel, the one with the music holder screwed to the bottom edge. Since this is a rather large panel it can be awkward to handle. You will have to remove it from behind by taking out the screws from the pivot mechanisms at each side. You might wish to wedge the panel with some paper when you take out the hinge on one side so that it doesn't come crashing down when you take out the pivot on the other side. A helper here is good insurance.

Basic pumping is done from the two outside pedals which are connected to the exhausters directly with block and rod linkages, instead of the straps used with the standard organ. Small, fairly light-pressure, caliper-type springs are anchored between the exhauster bellows and the vertical piece of wood that sticks up beside the rear portion of each pump pedal. (The left caliper is damaged in Fig. 20-3.) The safety valve on the

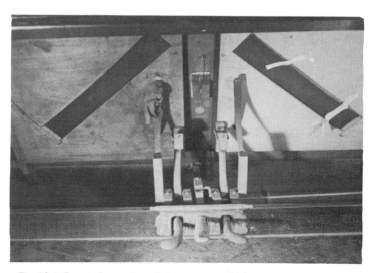

Fig. 20-1. Front of unrestored piano organ with bottom panel removed.

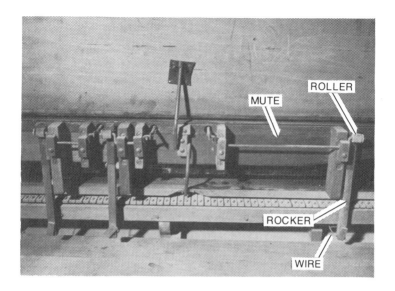

Fig. 20-2. Inside of unrestored piano organ with upper back panel removed.

bellows is located between the exhausters, and the exhauster valves are clearly seen positioned slant-wise on each exhauster.

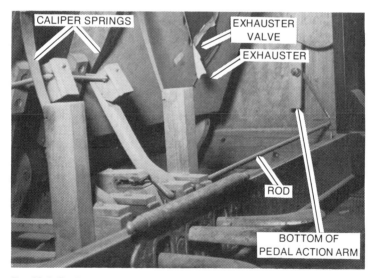

Fig. 20-3. Rod connecting center pedal of unrestored piano organ to bottom of pedal action arm.

The center pedal is a real curiosity. Had I not seen the catalogue ad I honestly doubt that I would have figured it out, since a part in the chain of its operation was missing. The pedal pivots at the end of a shaft that goes through to the back of the organ case, also having a spring of sorts on the bottom of the pedal, just inside the case. The pedal connects, via a wood block on top of the pedal, to a rod which then runs to the right side of the case. This, in turn, bends at right angles and then connects to a vertical piece of wood having a spacer attached to keep it in place. All of this can be traced out in Fig. 20-3. Now look at Fig. 20-4. This photo was taken of the same rod from the back of the case and shows the light screen-door type of spring that keeps the shaft in place. On top of this shaft is the "shepherd's crook" that will be referred to as the *pedal action arm*.

While we will discuss the exact method of operation later, try the instrument now to see if it works. Pressing down the pedal should cause the coupler tables to rise into proper position to work. Pressing the pedal again should kick the couplers out. If it doesn't, read the section on the coupler (a few pages later), before proceeding with disassembly, and restore it to where it works. It is likely to take some thorough thought before you figure the whole thing out.

While only three stops are visible on this instrument, the manufacturer very ingeniously managed to achieve multi-stop performance. For instance, there is no *off* position; the rear rank of reeds is always open. Why bother with enough stops to turn things off? The three stops are rather simple in operation. Look back at Fig. 20-2. The conventional mute is connected to the wire which goes to the back of the action and then hooks to the bottom of the rocker (as I will call it). When you pull one of the stops out, it causes a small roller to press forward on the top of the rocker causing the bottom of the rocker to move out and pull open a mute.

Another ingenious mechanism is that which controls the swell shutters. Here there is no connection to the front whatsoever. At the side of the bellows you will note not only the large caliper-type springs but also a bent-wire mechanism extending from the moving back panel of the main bellows chamber up and over the top of the back of the reed pan (Fig. 20-5). Note that the rod sits quietly at rest on top of the reed pan under an arm connected to the front and rear shutters.

Fig. 20-4. Spring holding pedal action arm, viewed from rear of unrestored piano organ case.

(Fig. 20-6). When the bellows is pumped up a bit, the back of the bellows moves forward causing the rod to push up on the arm that pivots and operates the swells it is connected to. Thus all one has to do to get the swell in action is to pump hard enough to get the bellows about half exhausted of air. (You will notice that the bellows is upside down compared to the usual upright organ; this one has the main bellows hinged at the *bottom*.) Momentarily stop pumping, letting the back of the bellows return closer to open condition, and the swells close. I suspect that this feature, for all its ingenuity, may have been less than popular. One really has to judge exactly how much to pump or he gets a swell effect possibly not desired. Or, conversely, if he pulls out an additional stop, logically enough requiring more air, he had better know how to increase his pumping in order to keep the swell from dropping out. It was a clever idea, though.

DISASSEMBLY

Now that you have determined how things work, proceed with the disassembly. The keyboard cover comes off with removal of two nickel-plated screws from either end. You should not lower or raise the keyboard cover with any of the stops pulled out; they make contact. My guess is that your organ, like mine, bears scars from that very thing having happened many times. The keyslip below the keyboard is removed by taking out three long screws which are inserted

Fig. 20-5. Piano organ automatic swell mechanism attached to restored bellows.

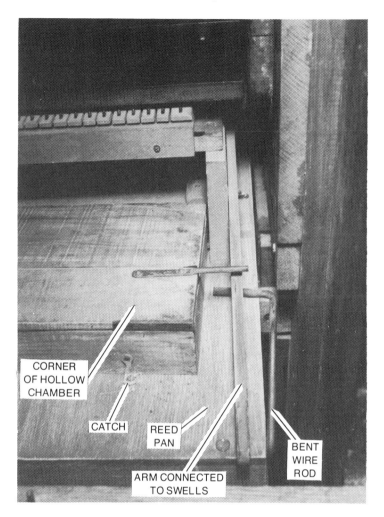

CORNER
OF HOLLOW
CHAMBER

CATCH

REED
PAN

ARM CONNECTED
TO SWELLS

BENT
WIRE
ROD

Fig. 20-6. Actuating arm from swells located on top of automatic swell rod.

from below. You can remove the cheek pieces at either end of the keyboard now since the screws are visible from the top. They are far enough back under the case cross-piece, however, to require a stubby or right-angle screwdriver.

The Keyboard

The method for removing the keyboard is much like that required for the standard organ. Two screws at either end, and one center screw under a key, hold the frame. In addition, there is the usual bent-wire brace holding the front of the key frame to the reed pan. Mine was difficult to get to, for some reason, so you may have to use an angle screwdriver here also. You will, as with other organs, have to remove the rear keeper to get the center key out to remove the screw under it. Once this is done, replace the keeper and screws. The keyboard is now free for removal except for one thing: the rod that activates the octave coupler. Unlike rods of other organs, this rod is fastened to the bottom of the keyboard. You will note that the rod goes to the side and out via a slot. To remove the keyboard you will first have to rotate the "U"-shaped rod that fits under the little wood piece extending from the hinged platforms of the two sides of the actuating mechanism of the octave couplers (Fig. 20)7). You will also have to lift off the hook-like wood connector that goes from the side of the keyboard back to the actuating mechanism at the rear. This all sounds more mysterious than it really is. Compare the photos with your organ and you will find the operation as described fairly easy to do.

The Pitmans

Check the pitmans for signs of damage or short sticks. If all are OK, tape both sides of the pitmans and try to get them out still in the guide strip. Usually all you have to do is pry the guide strip up (or unscrew it if it is not nailed) and take out a

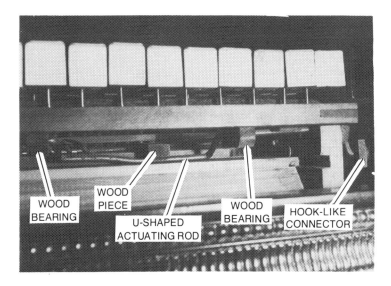

Fig. 20-7. Close-up of coupler block with actuating rod under it.

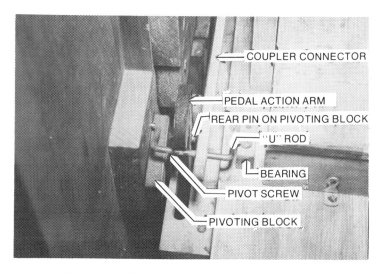

Fig. 20-8. Action of foot-pedal mechanism to operate couplers.

center screw, easily reached. Set this aside intact. This saves grief later.

The Reeds

Removal of front reeds is accomplished by taking off a strip from the bottom of the reed pan, then rotating the keyboard brace so that it is completely out of the way. Then you can open two catches at the side of the piece to which the front swell is hinged. The whole swell will slide forward and out. You will notice that there are two ranks of reeds in front and one in back. As mentioned earlier, there is no mute on the rear set of reeds.

Before you can remove the rear reeds you have to disconnect the wires between the rockers and associated mutes, and remove the rockers by taking out the pivoting screw in the center of each. This is not really difficult, nor does it take a lot of time, but it is inconvenient compared to the ease of getting to the older style organ reeds. You should indicate on each rocker whether it is 1, 2, or 3 from the left, unless you plan to replace these right away and lay them on top of the cross-piece just above the keyboard. Since you are now disassembling for restoration, be sure to label them.

There is a hollow chamber behind the reeds at the rear which you must now remove before reaching the reeds. The advertising claims that this box makes the instrument sound more like a pipe organ. To remove it, unhook three catches holding the box at the rear. The corner of that chamber can be seen in Fig. 20-6, with one catch showing.

Now look at the rear of the reed pan and the mechanism associated with the octave coupler (Fig. 20-8). Note the bearing that fastens with two screws on the edge of the reed pan. When you remove this, the "U"-shaped actuating rod will slide out of its bearing hole on the side of the case. Be sure to remove this bearing and rod before attempting to remove the action. It is easy to overlook. You can now remove the screws holding the action to the bellows platform and remove the action. It may be easier for you to take it out from the front because of an offending brace at the back of the case. Or, remove the brace next.

Across the back of the case is a brace having three air holes at each end (Fig. 20-9). First remove the screws that are inside the brace, running through a glue block to the top of the back of the bellows platform. Then remove two screws from either end of the brace itself and remove it. Take out the screws holding the side of the bellows platform to the case, unless you are adverse to lying on your stomach to remove some bottom screws holding the bellows to the bottom of the case. You can tip the organ on its back to get at these, but if you do, be sure that the top screws are still in to prevent the

Fig. 20-9. Rear brace, glue block, and pedal action arm.

Fig. 20-10. Removed leg of piano organ. Pedals have also been removed.

bellows from falling out. Also disassemble the linkages associated with the pedals so that the exhausters are free. You can then lift things out.

The Pedals

Now remove the pedals themselves and their associated hinge blocks. If any repair needs to be done to the pedals, now is the time to do it. You may find the pin the pedal hinges on has been broken or worn; take it to a good welder and have things brazed. If the plated surface is in poor condition, have it redone at a competent plater's shop. Any large city will have plating facilities available. If you don't know where to find a plater, ask at a good auto parts store or talk to someone who is active in an antique car club. This organ originally had nickel-plated pedals so that is what I had put back on. If you contemplate much playing, you might consider chrome, which is harder than nickel. It does have a different sheen but I doubt that many people would notice the difference.

A final note: Be sure that the pedals are properly sanded and ready for plating. I have had some difficulty (though not with organ parts) when I was given to understand that the plater would do certain grinding and shaping operations that were not done.

You may not be done removing things. The front legs of this organ also come off (Fig. 20-10). By now the case is light enough to be easily tilted back so that you can get at the screw that goes up from the bottom of the front leg. Check here for possible problems. I thought it funny that there was a pad of paper between the bellows platform and the top of each leg. Why they were there I still don't know. I left them there when I reassembled the action on the bellows. As a result, the keys were too high. They extended above the facing of the keyslip. I had to remove the action, remove the screw between the bellows and leg, take out the paper shims, then replace everything. I don't say that all such shims or additions made in years past were not necessary, but it would be well for you to question any such additions before blindly putting them back. You are now ready to start correcting things.

CASE WORK

As with other organs, you should do whatever case repairs need to be done before you strip or otherwise refinish the piano-cased organ. In this case I had to reglue a couple of questionable joints, reproduce a few inches of decorative border missing from the lower panel, and that was it. The missing decoration consisted of a rather simple strip pattern so I reproduced it from a short piece of mahogany (the original wood), proceeding to carve it with my trusty X-acto knife. When I was satisfied that it would pass muster, I glued it in place.

The original finish was not really bad. A prominent feature of an otherwise rather plain case is the floral design painted in the center of the upper panel. The main problem with the finish was that it was crackled, dirty, and dull in spots. I decided to try an old trick called *furniture finish feeding* and go from there.

To do this, first clean the piece well with turpentine. Then every few days put some raw linseed oil on the case. Few finishes really deteriorate completely; they dry out and lose their oils. If you want to keep up the feeding job, you can do so every few days for months. I am told that this is the technique used on museum pieces and that it does wonders in gradually getting rid of the crawling of old finish. I have also heard of other preparations designed to soften crackled finishes, but I have no specific information available. If you are interested, do some checking; it could pay off. Well, I fed the finish for three weeks. It noticeably helped the original finish, though it certainly did not make it like new. I let it dry out for another week, wiped it clean with turpentine, then gave it all a coat of clear gloss varnish. When this had cured for a few days I rubbed it down with steel wool and oil, giving it a reasonably uniform finish that was still obviously original but noticeably brighter than it had been.

What if the finish had not been salvageable, yet I still wanted to save the front painting? That too can be done, though the job is much more ticklish. The method I am going to describe is also useful when you must take off all the black around a gold stopboard badge, yet want to save as much of the badge as possible.

First use stripper very carefully (not letting any run or splash on the painting) ; take off the paint or varnish all around the decoration to within an inch or so. Then, with a very small brush, lightly loaded with stripper, brush over the painting and *immediately* wipe it off with a clean rag. Have several handy. This will take off surface clear varnish without disturbing the painting. When you notice the slightest effect on the painting or badge, stop. Then, using a very fine brush, put stripper on the surrounding old finish as if you were painting around the decoration. Carefully scrape unwanted finish off with a knife blade (X-acto would be very good). When you are done, thoroughly wipe off everything with turpentine, not allowing even turpentine to stand on the painting or badge since it can soften things.

I won't promise that this technique will allow you to get by without having to do some touch-up of the decorative design, but it will let you get rid of all of the old finish. All of this takes much more time than my telling indicates, but it is worth it. Since toll painting has come to be such a modern skill, you might get such a craftsman to look at any decoration your organ may have where the design is too far gone to save. Get the artist to copy what's left of the original, and then, after you refinish the whole thing, repaint it the way I had the Cornish badge relettered.

I haven't said anything yet about matching the old finish to the new carving I had to reproduce. This is a particular problem when you must match an old, darkened finish. The finish on this organ still showed the mahogany under it, but way under. I mixed my concoction in an old spray can lid, starting with about 1/4 inch of walnut stain in the bottom. Alone, that was too brown, so I added Prussian Blue, making things too black. Some Alizarine Crimson brought the goo up to match fairly well. I then applied the oil and stain with a brush. Wanting to duplicate the reddish-brown show-through of mahogany, I got some Alizarine Crimson on my finger and, while the new stain was still wet, rubbed just a faint trace of the red on it in spots. This slimy mixture takes a while to dry, so I left all alone for a couple of weeks while I did other things. You will notice that when something like this finally dries it is quite evidently duller than the surrounding finish. However, when I sprayed everything with gloss varnish, the match came out quite well. I won't say that the new piece and its pseudo-old finish are perfect, but you have to look a bit to find it.

Chances are that my mixture won't do you any good. The best bet for you is to have handy a set of artist's oils (a cheapie set from the discount house will do) and several small cans of oil stain. Start with some of the stain that seems nearest in color to that which you want to match, then experiment by adding oil colors as above. You don't have much involved so if you wind up with mud, junk it and start over. Add very little oil paint at a time; a little goes a long way. Try things occasionally on scrap wood, preferably like the piece you are staining, since the applied appearance will differ significantly from what it appears to be in the mixing can. One suggestion: Don't use black oil paint even when black is what you want. Black in artist's colors is usually lamp black which tends to be very dull. Better use a combination of blue and dark brown (such as burnt umber) to make black. It is a richer color by far.

After the case is finished, and sometime before you reinstall the bellows, put back the chromed (or nickeled) pedals. If you want to keep the pedals from being scratched, cover them with masking tape while you are working on the instrument (Fig. 20-11). You may now rest your case.

THE BELLOWS

Begin bellows disassembly by removing the automatic swell mechanism then removing the main springs (taking appropriate precautions). Now remove the valves from the exhauster bellows, taking care to save the valve, the music-wire spring, and the small staple that limits its travel. Look around the edge of each exhauster bellows and remove all the tacks you can get out. Using techniques described earlier, take off the old bellows and keep it as a pattern. Again, take precations against the stink.

After all bellows cloth is off (the top of the hinges as well) examine the bellows wood and cloth hinges. Repair anything suspicious. The rest of the process of replacing the bellows is

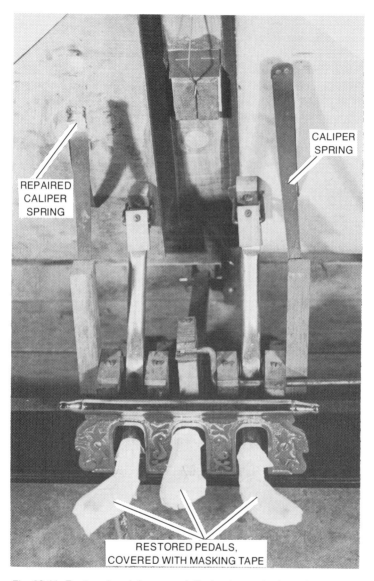

REPAIRED
CALIPER
SPRING

CALIPER
SPRING

RESTORED PEDALS,
COVERED WITH MASKING TAPE

Fig. 20-11. Restored pedals covered. Spring is repaired on piano organ's left side.

exactly like that mentioned earlier concerning the older type of organ, and need not be repeated here. The one difference concerns the interesting innovation with exhauster valves. The material used is no longer leather—it is bellows cloth with the rubber side face to the wood. The problem of a bellows valve stretching is ingeniously solved by using a music wire spring inside a pocket at one end of the valve, the wire having just a small 90° bend to keep it from slipping out of the pocket. The other end of the wire first goes through a small staple half-way along the wire's curve (Fig. 20-12). The staple is not driven clear in but is up just enough to allow the wire to move a bit. The other end of the spring is driven securely into the surface of the exhauster. It works quite well.

As with earlier bellows, be sure to mark where the screw holes are that hold the blocks that in turn hold the springs and the automatic swell. It might be a good idea to make a paper pattern of the holes in relation to the edge of the bellows platform. Then when you are ready to install the blocks, you can use the pattern and an awl to prepunch the holes.

After completing the main bellows and installing the valves that will be inside the exhausters, you can test by installing the springs, sealing the main bellows opening as

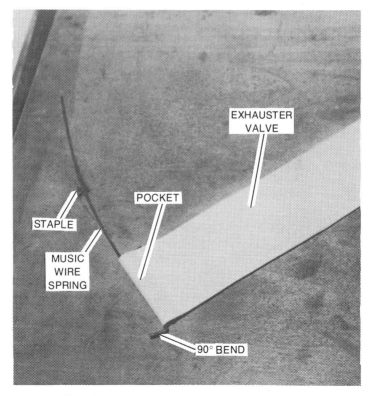

Fig. 20-12. Restored exhauster valve of piano organ.

earlier described, and compressing the bellows almost flat. It should hold quite well with just the inside valves holding. Now complete the bellows by installing the exhauster valves and the swell mechanism on the side. When done, install the bellows in the case in reverse of the way you took it out. You may have to install the center pedal before putting in the bellows because of the way it hinges at the rear. Installing the pedal first would, at least, be more convenient. Then put back the other pedals.

Connect the linkages from pedals to the exhausters and reinstall the caliper springs. What if you have a broken spring? The best thing is to get a new one from one of the suppliers listed. However, having a broken exhauster spring with this organ, I decided to use my principle of trying anything on something that is shot anyway, and I got away with it. This spring was broken right at the rivet at the top where the two parts of the spring were held together. I scored the part with the rivet still in it, marking across it just below the rivet. I then put it in a vise and broke it to match the front piece. Then I clamped both together and with my little 60-amp electric welder proceeded to use a 1/16 inch rod to weld across the top and about an inch down each side. It worked fine. I notice that it doesn't seem to be quite as stiff as the other, but really very little less. Who says you can't weld a spring? See the left spring in Fig. 20-11.

THE ACTION

Insofar as the action is identical to that of the standard organ, proceed with disassembly as previously described: keyboard, mutes, swells, associated parts. Remove, inspect, reface, and rebuild as needed. I will concentrate here on differences between the two organ types.

The first is rather inconsequential. Under the reed pan, by the rear pallet guide pins, the older organs had a strip of felt glued *behind* the pins. For some reason the piano organ felt was laid down first and the guide pins evidently pushed through it. If you wish, you could just restore by using the older method; it would be easier, and no one would know. If you want to restore it as it was originally, as I decided to try, cut the new felt the right width and length. The problem is that of getting the guide pin, which is blunt on top, to go through the felt. I find that it can be done easily if you hold the felt on top of the pin and lightly cut the felt with a knife directly on the top of the pin (Fig. 20-13). Push the felt down about 1/8 inch or so (*not*

Fig. 20-13. Installing new felt over rear pallet guide pins.

all the way down yet), stretch very slightly to the next pin, and repeat down the line. When all the felt is on the pins, you can spread some white glue on the wood beneath and push the felt down to it. Clean off any glue seepage.

Inspect the whole reed cell block as suggested before, paying particular attention to the bleeder holes communicating with the very highest treble reeds. When you install the reeds you may find inspection of the tiny ones facilitated with the use of a plastic jeweler's eye loupe as earlier mentioned. After installing the reeds again, put back the pallets (with new leathers as earlier discussed), and reinstall the mutes. Again, be sure that the springs are in good shape and of the proper length to give good snap action to the mute.

Renew the felt seals on the front and back swells and reinstall. Also restore the octave coupler. You will find it quite similar to those previously described, and restoration methods are identical. The only real difference is that both coupler tables have a small piece of wood extended out in front, and padded underneath with a small piece of leather. One can be seen in Fig. 20-14. The coupler actuating rod, pivoting from under the keyboard, slips under this wood piece and works by

Fig. 20-14. Piano organ octave coupler, showing block of wood attached at front.

lifting the coupler table up. Note the rod back in Fig. 20-7, where it fits under the wood arm from the coupler table, pivots from a wood bearing on the bottom of the keyboard, extends out to the right beyond the keyboard where you can see the very end of the coupler connector.

Install the coupler using the same holes the screws went into originally. Flip the coupler small arm back so that you can now reinstall the pitmans. If the pitmans need new felts on top of them, make new ones as earlier indicated, and install. Then lower the small arm to where it just rests on top of the pitman collar. Check all adjustments. You may need to read the previous material about coupler adjustments again to familiarize yourself with the steps.

Be sure to check against any binding anywhere. One difference here is that there is a short rank of bass reeds that are actuated only when the octave coupler is operating. There was a crude connection made with a piece of leather connecting the mute of this rank to the bass coupler table. There is no separate operation of bass and treble couplers—they are both on or off at the same time.

After restoring the keyboard and the coupler rod, which is fastened to the bottom, reinstall them. You will have to put something temporarily under the coupler table to raise it about 1/4 inch so that you can then wiggle the actuating rod under it. Remove the temporary block, fasten the keyboard in (including the center screw), and you are ready to work on the octave coupler activating machinery.

As you can see in the accompanying several pictures, the "shepherd's crook"-like shaft floats rather freely in the slot attached to the left side of the reed pan. You need to look back at Fig. 20-8, so that we can get clear just what gizmos do what.

The coupler connector is fastened at one end to the actuating rod that goes under the octave coupler tables. The other end has a hook on it like a large knitting needle and always is hooked to the "U" rod. The pedal action arm is the "crook" just referred to. A good view of it, particularly of the back hook, was shown in Fig. 20-9. The rear pin on the pivoting block is a steel pin that functions as the means by which the pedal action arm throws the whole coupler out of operation.

The "U" rod is pivoted on both sides and carries the coupler with it at all times. The pivot screw is hard to see, but

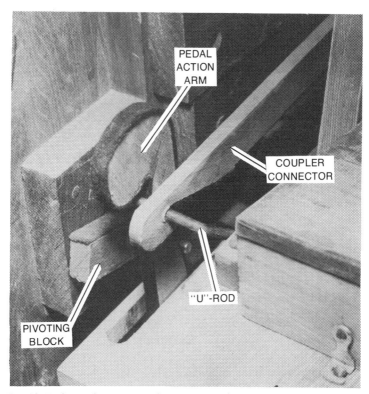

Fig. 20-15. Start of sequence of activating octave couplers in piano-cased organ.

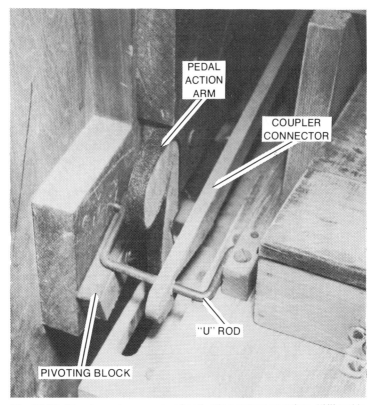

Fig. 20-16. Step two of sequence of activating octave couplers, "U" rod is down.

it is at the exact center of the pivoting block. The pivoting block is the felt-covered piece that rotates with the "U" rod when the rod is pulled down, then pushes it back up when the pedal action arm engages its rear pin.

Following is a step-by-step account of the way it works. With everything at rest, and the coupler not in operation, the coupler shaft hook rests on the "U" rod with the rod elevated at about 30° above its pivot points. The pedal action arm is resting loosely with its back against the pin of the pivoting block but with the rear slot on the arm well above the pin. The arm is held loosely in this position by the spring seen in Fig. 20-4.

When the pedal is depressed, the following sequence takes place. The front hook of the pedal action arm contacts the front of the "U" rod, the rod sliding up into the pedal arm hook, (Fig. 20-15). As the pedal pulls the pedal action arm further down, it pulls the "U" rod down with it until the front of the rod comes to rest *below* its pivot points. This carries with it the coupler connector which is always hooked to it and, of course, pulls the arm of the rod that goes under the coupler tables, raising them. Since there is also some resulting tension on the coupler connector, it holds the "U" rod in the down position. See Fig. 20-16. Note that since that tension holds the "U" rod, when the pedal is released the pedal action arm can return to its original position but the couplers will remain in active position. Note also that when the "U" rod went down it pivoted the pivoting block with it so that the rear of the block, with the pin in it, is now much higher than it is when at rest.

When the pedal is depressed again, the pedal action arm starts down as before, but since the "U" rod is now much lower down, the front of the pedal action arm does not contact it. Instead, the *rear* hook of the pedal action arm contacts the pin on the rear of the pivoting block. As the pedal action arm continues down, it causes the pivoting block to rise at the front, bringing with it the "U" rod. When the rod passes its pivot point the back pressure on the coupler connector pulls things the rest of the way back to off position (Fig. 20-17). Neat. It works every time.

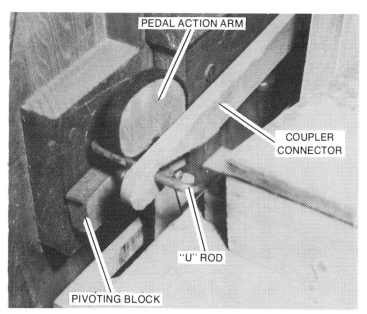

Fig. 20-17. Step three of activating octave couplers; pivoting block raises "U" rod.

The only objection I have with the thing so far is that I haven't been able to get the coupler action to operate without a noticeable "clunk." I have replaced all the felt padding as it was originally, but still the sound is quite noticeable. I have a hunch it was present when new, too.

This completes restoration of the piano-organ. There may never be a great rush to buy them, but they are certainly an interesting part of organ history.

PIANO-ORGAN DISASSEMBLY NOTES

CASE NOTES

BELLOWS AND ACTION NOTES

Chapter 21
The
Melodeon

The name "melodeon" is most commonly given to the earliest suction organs produced after Carhart got his patent in 1846. A variety of brands soon came out, each with its unique method of operation, but virtually all working on the same principle. The case is about writing-desk size, most often rosewood veneered (though other types of wood often were used for legs). Frequently there were folding legs for portability. Just a bit later in their history, melodeons had cases looking like miniature square grand pianos with beautifully turned and carved legs. The Carhart, which is the main subject of this restoration section, is a good example of the early style (Fig. 21-1). By far the most common mechanical arrangement is for the instrument to have a single rank of reeds, pumped with a single pedal, and a single swell stop, operated by another pedal.

OPERATION

The general operation was as simple as the design. The pedal was linked by either a strap of leather or a tapered rod to a single exhauster bellows that sat on top of the main bellows. The valve action was identical to that already covered by the section on later organs. The action sat directly on the front of the main bellows over a large opening into the bellows. In Figs. 21-2, 21-3, and 21-4 you will see three different methods of operating the exhausters. In the little Prince (Fig. 21-2), a

Fig. 21-1. Carhart melodeon, restored.

sturdy spring holds the exhauster closed until operation of the single pedal pulls it down. The pedal is located on the end of a wide leather strap and the organist must hold down the pivoted heel portion of the pedal while pumping the front part (see Fig. 1-1, Chapter 1).The Eldredge has two sickle-shaped pieces of strap metal, one along each side of the exhaust bellows, pivoted at the extreme front of the reed pan (Fig. 21-3). A bracket in the very center of the top rear panel of the feeder

Fig. 21-2. Spring in restored 1847/8 Prince that pulls exhauster back up.

has a shallow receptacle for the point of the wooden shaft that connects it to the pedal. In this case, the operation is reversed from the Prince; here the pedal pushes the exhaust bellows up and it returns by gravity.

The same principle is used by the Carhart but with a different mechanism. In Fig. 21-4 you can see a large forked cast piece which pivots from the right side of the case. A receptacle under the back prong of the fork attaches to the

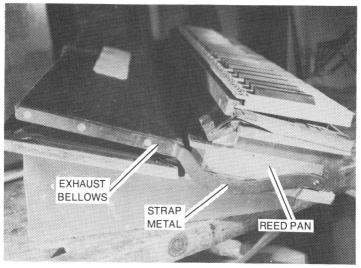

Fig. 21-3. Restored Eldredge action, showing operation of exhauster.

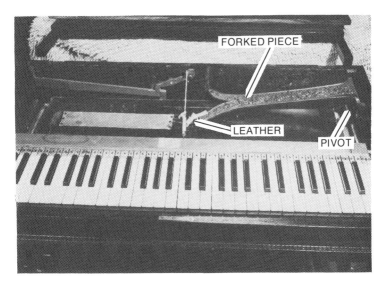

Fig. 21-4. Interior of restored Carhart showing exhauster and swell mechanism.

upper end of the pedal rod, while the prong to the front is tied to a piece of leather which in turn fastens to the center top of the exhaust bellows. In operation, when the pedal is depressed, the cast fork is moved up, pulling the exhauster with it. It returns by gravity.

PROBLEMS

Note here a problem common to melodeons. With a relatively small main bellows and only one exhauster, the organist has to pump in a fairly lively manner to keep things going, particularly if he is to avoid a kind of quaver that keeps time to the pumping.

In all probability, any melodeon you find is pre-Civil War. I don't know exactly when manufacturers ceased making them, but the dates I have been able to verify and the guesses I have heard all are in the 1850s or even earlier. This means that the wood is very old and so is the glue. Further, there were parts on them, particularly the folding instruments, that could easily get lost. It is common to find pump shafts gone (they are easily replaced), reeds missing (these are *not* so easily found, though it is possible to find some), and cast pedals missing (this is a real problem.) If you are contemplating purchase of such an organ, be sure that you can live with (or without) its problems since there is less opportunity to replace parts. You may be able to do with some substitutes in some instances. If the caliper-type spring from the main bellows is broken you won't find one exactly like it but you may be able to modify one designed for a later type of organ. Figure 21-5 shows the typical spring to be found in the main bellows.

The ivories frequently appear in two parts, just for the top of the key (usually there is no ivory on the front vertical part). This might make it a bit easier for you to match one or two if you have access to some old ivories from a later organ or even a piano. Chips in the rosewood case can be troublesome though not insurmountable since such veneer is available. Be warned, however, that rosewood is quite brittle and difficult to work with.

As was suggested concerning evaluation of the standard reed organ, be sure to check everything over very carefully. Particularly check the reeds since you may have a type not readily replaceable. Fortunately, although styles of reeds changed over the years, there seems to have been maintained a uniform size for the reed frame so that reeds from much later organs will often fit the reed cells of melodeons. Since there is only one rank of reeds on the melodeon you may well be able to pull them all for a thorough check before deciding to buy the organ.

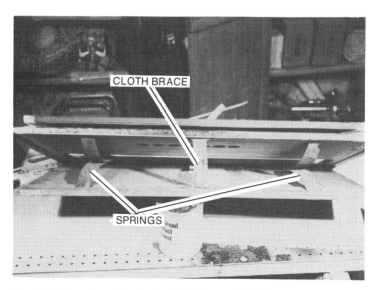

Fig. 21-5. Unrestored Carhart main bellows with cloth removed, showing springs and cloth brace limiting bellows opening.

As before, make sure you thoroughly understand the operation of the organ and have ample pictures of the disassembly process. Don't be mislead by the relative simplicity of the melodeon; parts still have to go back in rather precise fashion so don't trust your memory.

DISASSEMBLY

Remove the lid, taking off also the brass hinges and all screws. Keep the screws and hinges together with masking tape, indicating on the tape exactly which hinge went where. In many of these early organs the parts were handmade and therefore are not identical to similar parts used elsewhere. In the Carhart the hinges had slight differences between them, as did the screws.

The Keyboard

To remove the keyboard you are going to have to remove a number of keys since the screws in the frame (there are several) are under the white keys. It may be a good idea simply to number each key at the back and then take them all off, storing them in a box. You can then easily remove the frame.

You may need to remove the pitmans first. In some cases you may be able to lift the keyboard frame off and leave the pitmans in the holes, thus enabling you to tape down the whole bunch so that you can then lift them all out at one time, keeping them in order. If you can't conveniently get the keyframe off first, I suggest that you lay out a piece of tape and place the pitmans on it, in order, as you do with reeds.

The Action

You will now remove the action from the bellows platform. Here you will find some large screws going from the front of the action down through the bellows platform and some shorter ones at the rear. Unless there has been a corrosion problem, you will probably have no difficulty with the short rear screws, but the longer front ones may be another matter. They go through a lot of wood and the presence of any corrosion at all makes for real problems. On the Carhart I had to get under the bellows platform and pound up on the screws which, fortunately, went all the way through the platform to where I could get to them. Otherwise they just sat imbedded in their sockets and turned. One screw still didn't come (its slotted head was broken as well) so I had to drive it out with more force and damage to the bellows platform than I was happy with. When this situation exists you have no alternative but do some extensive repair of screw holes.

Next remove the side levers from the swell mechanism, taping the pivot screw to the lever for safekeeping. There aren't many of these pieces, so keep them all together; they can easily get lost.

Improvisation

You will have to keep improvising on these instructions if you have a different instrument. For instance, I had to remove the Eldredge exhauster before I could remove the action since it was pivoted to the side of the action. This entailed a bit of a cramped job with an angle screwdriver. You will frequently feel that the melodeons were supposed to be indestructible since no provision was made for normal servicing. Thus glue blocks often held major items in place. Some were even glued over screws. The Carhart, however, did not have such connections between action and exhauster, and this allowed me to remove the action and then take the bellows all out intact.

Now remove what mechanism is present for connecting the exhauster to the pedal shaft if it gets in the way of removing the bellows. This presented no problem with the Eldredge; but in the Carhart the cast iron fork was obviously in the way. In order to remove it I had to cut the leather connecting the fork to the exhauster and remove the small pivot block where the fork was anchored to the side of the case (Fig. 21-4). I might add that the block was both glued *and* screw-fastened to the case. Since there is no way to get the fork out with that block in, it had to be broken loose.

The Bellows

Likewise when you start to remove the main bellows (with the exhauster still on it) you are liable to run into blocks glued in so that they must be broken loose before the bellows can be unscrewed from the side mounts and removed. Unless the organ has been worked on more recently or someone has used modern glues on it somewhere, you will find that the blocks will come off fairly easily if you work carefully with a hammer and chisel. They also usually have nails in them and sometimes screws. When they are all out, lift out the bellows and set aside.

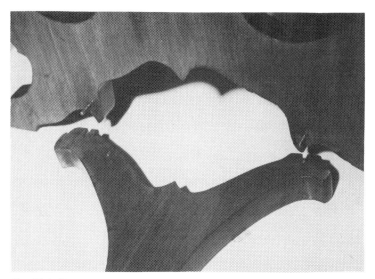

Fig. 21-6. Close-up of restored Carhart folding leg arrangement for fastening in the bottom cross-piece.

The case is now light and manageable. If your organ has folding legs, remove the cross-piece at the bottom. Unless something is missing or someone has tried to make the organ more firm by fastening the cross-piece in, you are likely to find something like that in Fig. 21-6 as a means for the legs to connect to the cross-piece. To show the relationship of the pins in the legs to the slots in the bottom of the cross-piece, the latter is shown upside down. The folding legs usually work from some mechanism at the top similar to that seen in Fig. 21-7. You will find that the cast brackets are not identical in length for both sides, so that one set of legs can fold on top of the other. Be sure you indicate which bracket goes where.

When you have disassembled everything examine the case and legs very carefully for any repairs or regluing of joints that may be needed; then do these jobs before stripping for finishing. The practice of letting old finish drippings stand on new wood is useful here also.

CASE WORK

The lyre-shaped legs of the usual parlor melodeon are a joy to behold—and a job to repair. They were cut from solid wood and, as a result of a century and a quarter of shrinkage, usually have developed many cracks. Do *not* just clamp things together. All you will do is promote more cracks elsewhere.

You are going to have to fill in with new wood, as carefully matched as possible, then carefully use a brush and stain to improve the match. Also be on the lookout for hunks of plastic wood inserted by someone a few years ago. On the Carhart there were several such locations. As Fig. 9-2, Chapter 9 shows, the cracks can be filled in a manner that makes them virtually invisible. The legs shown had a number of cracks that were filled. While looking at that picture, note the difference in shade. No stain was used on the leg on the left. It just has a clear finish on it while the right one is unfinished. That is the difference finish makes.

Before you start to use stripper, do a very careful check of each piece of wood; it may not be what it appears. For some reason I was cautious with the Eldredge and upon careful examination I found that the legs and cross-piece (which is not removable, by the way) were in reality a very light-grained wood, possibly ash, and that the manufacturer had done a beautiful job of handgraining to make it a strikingly close match to the rosewood of the main case. Had I poured stripper on it I would have been one sick cookie. There was no such problem with the Carhart; the case is rosewood veneer, the legs and cross-piece solid mahogany.

Fig. 21-7. Restored folding leg mechanism of Carhart.

If you find that your organ has some graining that you wish to preserve, you have a couple of alternatives. You can just lightly sand the finish to the point that you have smoothed out varnish chips and the like and therefore need not use stripper at all. If you do go into the graining somewhat, or there are damaged spots, you can experiment with thinned artists oil paints, and restore the graining. If someone has slapped on several coats of varnish, you can use stripper cautiously; flow some on thinly with a brush and *immediately* wipe it off. Do this again until you seem to have most of the junk off though the graining is still intact. Then wash it down with thinner, let it dry, and lightly sand until you are satisfied. All of this will take time, particularly in cases of organs with elaborately cut legs, but I assure you it's worth it. I wish I could do graining like those old craftsmen could.

The finish you use is, again, a matter of some arbitrary choice. For some reason, rosewood seems to call for a gloss finish so that what I use. When it is rubbed down, the case looks just gorgeous with that beautiful graining.

Restoration of the pedals is a real problem. What if you have only one pedal? You can't even use that to make the other since the two were usually not alike. In the rare instance where you could find one like yours in a museum, you might take photos and measurements (with permission, of course), make a wooden pattern of the pedal, and have a new one cast at a foundry. Of course that route is costly and time-consuming. For those needing to know what typical pedals look like, Fig. 21-8 shows the Carhart pedals from the underside with the bracket which holds them. These pedals are made of cast iron though often you will find brass as on the Eldredge. What should you do if it is not possible to reproduce a metal pedal? Make wooden ones. In fact, I have seen pictures of some with wooden pedals, so you wouldn't be entirely out of line (assuming that the ones I saw were original.) And besides, so what if everything isn't authentic? Just don't make any alterations to the existing equipment that you may be sorry for later.

BELLOWS

In some cases removal of the old exhauster is just a matter of lifting it off; frequently the leather or bellows-cloth hinges have completely torn or rotted off. In most cases it will still be an easy job to remove the old hinges since they almost always have deteriorated. Before you remove anything,

Fig. 21-8. Underside of Carhart pedals.

however, take several pictures and exact measurements concerning where everything goes. While the position of the exhauster bellows may not be quite as critical as it is with later organs, it must be fairly closely positioned or it will not work properly. This is more the case with melodeons using the system like the Eldredge than is the situation with the Carhart. You need to match screw holes in the Eldredge but not the Carhart.

As you disassemble the exhauster be careful not to just tear things off even if they are ratty. You may have some real problems with wood strips at the edges of the bellows; they seldom come off in one piece. No need, though, for you to try to do so since you may not need to replace them at all unless you are aiming at completely authentic appearance even inside. I used the miniature prybar here to good effect in getting the strips off. You will notice that the exhauster is comprised of not just bellows cloth; it usually has cardboard folders the full width of the sides with just hinges at the top, bottom, and middle. Some melodeons used bellows cloth to cover the whole thing while others used a kind of silk-finish cloth on the cardboard folders, and leather strips for hinges. In any case,

WOOD STRIP

Fig. 21-9. Carhart main bellows, upside down.

save everything, marking exactly which side the bellows part came from.

Next remove the main bellows cloth which usually consists of just cloth (no cardboard). Some bellows may have a groove on the bottom of the bellows platform into which the bellows cloth is inserted, and a strip of wood nailed in the groove to hold things. Getting this out can be a chore since there are usually a jillion brads in the thing. The strip can be seen in the restored bellows, Fig. 21-9. You can usually chew it out with a narrow chisel or sharpened screwdriver. After getting off one side, look in to see what kind of spring is in there and remove the one nearest (provided other beasties don't object to your intrusion.) Do the same for the other side. You will then have to put a block of wood inside the bellows to hold it open while you take off the cloth from the front edges.

You now have just two flat pieces of wood hinged at one end. In the Carhart bellows I found a flexible brace at the center which holds the bellows at the right distance even with the springs installed and the bellows cloth off. If you know that such a device is in your melodeon, you may take off the bellows cloth without removing the springs first. The danger, however, is that you don't know for sure what condition that brace is in (See Fig. 21-5) and if it breaks at an inopportune moment you are in trouble. I prefer to be safe and remove the springs as previously indicated.

The Hinge

The hinge of the main bellows is probably completely shot. Frequently you will find that the original hinge was a leather strip thoroughly tacked to each panel of the main bellows with a cardboard tack strip. If you wish, you can replace it with the same. I suggest that you use heavy-duty bellows cloth, properly glued in with contact cement and either tacked or stapled thoroughly. It will be stronger and give a better seal than the leather, (Fig. 21-10). Before installing this hinge, however, be sure to inspect carefully each part of the bellows. If you find small cracks, clean them out with strips of sandpaper, fill with glue, and thoroughly clamp with bar clamps.

A caution here: Use protective blocks on the edges to keep the bar clamps from cutting into the edges. Also use scrap boards along each edge parallel to the bars of the clamp, the boards clamped every few inches, to prevent the bar clamps from warping the main bellows panels. Dents or bows can lead to nasty things. Of course, don't use any more pressure on the bar clamps than absolutely necessary to get the crack back in

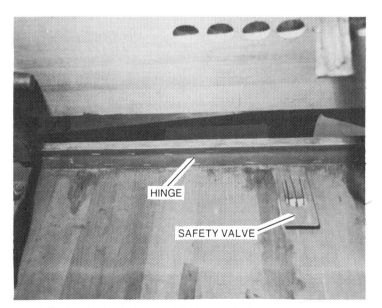

Fig. 21-10. New bellows-cloth hinge in Carhart main bellows.

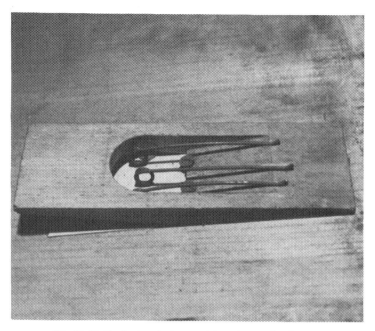
Fig. 21-11. Typical melodeon safety valve, on the Carhart.

place. After all is glued and ready to go, you can use a power sander very lightly to smooth things up prior to a coat of sealer.

Before installing the new hinge also check the operation of the safety valve since on the melodeon it is usually on the inside. A typical safety valve is pictured in Fig. 21-11. You will notice that it is cut and positioned so that when the bellows is pumped up too much the raised part will contact the opposite panel, causing the valve to rock, or pivot backwards, opening the portion that is held flat by the springs. This then uncovers a hole in the main bellows panel. If the springs are bad, make new ones of piano wire of comparable diameter. You may also need to resurface the bottom of the valve with chamois skin. Once you are satisfied with the safety valve, reinstall the new hinge on the main bellows.

Before installing the exhauster, be sure to install the valve on the main bellows. This is virtually identical to those on later organs previously described, so use the techniques already discussed. Ordinarily you will find that the exhauster should be restored first. In the Carhart it was a necessity since the bellows cloth hinge had to be applied first to the back edge of the main bellows before the latter could be covered.

264

The Cardboard Folders

Examine the cardboard folders very carefully. They certainly are old, but they may still be in good condition, excepting only the hinges. Sometimes they are covered completely by leather, folders and all; this will be a costly recovering job if you want to go that route. Since they are out of view inside the case, I suggest that you take off the rotten leather, clean the folders carefully, and recover with light-weight bellows cloth. Don't use heavy cloth here since it will be too stiff for easy exhauster operation. If the folders are covered by the silk cloth and, particularly, if the patent label is on them like it was on my Prince, by all means try to restore the folders without recovering them. In this case just replace the hinges with either bellows cloth or leather.

If the folders are not in usable shape, make new ones out of cardboard of comparable thickness. Otherwise clean the old ones up and lay them out in proper fashion exactly as they will fit when restored. In Fig. 21-12 they are laid out on the reversed top panel of the exhauster bellows. Note that the corners do not meet; they don't need to. The leather corners you will install later take care of that problem.

Prepare the folders for each side first by gluing on new inside hinges (Fig. 21-13). The strip in front is a folded side with four new hinges installed. Be sure to install those hinges

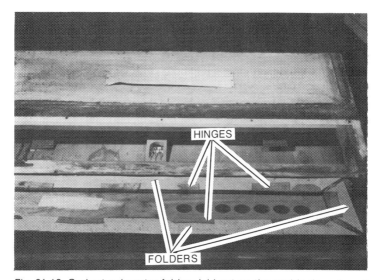

Fig. 21-12. Carhart exhauster folders laid out on the upside-down top of the exhauster.

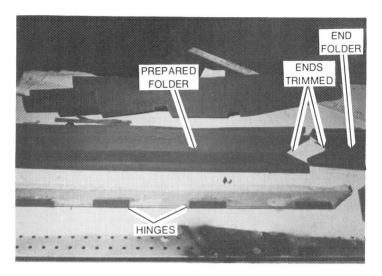

Fig. 21-13. Carhart folders in process of having bellows cloth applied; hinges recovered.

(made from bellows cloth) with the folders *folded*. If you install them with the folders flat they may not fold properly. Then apply lightweight bellows cloth to the outside, leaving about an inch extra on each side to glue to the edges of the bellows panels. In Fig. 21-13, see a folder so prepared and left unfolded just above the folded exhauster side. At its right is a completed end folder.

If you apply all of this with contact cement, you will note a real problem when you use lightweight bellows cloth. It tends to curl up once the contact begins to dry (that will happen fast!) An easy way out is to spread the contact liberally on the folders as they are spread out, then put the cloth on the contact while it is still wet. You can then do some smoothing out, but some wrinkles in the lightweight stuff may stay in spite of your efforts.

Attaching the folders to the bellows platform and to the top of the exhauster is fairly easy if you make sure that all is in the right place. Before laying things out for final installation be sure to trim the ends of the folders (the diamond-shaped cuts) as can be seen in Fig. 21-13. This is where the corner leathers will go. You don't need to worry about trimming the top and bottom edges now; they can be trimmed after installation.

Place the folders in the exact position that they will go when completed, the wood top to the exhauster also in place.

There should be enough cloth extending from the top and bottom edges of the folders to cover the edges of both the top of the exhauster and the appropriate area on the bellows platform to which the bottom of the exhauster fits. So far, though, no glue is on the edges—again, do *not* put glue on that approximately one inch edge of cloth; it will curl badly and you will be in trouble. Apply a very liberal coat of contact cement to the back edge of the main bellows platform where the exhauster folder is to attach. *Immediately* apply the cloth to it, rubbing it in thoroughly. Watch it for a couple of minutes, and prevent it from curling off. The moment you see such curling signs, smooth it back. It will soon stay in place. Do the same for the top and bottom edges of the exhauster sides all around. After a while, maybe half an hour, you can trim the cloth.

Leather Corners

Next is the installation of new leather corners. Here you need a supply of New Zealand lambskin (or equivalent) the same as you use for pallets. In order to be able to cut a pattern to fit the corners, you need to have the exhauster bellows held up. In the case of the Carhart, that was very easy; just insert a stick slantwise through one of the exhaust valve holes and it will hold the bellows up at any level you choose (Fig. 21-14). That brush through the exhauster hole is my glue brush! I

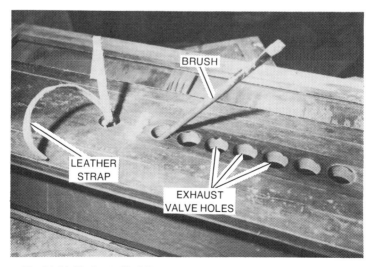

Fig. 21-14. Method of holding up exhauster while corners are applied.

Fig. 21-15. Corners ready for leather to be applied; trimmed folders installed.

later changed to a stick. Figure 21-15 shows the end of the exhauster ready to measure for leather corners. It is also a good shot of what the installed folders look like, all trimmed.

Make paper patterns for the leather corners. Allow about 3/4 inch all around for gluing. Note that you may find that each corner will vary a slight bit. In the two corners shown in Fig. 21-15, the leather will come down the front edge of the main bellows at the right corner but must flatten out at the bellows platform at the bottom of the other corner. Why not use bellows cloth here? Because you must be able to stretch the material in several ways and bellows cloth won't do it. The lambskin does a beautiful job here.

After you have cut the leather to fit, prepare it by applying contact glue all along the edges of both the leather (rough side in) and the edges of the corner openings where the leather will

268

mate. The easiest way to apply the leather while the glue is still tacky on both is to fold the leather right at the point where it will fold in the bellows, apply it first to that central portion then, opening up the fold, apply it top and bottom, lightly touching it to where it goes around the perimeter. If all seems to be in place, smooth it down all around. Don't hesitate to stretch it a bit where such seems to be called for. When smoothing it down, do so evenly but don't worry about not being able to apply much pressure. It doesn't take much. Just as soon as you have applied the corner, before you do any trimming, take the stick out of the valve hole and lower the bellows to full folded position. If something seems to be binding, try to move things just a bit to where the exhauster folds OK. Now do the same for the other three corners. This should complete the exhaust bellows except for the valve; leave that off for now. Figure 21-16 shows the corners installed and trimmed.

If your bellows platform has the slot for inserting the side edge of the main bellows, you could save yourself some grief

Fig. 21-16. Lambskin corners on opposite sides, installed and trimmed.

by just filling the slot in with wood and applying the bellows cloth to the surface of the platform as described in earlier pages. In this case, I decided to go with the original and put cloth in the slot, though not for very good reason. Examine the edge of the bellows platform also before putting back the new bellows. You may find that the area where the corner screws hold the action to the platform is not in good shape. If you have to replace wood where screws go near the edge, be sure to taper the wood insert to where it appears from an edge view like a single dovetail, the widest portion on the opposite side of the bellows platform from where the screw enters it. In this way the pull of the screw can only tighten the plug rather than pull it out.

Some bellows have a strip of cloth inside the front edge of the bellows to act as a limit to the opening travel of the bellows, as was seen in Fig. 21-5. In this instance it is attached by means of a metal strip at top and bottom. In other cases the strip is simply glued and tacked to the front edges of the bellows and the bellows cloth is glued on top of it. If yours doesn't have such a device, you may wish to add one. It certainly helps in that you can install the springs right away without having to go through the wood-block routine to hold things open until the front of the bellows is installed plus the springs.

From here on out the installation of this portion of bellows cloth is identical to that of the standard organ. Even normal, heavy-duty cloth is used here. So, the previous instructions on measuring, cutting, applying glue (any of the methods described) all apply here.

A final note: You removed a strip of wood that was originally holding the bellows cloth to the edges of both the main bellows and the exhauster top. If you are using the contact cement method of application you do not need to replace the wood unless, of course, you are looking for completely authentic appearance even inside. It was on originally just because it was necessary to hold things while the old hot glue took hold.

Testing

To test the bellows (with the exhauster valve still off), tape a piece of sturdy cardboard over the large opening in the bellows over which the action fits. Be sure that the masking tape covers all edges and even the holes where the back edge of the action is screwed to the bellows platform (Fig. 21-17).

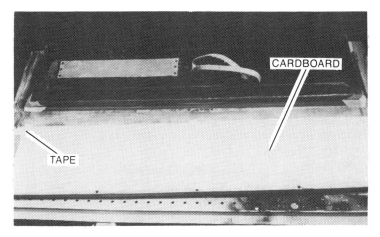

Fig. 21-17. Cardboard temporarily taped to opening in main bellows for testing.

Carefully lay the bellows on a flat surface and press down until you feel the safety valve being touched inside. Let up on the pressure and time the bellows to see how long it takes to come back to full position; it should take in the neighborhood of twenty seconds. By not having the exhauster valve on, this tests the inner valve alone.

Now install the exhauster valve. Test by taking hold of the top of the exhauster and pumping the whole bellows up with it by rapidly raising and lowering it several times. Time things again; times should improve ten seconds or so. Your bellows will, of course, vary some but if you are in this general ballpark you are OK. Since these are much smaller bellows than the later standard organ used, you can't expect the melodeon to achieve the performance of the larger organs.

You may find the original bellows did not have a strip of anything glued over the outside of the hinge of the main bellows. For my part, I just feel better if I don't have to rely on the hinge to perform its main function and be airtight at the same time. Such an added strip probably will not be visible and is good insurance. Do not replace the bellows permanently in the case yet since you can do some action testing with it out. You may wish, however, to place it in the case as a convenient storage area.

THE ACTION

Since you have already removed the melodeon's keyboard and pitmans, next take out the reeds. If your organ has an easily removable swell shutter, remove it. Otherwise open and put a block of wood under it to hold it there.

Checking The Reeds

Pulling reeds is a bit of a problem with some melodeons since these reeds did not have the slot in the heel of the reed frame as later reeds did (See Fig. 2-4, Chapter 2). Some have just a small projection so that a reed hook can get a small hold. Here the paint-can opener discussed earlier makes a good reed hook. Be sure to bend the end to a full 90° angle. Some melodeon reeds don't have even this aid to pulling and you must carefully put the reed hook over the protruding rivet and pull. If this just doesn't work you can, in desperation, grind the points of a needle-nose pliers so that you can grasp the reed by the end and pull it out. In all cases, be sure you don't get anything in far enough to catch the free end of the reed.

While you are pulling reeds, check for anything that appears unusual. The Carhart, for instance, had an unusual problem: the reeds were just falling out. This could indicate badly shrunken reed cells or, as it turned out, it could indicate that the reed cells were badly unglued from the reed pan and many were broken. Place the reeds on a piece of masking tape and roll them up for protection.

Remove all pallets, taking precautions as indicated earlier. Be sure to number them and know which end you started numbering from. Strip off the old felt and leather; it probably is shot. Put the pallets in a box after you have sanded each one smooth. Also be sure that you have the exact measurements of the felt and leather of the original and know exactly where it was glued to each pallet.

Now check over the wood of the action. Be prepared to find just a bunch of small cracks in the reed pan and elsewhere. Very carefully examine the block of wood the pallet springs are fastened to. If it shows any sign of glue separation, remove all the pallet springs and get the block glued properly. This piece has a lot of tension on it and over the years, as glue has dried out, it might have begun to separate and warp.

Check the condition of the pallet springs. Don't be at all surprised to find at least a few of them breaking as you flex them in removing the pallets or in testing them. Many such springs were made of spring brass and as such are quite subject to corrosion. If they break as you handle them, be thankful; it happened at a time you can easily fabricate another out of music wire. Again, take the spring with you and get some music wire of the same diameter at a model airplane supply store. By holding one end of the music wire in a vise, clamped with a small bolt or rod of a smaller diameter than you want the finished loop to be, you can easily wind a new spring.

Checking the Reed Cells

The reed cells of any organ can be really troublesome, those of the melodeon particularly so because of its age. Use a small light to probe into each cell from both above and beneath. In addition, I also made a small, simple probe from a piece of very thin aluminum bent at one end so that I could get it in the joint where the reed cell meets the reed pan if it has come unglued. I was unpleasantly surprised to find out how many such places were open. Be particularly careful in checking the treble cells. If there is the slightest crack between cells you will get the inevitable cypher, and will have to strip things down again and do the job over. To give a blow-by-blow description of what was done to each cell of the Carhart would be quite lengthy. I recommend using the following procedure (which I followed):

1. Check all joints, particularly those between reed cells and reed pan, and glue where necessary. I wound up running glue along the joints of all the cells since so many needed it. I figured that even those for which the glue seemed to be holding would probably be about to loosen. Use the small aluminum probe to work the glue into the joints (Fig. 21-18).
2. Replace wood missing in the front of certain cells, making sure not to fill in the slot that the reed slides in.
3. After all is dry, fit each reed to its cell. Here I made very good use of those cheap files discussed much earlier. I found one, happily, that was exactly the width of the slot in a reed cell. I ground it to a circular shape at the end to match the shape of the reed-frame front, then used the file to test reglued cells for size. My biggest problem was that of glue that had seeped into the reed slot in spite of my attempts to keep it out. I also ground down another file to use just in the slot of the reed cell. Walt tells me he often uses two small hacksaw blades taped together for the same job. This task is a ticklish one for which you may have to devise other tools, depending on the demands of your particular instrument. The main thing is, don't get in

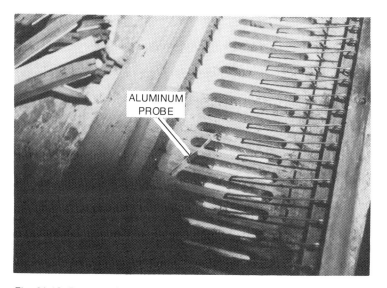
Fig. 21-18. Bottom of reed pan showing openings to reed cells and small tool for getting glue into cracks.

a hurry while working with reed cells. Check each cell as you finish with it and try to keep glue out of the slots.

4. After the cells are repaired, and the reeds all fit properly, check the guide pins for the pallets. Chances are some rust will have built up around some of them or some will be missing. Be very sure to clean those things off thoroughly. It gets to be a chore when the pallet springs get in the way of your getting to the front row, but I assure you that you had better do it. If they are not smooth they will be a main source of cyphers where the pallet hangs up, and the pallet won't return properly to position. Now apply felt as needed behind the guide pins. While you have the felt supply out, apply it also in front of the reed cells.

5. Check the condition of the hinges, springs, and anything else associated with the swell shutter. I must confess to some suspicion concerning the Carhart; rather than the usual springs on the swell shutter it had three strips of rubber so tacked on that the swell was kept well in place. I was more suspicious when the rubber was in such good condition, while so much of the rest of the organ had deteriorated. However, the cuts in the top of the reed cell block necessary for the

installation of the rubber did not seem to be later work nor did the locations where the rubber was anchored on the underside of the swells. Since the system works well, I just put things back. More commonly you are likely to find some springs, similar to large pallet springs, positioned at each end of the shutter to keep it in place. If the cloth and felt of the swell hinges and seals are bad, replace them.

6. Measure carefully the leather and felt needed for the pallets and restore them. The melodeon pallets are quite similar to later organ pallets, only smaller. When this is done you can begin to reassemble the action.

Reassembly

Install the reeds, cleaning them one at a time in Lysol Toilet Bowl Cleaner. After you have them all in their cells you can test to a degree by blowing into the cell through a straw. Be careful not to let saliva get in the straw. Next install the pallets, checking each one before putting it in.

Now comes the keyboard frame. If there are warps, as mentioned earlier, correct them. The melodeon frame does not have the felt strip between guide pins but it does have small circles of felt around the bottom of each pin. Also, the key does not have felt up in the guide-pin hole, If the wood around that guide-pin hole seems worn, you may need to fill some in, though it must be done without causing any binding. Keyboard and frame can be seen in Fig. 21-19. Installing the keyboard is different with the melodeon since there is no separate guide strip for the pitmans; they go through holes in the keyboard frame. They can be seen in Fig. 21-19 just ahead of the second row of guide pins. Thus you must install the frame, the pitmans, and the keys, in that order. After setting in the frame, but before installing keys, put the pitmans in and test each one for completely free operation. Since the normal operation of the key pushes the pitman even with the surface of the keyboard frame, you are in no danger of pushing it too far.

If pitmans are missing you probably will have an easier time of replacing them than is the case with later organ pitmans since there are no octave coupler collars to bother with. You can try a pitman in any hole and put a key on top of it. The dip of the key at the front is less than that of the standard organ.

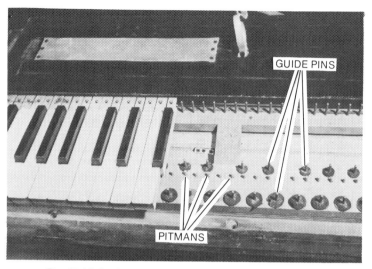

Fig. 21-19. Carhart key frame with keys partially installed.

Mark the location of each of the screw holes in the bellows platform where the action fastens down so that you can find them after new felt seals are put over them. Apply felt seals about 3/4 inch wide where the bottom of the reed pan mates with the bellows platform. Let dry thoroughly and then punch holes through the felt at the screw holes with an awl.

Put the bellows on a low bench so that you can now sit the action on it. Put about three or four screws in to fasten the action down a bit and then, reaching over the action, operate the exhauster. There should be no sound whatever. If you hear some reeds sounding, try to find the right key and operate it rapidly several times, then stop and see if the sound stops. If there is no sound when you pump the bellows several times, try the keys one at a time. Do all reeds sound? Is there any other note sounding at the same time? If problems arise, run them down one at a time. By now you shoud know the organ well enough to track things down. When all seems OK with the action, take it back off the bellows platform so that you can install the bellows in the case.

Install the bellows, making sure that you screw it down to the exact spot it came from. Make sure that you put the screws in their original holes. If a screw of the proper length just seems to be reluctant, try another. Melodeon hardware was often handmade and even screws may need some juggling to get them in the right places.

Before you can install the action you will have to remove the keeper at the rear of the keyboard and take out several keys in order to get screws through the action and into the bellows platform. Once the action is securely fastened, replace the keys and keeper. Next install the levers on the rear and side of the case; these operate the swell shutter. There is often a spring on a small cord that keeps downward tension on the swell shutter pedal (See Fig. 21-4). In Fig. 21-20 you can see the Eldredge has a small brass spring fastened to the rear of the case so that it constantly bears down on the lever, performing the same function.

Figure 21-14 shows the leather strap that will connect the top of the exhauster to the front fork of the cast iron arm of the pumping mechanism. First install the cast piece by inserting one end in the hole in the back of the case. The other goes in the bearing block that attaches to the side of the case. This bearing must be glued and screw-fastened to the case. Before you install the arm it would be a good idea to give a generous shot of silicone spray inside these bearing holes. Once the fork is in, tie the leather strap to its proper spot, which should leave only about an inch or less space between the fork and the top of the exhauster. If you allow the leather to be too long you may limit the pumping travel of the exhauster.

BRASS SPRING

Fig. 21-20. Eldredge swell mechanism.

Fig. 21-21. Lathe attachment for turning long shafts.

Often you will have to replace the rods that connect from the pedals to the action above them. If you can, find wood like the case or nearly so. The Eldredge rods are walnut, about 1/2 inch diameter at the center, tapering to about 5/16 inch or so at each end. You could make them in a rather crude fashion by just planing down a 5/8 inch square strip; that seems to be the way those on the Eldredge were made, though I have no way of knowing if they are original or not.

If you wish to do a little more polished job and turn them on a lathe, you will have a problem turning something this length without the thing vibrating like a bowstring the moment you touch it with a chisel. Figure 21-12 shows an easily made device that provides a moving center rest for such turning jobs on chair rungs and the like. I made this one from plans I found in a home craftsman's magazine some years ago. The photo should provide a sufficient pattern for any lathe enthusiast to use in making one. Don't skimp on that piece shaped like a question mark. It must be made of 3/4 inch plywood. The width of the 3/4-circle part must be no less than 1 1/4 inch. The three adjustable pieces must be of good hardwood; I used oak. With this device it is just a matter of minutes to chuck in a 1/2 inch dowel rod and taper both ends. Sand the rod while on the lathe; then, after removing it and cutting to fit, hand sand the length with fine sandpaper. If you have used the usual birch dowel available at most lumber yards, you will have to stain it to

278

match your melodeon, though you could use a square of walnut if you wished.

Carefully cut the ends of the rod to match the receptacle in your organ. Some will have a tapered hole for the rod to fit in, others will require that you put a pin in the end of the rod. The pin then goes through a small hole in the action arm of the exhauster or swell control rod. When you cut the rods to length, leave a bit more than you think you will need because you will need to round the ends off, usually, so that the rods can fit into cups on the action pieces. You need a bit of sanding room here. You can always take a little more off if need be.

Final Checking

After inserting the shafts in their proper places, try both pedals to make sure that they work without binding and that the bellows pumps properly. Do not be surprised to find that the bellows does not hold as well as it did when you tested it with the action off. As you will find out, your right leg will get a vigorous workout if you use more than three or four notes at a time. Now you know why the double pedal exhauster bellows was developed.

This completes this section on melodeons but by no means does it cover all possibilities you are likely to encounter. In those very early days of organ development all sorts of experiments were tried and I am quite sure that there were many melodeons made using mechanical contrivances I have never heard of. I hope, however, that at least the method of approach described here will enable you to deduce what is needed to make your little instrument sing sweetly again.

MELODEON DISASSEMBLY NOTES

MELODEON CASE NOTES

MELODEON BELLOWS NOTES

MELODEON ACTION NOTES

Chapter 22
Organ Stools

Very seldom does anyone find an organ with the bench or stool it originally came with. In fact, there is some question concerning what actually came with some of them. For the serious organ player, a type of bench seems to have been preferred, the seat slightly slanted forward to give better support for pedal work. Those are quite rare now, two being shown in Gellerman's book. They didn't seem to catch on, however, for the casual parlor organ user, possibly because they were not adjustable. As a result, the most common stool to be found now is the screw-adjustable seat commonly known as the piano stool.

For some reason one will hear that a three-legged stool is for organs and the four-legged ones are for pianos. I have heard this distinction many times, getting it again from Walt just the other day; but no one, including Walt, can give me the reason why. I can find no such distinction anywhere in organ literature. The fact remains that one can use just about any kind of stool with an organ. All of the stools mentioned in the following discussion can be seen in Fig. 22-1 except for a type of claw-and-ball stool with a high, comb back. They are very decorative, they are getting rare, and they are high priced.

Possibly the oldest variety is the completely cast-iron stool. I have one with a patent date on it of 1869. It is the far right stool in Fig. 22-1. These are quite attractive with the older organs. The difficulty you are likely to encounter with them is that the threads inside the cast frame are cast integral

ALL WOOD

WOOD TRUNK, FITTED IRON LEGS

TURNED-WOOD SEAT (THIS IS THE ONLY RESTORED STOOL OF THE 4)

COMPLETE CAST IRON

Fig. 22-1. Organ stool collection.

with the trunk and therefore are almost impossible to repair if worn out. As you may know, a stool with a worn screw or threads requires quite a balancing act from the organist trying to sit and pump at the same time. I took one such stool to my friendly welder who reamed out the central portion then welded inside the inner screw of a defunct wood organ stool. This meant that the screw that had to be used with it is smaller than the original, but that is no problem.

Another more commonly possible repair involves taking a portion of about 5/8 inch OD threaded rod (to use for the rod) and using a floor flange to fasten it to the seat bottom. Weld two matching nuts inside the cast shell. This idea came from John, who has made many wooden organ stools from scratch using such rods and nuts for the adjustable mech- anism.

A problem very often encountered in a wooden stool is that of the threaded metal insert down in the trunk of the stool coming loose. In such cases the stool wobbles and cannot be raised or lowered. It may be possible to take off the top metal cap of the stool trunk, and by some means wedge slivers of wood, saturated with glue, down around that loose element, to fix it in place. I haven't had much luck with that approach. Since usually the wood trunk is battered and often poorly finished, I have carefully split the trunk open. Then, when regluing it back together, I also get the threaded portion of the screw mechanism firmly fixed in place.

Since so many of the organ stools used rather soft wood for the trunk, getting them properly stripped is not easy. A great deal of edge grain shows, and the wood may be badly dented. Often, stain or enamel was applied to the raw wood. I have found that the easiest means of refinishing a rough stool is simply to chuck the thing in a lathe and take a shallow cut all over it to take off the surface material. In order to do this you will have to make sure that the trunk is properly repaired, with all cracks filled. Then, on the lathe, make a tapered plug that will fit into the top opening of the stool trunk. By centering the lathe in this plug you will come up with a reasonable centering of the stool. I fully realize that the practice I suggest really falls into the "skinning" category so anathema to many furniture restorers, but if all else proves impossible, I do what needs to be done. After you have properly turned and sanded the trunk on the lathe, it can be filled, sanded again by hand, stained, and finished to match the organ it is to go with.

One caution: If your stool has a wood trunk with fitted iron legs (like the unrestored one second from left in Fig. 22-1) be very careful not to turn the trunk down any more than is abolutely necessary. If you go too far you will have difficulty refitting the legs since they have a curvature to match the original diameter.

Because stools are hard to find and increasingly expensive, you may wish to make one from scratch. If you take measurements of an all-wood stool such as the unrestored one at the left of Fig. 22-1, you will see that making one is not a difficult job with a lathe and maybe a router. John has made many, using the new rod and matching nuts for hardware.

Stool seats usually fall into two categories: the turned wood tops most often seen on claw-and-ball stools (turned wood can be seen on the only restored stool in Fig. 22-1 second from the right), and the upholstered variety. The most common problem of the turned wood tops is warping. Frequently the top has been lathe-turned from a blank glued up from two or three plies of wood about half or three-quarters of an inch thick. Occasionally the top ply will crack and begin to curl. The solution is by no means easy. On one job I was able to get the top ply off, sand it flat, and reglue it back so that it looked reasonably OK, though the crack still showed. In another case, however, the wood had shrunk and warped to such an extent that clamping it down to reglue in one area just caused it to come loose in another. I finally gave up on it and just padded the warped top. I might add that it was not a claw-and-ball stool so the padding did not appear out of place. If you really want to have the turned wood top you might try your local high school shop to find out if you can use a wood lathe with enough swing to turn a new one.

Many of those that were originally upholstered used as a base just a hunk of rough wood, so if the original wood is about shot don't worry about saving it. Cut another slab from plywood since the whole thing is to be covered anyway. A simple padding can be made from extra-firm foam rubber, but that still produces a seat really much softer than the originals were. Better to go to an upholsterer's shop and get some rubberized horsehair, use it for the base, then add carefully tapered layers of cotton. This will produce a firm but properly resilient seat. If you cover it first with a layer of muslin, very carefully positioning the padding to avoid lumps, you stand a better chance of getting the final material on smoothly. If you need further information on upholstering, there are a number of books on the subject, probably available through your public library. A decorative fringe, obtainable in a wide variety of styles from fabric stores, lends a frilly, Victorian touch for those so inclined.

Finally, you can go all out and use needle point (as was originally common) or the new Speedtufting techniques to produce custom designs that will really make your stool distinctive. You can put initials on it, special designs, or whatever. As suggested concerning custom pedal pads, this is where you can get someone else in the act. The more the merrier.

A final note: If you have a claw-and-ball stool with bad feet, check antique shops and flea markets for sets of feet. I have seen several lately at prices that make it practical for you to repair an otherwise good stool. At any rate, don't throw anything away; things do turn up, you know.

STOOL NOTES

Chapter 23
Notes on
Professional
Restoring

This book is written primarily for the hobbyist who simply wants to restore an old organ. Considerations of time or value (present or potential) do not enter into the matter. When asked why I want to spend several hundred hours working over one of these smelly old trash bins, I usually come back with some crack about old fishermen never die, they just smell that way. (Scratch almost any carping critic of antique restoration and he's some variety of fisherman or hunter.) The fact is that any hobby is its own justification.

But—once you successfully restore an organ, insidious things happen. Other people hear that you can do the job and they want you to restore Grandma's old jewel for them. Or, you go to an auction, and there is that piece of *junk* that just no one would buy because of its horrible condition (except you, of course.) Should you get it for restoration and resale? (I got the Packard after it failed to sell at auction twice.)

EVALUATING COST

Once business rears its ugly head, a lot of things clamor for attention. How much do you really think your time is worth? That in itself isn't easy to anwer. If you are considering going into business, with the expenses of a shop, tools, insurance, utilities, and the like, your hourly charge may easily reach $20, the charge I know is currently being asked by a player-piano restoring company. Since an organ can easily take several hundred hours to restore, you know what that fact alone would do to most contract jobs. On the other hand, although you don't need or want any more organs, you might just want to have the opportunity to work on organs. A dollar an hour is a heck of a lot more return on your time than most other hobbyists get back for the time they put in. Furthermore, before you can really answer any such questions you should have restored enough organs to have some sort of idea of the time required for various jobs.

Time and Materials

For instance, here is the time breakdown of a job I did, without case work (the owner did his own.)

Function	Time
Initial disassembly	1 hr.
Bellows (remove, strip)	1½
(clean, sand, treat wood, repair wood)	3
(mark new bellows, cut, install)	4½
Install seals on platform, install pedal straps	1½
Strip action; clean, renovate wood	9½
Clean and repair keyboard	3
Repair vox humana (bad shape)	3
Remake several pitmans, adjust and level keys	4
Reinstall stopboard and adjust (no repairs)	2
	33 hours

This was a simple job; the only complication was the vox humana, which ordinarily can be restored in an hour or less. The fact that the stopboard took no work lessened the time by at least ten hours. If you charge what any other craftsman gets, say a plumber or electrician, see what even this small job could amount to?

Oh yes—there's also the cost of the materials. You have glue, wood filler, dowels, felt, bellows cloth, pedal straps, piano wire, ivories, screws, and so on.

Obviously there are other considerations. Case work is almost impossible to estimate since you never know just what you are going to get into. If there are parts to reproduce, don't be fooled into thinking that it looks simple unless you have done that job before. For instance, the carving I had to reproduce for the Packard in Fig. 7-1 took me 35 hours to do. An expert carver could do it in less time, true, but are you sure you are an expert? The organ restorer has to be a little bit of everything but he seldom is highly efficient in all. Now you know why that organ did not sell at auction.

Upon being stripped, an organ may display hunks of plastic wood someone had used to cover up rot; you must now find and fit something better. Pitmans may be non-standard (oh, the sucker sticks and whittled sticks one finds in these things!) and you will have to buy a special bit and make a die to size them correctly. I once spent several hours doing that job. Myriads of unseen cracks will fiendishly open up in the case and action, all of which must be laboriously cleaned out, sanded, either filled with additional wood or glued and clamped. That takes chunks of time plus the expenses of bar clamps and the like, unless you already have them on hand. For you tool nuts this can be a blessing: It justifies your purchase of tools you would get shot for buying otherwise.

Be careful when estimating how much time such case work will take. I have taken as much as 200 hours on a really dirty case. Just don't be too quick to make an estimate that you think would be pleasing to a customer. Remember, you have to live with that estimate too.

Until recently, organs in bad shape were hardly marketable and could be picked up for very little. No longer. Even very poor ones, with many parts missing, are appearing in antique shops with prices of several hundred dollars on them. I find that most dealers have absolutely no idea of what restoration involves or what it can cost. Particularly, if the organ will play at all under furious pumping, everyone concerned (except you) seems to think that any work needed must be minor. I once heard an antique dealer estimate to a potential customer for an unrestored organ that it would cost about $25 to get it fixed up. Deliver me.

All of this means that if you are going to do restoration work for someone else you need to take steps to protect yourself. In the first place, be sure that those who need the information know just what is involved in restoring. That may prevent many from even bothering to ask you to do the job. Those who still want the work will be much better prepared to pay any actual costs involved.

Insurance

Another protection you need: insurance against the loss of someone's old instrument while it is in your shop. Should some horrible thing happen to destroy your shop, even when you are not personally to blame, you might find yourself with a $2000 charge for the destruction of Grandma's irreplaceable heirloom, even though you honestly would not have given a hundred for the old clunker. Not that we should disparage the very real sentimental value of many of these old instruments. They have very cherished meaning to some people and that's fine; but when they start translating that into dollar values that you must pay, you had better be ready.

You can take out commercial insurance against such an event, but that's somewhat expensive. I doubt that your homeowner's policy would cover commercial work done in your basement and even if it did, it is highly unlikely that it would cover to the tune that may be demanded of you. For that matter, the organ owner's homeowner policy may cover it since such policies usually cover a portion of possessions off the premises, but I question again if the policy would cover the amount of antique value the owner may claim. My attorney says that you can have on a restoration contract (a sample is coming up), the agreement that you are not responsible for damage beyond your control. Most recently I wrote to the owner of an organ expressly stating that I expect him to have insurance adequate to cover the value of the instrument. A side note here: You may at times be dealing with pleasant people who do not follow the antique market but simply want the old heirloom fixed so that the grandchildren can play it. If you tell them the potential value of their instrument for insurance purposes, they will be delighted! Not that you should always do that kind of estimating; don't do it if you are not so inclined. You can simply say that you don't really know but that you expect them to insure it for whatever value they think it has.

In any event, no matter *what* you say in the contract, you are responsible for negligence. Don't bite off a job you can't do satisfactorily and be sure that you use the utmost care in handling the organ while you have it.

WRITTEN CONTRACT

Why have a written contract? I learned the hard way. An out-of-town owner wanted her cottage organ restored and heard of me from a nearby antique dealer. She called me and asked the price of restoration. My first mistake: I estimated without looking at the organ, trusting her description of it. Don't *ever* do that; no one really knows what's inside the organ and seldom will an owner admit how bad off it really is even if he suspects. My second mistake: I gave two prices; one for the bellows restoration if that was all the organ needed, and double that amount if the action needed full disassembly but no custom rebuilding of parts. You know what happened. The organ needed everything, including some replacing of interior parts damaged by mice, but for some reason she heard only the first price during our phone conversation. I work on organs because I enjoy them. Experiences such as the one I just recounted are no fun.

Because of that early experience several years ago I now give a customer a written account of what is to be done and get in writing his approval. Since I do so few organs commercially (I am not in the business at all) I haven't bothered to make up a printed contract, but the letter I send usually contains at least the following:

1. The exact work to be done on the case, including the type of finish the customer has desired, or a statement that it is to be left up to me. Be sure that you indicate satin, gloss, lacquer, the new tung oils, or whatever.
2. The exact work to be done on bellows and action, including the replacement of damaged parts, felts, leathers.
3. The *exclusion* of restoration of reeds unless you have had opportunity to pull all of them and know that they are all good. Cracked reeds will not show while in the cells, so be very careful here. If you have a source of supply of new reeds, your contract should state a total price for restoration *plus* what the replacement cost of reeds may be.
4. Other possible exclusions (these may or may not be needed): the condition of reed cells can be very deceptive, taking possibly ten or more hours of work more than you might have anticipated. If you even suspect cell troubles, an insurance clause for more labor cost may be wise.
5. Delivery time. Be wary of promising very quick delivery unless you know for sure that you can really clear the decks and stick at it. Even here, be careful. My wife asks me how long I need to do a given job (*any* job), then triples my answer so that she knows in practice how long it is going to take me. Better allow a generous buffer time to test the finished product, preferably in your home, out of the basement. Your customer will obviously be delighted if you can deliver earlier than promised but seldom is happy to have a delay.

6. Guarantee. Be careful here; as will be noted in the little statement that I suggest you give with a restored organ, improper care by the owner can cause damage or problems that are not your fault. It is best, of course, if you can state that you guarantee the organ only to be in good working condition when it is picked up by the customer at your shop where you will demonstrate it. If it is to be kept nearby you might specify some short period, say 30 days, of guarantee in which you will come to make adjustments. If it is to be taken some distance, specify that you will do repairs for problems due to faulty workmanship or materials for a given period if it is returned to you. The trouble lies in the fact that excessively dry home atmospheres can cause cracks in the reed pan; children can stomp on pedals and tear loose hinges and pedal straps; movers can jar things so that elements get out of line and stick; and much more. I know that you don't like to sound as if you don't trust your work, but you do have to protect yourself. Decide on the limits of your guarantee and stick to them.

7. Payment. Make this due upon delivery, particularly if the organ is going out of town or is done for someone who is a total stranger to you. If you are going to do the delivery (I suggest it—I don't trust movers), then include a reasonable fee for your time and equipment. In this case, you can then set the organ up in the home, test it out, and make suggestions for its continued good health.

8. A statement that you are not responsible for the organ's damage while in your shop if damaged by conditions beyond your control.

9. An indication that with the completed organ will come an account of what was actually done to the organ plus details of anything special found inside.

Following is the account of restoration I did to a Prince for my friend Richard Turner (see Fig. 1-3). It is headed "To Whom It May Concern" because the organ was originally intended for resale by Turner's Antique Shop. Marion Turner fell in love with the little beauty when it was done and has since refused all offers to buy it!

February, 1972

To Whom It May Concern:

This is an account of the work done on the Prince Organ no. 51781.

    CASE: Original finish in good condition, needing only clean-up, some light sanding and finish touch up; done by Mr. Richard Turner.

    INTERIOR ACTION. In very good condition for its age. Slight mouse damage on the interior, corrected by replacement of a piece of wood about 1×4 inches. I believe that I am the first to disassemble the organ since it was built. There is no indication that any repair has ever been needed before now. The interior chamber was like new. The pallets showed no evidence whatever of insect or moisture damage.

        All parts were disassembled and inspected. Reeds were cleaned individually. New cloth hinges were put on all swells. New piano-wire springs were fabricated. New heavy-duty bellows cloth was used to restore the bellows completely. New pedal straps were installed.

    KEYBOARD. All ivories are original. They were polished individually with steel wool. On the rear of about the tenth key from the left (under the stopboard) is a faintly visible pencilled date of 1875.

    OTHER MARKINGS. The case was apparently built by A. Schmidt whose name appears twice on the edge of the case on which the bellows support board rests: once with a metal stamp, once signed in pencil.

    RESTORED BY
    Horton Presley
    114 Shallowford Road
    Dalton, Georgia 30720

PROFESSIONAL NOTES

Chapter 24
Organ Care

Heretofore I have simply bought copies of the little pamphlet *The Reed Organ: How to Give it the Proper Care,* and presented one with each organ I restored. If you do not have one, I suggest that you get it. It is a Vestal Press reprint of the booklet Sears gave with the Beckwith in 1910 or thereabouts. You can save considerably on the list price by buying in small quantities. It has good information for any organ owner. In the event that the booklet becomes unavailable, or that you want a smaller handout that contains more modern instructions for taking care of an antique organ, feel free to copy the following:

Congratulations! You now have a restored reed organ. It has lasted these many years and now will continue to give you pleasure for many more years to come. As with any piece of fine furniture or with any musical instrument (this organ is both), proper care is a necessity. If you are careful to observe the following suggestions, you can minimize the problems that these organs have been subject to since they were first made.

CASE. Treat it as if it were your finest table. If you do set such things as flower pots or brass lamps on it, be very careful to use proper protection under them. Modern finishes and modern finish protectors are better than those available to the original manufacturers and organ owners, so use regular finish care and you should have no problems.

LOCATION OF THE ORGAN. Not only the case but most of the action of the organ is wood—old wood. Thus it is subject to three common sources of damage; dampness, dryness, and vermin. Place your organ where it will not be subject to the direct flow of air from a forced-air register or the close radiation from a hot-water or steam register. This is true, of course, of any piece of furniture in your home. Old books on the care of reed organs often speak of the problems associated with dampness, but the modern home with its forced-air furnace and air conditioner is more likely to be plagued by dryness. If you do not have a humidifier in your home you can expect, during very cold periods, your atmosphere to drop below the humidity of the desert if you have a forced-air furnace. Don't think nasty things about poor construction by modern furniture manufacturers; your atmosphere could be the cause of the rickety dining room furniture. Get a good humidity gauge and see for yourself.

For the organ, more than occasional looseness can develop. Cracks can open up in the reed pan (the flat area of wood you will see if you open up the back of your organ. The round box of the vox humana sits on it.) Since this must be airtight, any crack here makes your organ hard to play because you must pump madly to get any sound at all out of the organ. A humidifier on your furnace will help but even here you may find that it isn't enough to maintain the minimum 30 percent or preferable 40 percent humidity required for furniture health. As a sidelight, note how much better *you* will feel if you have proper humidity in you home.

Dampness is unlikely to be a major problem unless you must store the organ out of the normal living area or if you live in a location unusually subject to moisture. The signs will be those of stickiness; the keys will stick down, usually from swelling felts around the guide pins that go up inside the bottom of the keys to keep them in place, or from swelling wood around the little push-rods (called pitmans) that are between the bottom of the key and the valve (called a pallet) under the reed pan. Your only real remedy is to move the organ to where it can dry out. In extreme cases you might buy an electric damp-chaser for use in pianos. Your music dealer can supply one.

VERMIN PROTECTION. Vermin just love organs; the glue, some of the wood, the finishes, the felt, the leather. Insects find the reed cells (the holes into which each reed fits) ideal nesting places. You should periodically inspect the inside of your organ and spray with appropriate protective materials. One caution: Do not use powders except in the very bottom of the organ. Your organ operates on a vacuum principle, *not* air pressure, as is so often supposed. If you put powder inside the case on the reed pan, it can be sucked into the reeds causing all sorts of havoc.

REEDS NOT SOUNDING. Reeds work on vacuum or suction, drawing air from the outside through the reed and into the main bellows. If the slightest dust gets into the reed, it can stop the reed from speaking. If the problem has just developed, try pumping fairly vigorously, rapidly operating the key. This may dislodge the foreign matter. If not, you must pull the reed and clean it. This is usually not a difficult job but you must be very careful not to damage the reed.

First determine which rank of reeds the silent one is in. You probably have two sets, one in front, one in back. If the note doesn't sound with a given stop out, try another stop in the same general area. Since each key usually controls two reeds, the other stop may open another set and allow another reed to sound. Note the two stops involved. Close the stop of the reed which does sound and open the one involving the silent reed.

Now take off the panel immediately below the keyboard. It will usually come off when you remove the two or three screws holding it. You will then see a long, flat panel of wood, hinged at the top, covering the whole reed area under the keyboard. Open it up an inch or two (you won't hurt it) and see if a triangular piece of wood extending in front of the reeds is partially open. Test by pushing in the stop you opened and see if the piece of wood (called a mute) closes. If it is the right one, pull the stop out again and put something under the hinged panel (called a swell) to hold it open. Count the number of keys from the nearest end (both black and white) to the silent one. Then count similarily down from the nearest end reed (they are the little brass pieces you see sticking out of each reed cell.)

Now you need a special hook, called a *reed hook*, which should have come with your organ. The hook has a screwdriver at one end (for removing panels) and a rounded piece that sits at right angles to the shaft at the other end. In the middle is a loop about an inch in diameter. Place your forefinger in the loop, put the rounded end in the slot in the back of the silent reed, and gently pull straight out. *Caution:* Do *not*, under any circumstances, insert the reed hook into the

297

reed cell beyond the slot in the back of the reed. You can do permanent damage to the reed if the hook somehow gets hold of the free end of the reed.

Another word of warning: When pulling the reed do not try to pressure it from side to side. You can fracture the relatively fragile separation between cells, causing a cypher (a continuous sounding note), and necessitating a major repair job.

When the reed is out, look for small bits of dust, insects, or the like, lodged beside the tongue of the reed. Gently pick it out. You need a magnifying glass to see the obstruction in the little treble reeds (the high notes.) Concerning especially those small reeds, don't be too surprised that you can't find anything at all even though the reed may then play when you put it back in. Often small obstructions fall out in the process of reed pulling.

When you clean a reed with a cloth, be sure to clean in one direction only—from the rivet toward the tip end of the reed. Before reinserting the reed use a flashlight to check for more such dust or particles of wood in the vicinity of the reed cell. Clean the area carefully to minimize future problems.

Reinsert the reed with your fingers and push in as far as you can. This procedure minimizes the likelihood of your getting a reed in wrong. You will notice that there are small slots at either side of the reed cell near the bottom where the reed goes. Be sure the reed is exactly in those slots and is started straight in. After you have pushed it in as far as you can, use the blunt end of the reed hook to push it in the rest of the way. It should take no more pressure to insert than it did to remove. The reed should now sound normally. Use the same procedure relevant to reeds in the rear rank.

CYPHERS. When a reed sounds continuously even when the associated key is not depressed it is called a cypher. There are two common causes: a sticking key, or foreign matter under a pallet (this is the leather-padded piece of wood under the reed that controls the flow of air to the reed.) Keys stick either from some binding in the little pins that hold the key in place or from the small dowel that goes from the bottom of the key through a small hole down to the pallet.

You can sometimes stop a key from binding on its guide pins by gently rocking it from side to side , thus freeing it a bit. If that doesn't work, it may be that the dowel (the pitman) is sticking in its associated hole. Here the cause might be excessive moisture, the cure for which has already been described. If you can reach in and grasp the pitman without bending anything, try rotating it a bit. At times a pitman will warp slightly and bind in a given position. Some silicone spray may also help.

If the problem is foreign matter on a pallet, try pumping the organ fairly rapidly and also, as rapidly, operate the key up and down. Try also operating the keys beside it (the black keys also), both in unison with it and alternating with it. This often dislodges the foreign matter. *Caution*: Don't reach in to the pitman and push it down more than it normally travels when the key is depressed; you can cause a pallet under the reed pan to jump off its guide pins. When that happens, you may be forced to have the whole action taken out to get things back in place. An experienced restorer may be able to pull the associated reed and, with a wire, reach down to the pallet and get it back in place, but it is a ticklish job and should not be attempted by someone who is not acquainted with the underside of the organ.

WHEN NOT IN USE. When you are not using the organ keep all stops pushed in since this prevents possible warping of mutes and swells which are suspended from their normal resting places when the stop is out. Also try to keep the keyboard cover down so that dust problems are minimized.

NORMAL USE. While no instrument should be subject to abuse, normal use will in no way hurt this instrument. It was made to be played regularly. Indeed, one way to keep it in good condition is to play it often. It is not delicate. These gentle-toned instruments have given pleasure to their owners for up to 130 years; may yours continue to do so for you for many years to come.

Appendix

Appendix

Sources of Supplies

In addition to the regular commercial sources for materials contained in this section, you should be alert for other places to get things. For instance, you undoubtedly are aware of the fact that blue screws, used in much abundance in organs, are no longer being made. Whenever I go into an old-appearing hardware, I ask if they have any blue screws kicking around. By such means I have been able to buy a stock of several sizes. Another thing to look for is old wood, including veneered pieces, that are so far gone as to be unusable or even unrestorable. Such scraps often come in very handy for case repair.

I also ask every antique dealer I meet if he happens to have some organ parts lying around. In times past, organs were chopped up into tables, desks, you name it. Sometimes they surface in a shop or at a flea market. A couple of years ago at an antique auto parts swap-meet I was pawing through a pile of auto stuff only to find an excellent *matched pair* of bellows springs! You never know.

SOURCES OF SUPPLY FOR REED ORGAN NEEDS

Organ Supply Industries Inc., P.O. Box 8325, Erie, PA.16505-0325. Telephone (814) 835-2244. Good source of leather for organs as well as silicone solution for treating organ leather, also supplies rubber cloth and flake hide glue, No other reed organ parts.
Paul Toelken, PO Box 25017, Prescott Valley, AZ 86312 (only has reeds).
Player Piano Company, Inc., 704 East Douglas, Wichita, KS 67202. Telephone (316) 263-3241. Good

source of many reproduction items for reed organs: bellows, cloth, springs, stop faces, etc. Catalogue available (no charge).

Schaff Piano Supply Co., 451 Oakwood Road, Lake Zurich, IL 60047. Wholesale only. Order through your local music store. Good source for all that's available.

GENERAL CRAFT MATERIAL SOURCES FOR ITEMS USEFUL IN ORGAN WORK

Brookstone Company, Peterborough, NH 03458. Excellent source of small tools, leather punches, etc.
Albert Constantine & Son, Inc. 2050 Eastchester Road, Bronx, NY 10461-2207. Excellent source for all types of wood and veneers plus glues and tools for woodworking.
Craftsman Wood Service Co., 1735 W. Cortland Court, Addison, IL 60101. Telephone (708) 629-3100. Excellent source of wood, veneers, glues, woodworking tools, moldings, and hardware.
Tandy Leather Co., outlets in almost every major city. Good source of leathers for pallets and bellows.

CHEMICALS AND FINISHES

The Hope Co. 12777 Pennridge Drive, Bridgeton, MO 63044. Good refinisher and tung oil finish.

Bibliography

Works directly relating to reed organs.

Abbott, F. D. and C. H. Daniell, eds. *The Presto Buyer's Guide to the American Pianos, Player-pianos, and Organs*, together with a directory of their manufacture. Chicago: Presto Pub. Col, 1908.

Bryant, Niles. *Tuning, Care and Repair of Reed and Pipe Organs*. 1912. Reprint by Vestal Press, 1968.

Earl, S. G. *Repairing the Reed Organ and Harmonium*. n.d. Reprinted by Organ Literature Foundation.

Estey Organ Corporation. *Care and adjustment of Estey Organs*. n.d. Brattleboro, VT. Rpt. Organ Literature Foundation.

Faust, Oliver C. *Organs, Construction and Tuning*, Player Piano. Boston, Mass, 1949.

Gellerman, Robert F. *The American Reed Organ*. Vestal, NY: The Vestal Press, Ltd. 1973. Out of print; new edition forthcoming.

_____. *Gellerman's International Reed Organ Atlas*. Vestal, NY: The Vestal Press, Ltd. 1985.

Milne, H. F. *The Reed Organ: Its Design and Construction*. London, 1930. Rpt. Organ Literature Foundation.

Mustel, Alphonse. "L'Orgue Harmonium" in *Encyclopedie de la Musique et Dictionaire du Conservatoire*. Paris 1913-31.

Sears Roebuck and Co. *The Reed Organ: How to Give it Proper Care*. Chicago, 1910. Rpt. Vestal Press.

General craft books useful in restoring reed organs.
Garside, Jack. *Marquetry: The How-to-do-it Book.*
Vestal, NY: The Vestal Press, Ltd., 1992.

Gibbia, S. W. *Wood Finishing and Refinishing.* Van
Nostrand Reinhold Co., NY 1971. Prentice-Hall, 1986.

Grotz, George. *The Furniture Doctor.* Garden City, NY:
Doubleday, 1962.

Sources of organ information.
The Organ Literature Foundation, 45 Norfolk Road,
Braintree, MA 02184-5918. Telephone (617) 848-
1388.

The Vestal Press, Ltd., PO Box 97, Vestal, NY 13851-
0097. Telephone (607) 797-4872; Fax (607) 797-4898.
Catalogue of interesting publications, including helpful
reed organ items, is available.

The Reed Organ Society, c/o The Musical Museum,
Deansboro, NY 13328. Publishes an interesting
journal, four issues a year.

Index

Index

312

MAY 23 '94			